THE LOVECRAFT ANNUAL

Edited by S. T. Joshi   No. 8 (2014)

Contents

Abbreviations used in the text and notes:

AT   *The Ancient Track* (Hippocampus Press, 2013)
CE   *Collected Essays* (Hippocampus Press, 2004–06; 5 vols.)
CF   *Collected Fiction* (Hippocampus Press; 2014–15; 4 vols.)
LL   *Lovecraft's Library: A Catalogue*, 3rd rev. ed. (Hippocampus Press, 2012)
SL   *Selected Letters* (Arkham House, 1965–76; 5 vols.)

Published by Hippocampus Press, P.O. Box 641, New York, NY 10156
http://www.hippocampuspress.com

Cover illustration by Allen Koszowski. Hippocampus Press logo designed by Anastasia Damianakos. Cover design by Barbara Briggs Silbert.

Lovecraft Annual is published once a year, in Fall. Articles and letters should be sent to the editor, S. T. Joshi, ℅ Hippocampus Press, and must be accompanied by a self-addressed stamped envelope if return is desired. All reviews are assigned. Literary rights for articles and reviews will reside with *Lovecraft Annual* for one year after publication, whereupon they will revert to their respective authors. Payment is in contributor's copies.

ISSN 1935-6102
ISBN: 978-1-61498-112-1

The cover color, Pugmire Pink, is dedicated to our steadfast friend W. H. Pugmire.

Editorial

Later this year, Hippocampus Press will release the first three volumes of Lovecraft's *Collected Fiction: A Variorum Edition*, under my editorship. These three volumes will contain the entirety of Lovecraft's original fiction, arranged chronologically by date of writing. A fourth volume, containing Lovecraft's revisions and collaborations, will appear next year. I have undertaken a thorough re-evaluation of the textual sources (manuscripts, printed versions, Lovecraft's annotated copies of magazine publications of his stories, etc.) for Lovecraft's stories, and I also present a comprehensive set of textual variants for all textually significant appearances of the tales. This edition effectively replaces my corrected Arkham House editions of the stories (subsequently reprinted— each time with small revisions—by Penguin [1999–2004; 3 vols.], the Library of America [2005], and Barnes & Noble [2008]), and will henceforth constitute, in my judgment, as close to a definitive edition of Lovecraft's tales as can be assembled. Readers and critics who wish to examine the textual basis for my decisions regarding specific readings in the tales can now find all the information they require. While it is conceivable that another editor might come to slightly different conclusions in regard to certain textual decisions, I believe that the end result would not be significantly different from what I present.

I was particularly interested in the fact that, more often than I had previously realized, Lovecraft revised his stories (usually fairly minimally, but nonetheless in a telling manner) upon subsequent printing of the work. Several stories printed in *Weird Tales* in the 1920s were so revised when they appeared as reprints in issues of the 1930s. In the case of Lovecraft's second story of his mature period, "Dagon" (1917), I had previously neglected to consult the first *Weird Tales* appearance (October 1923), relying on the existing single-spaced typescript, which I believed to be definitive. But it became clear to me that, in the process of preparing a double-spaced typescript (which the *Weird Tales* editor Edwin Baird stated as a condition for acceptance of that story and others submitted to him in mid-1923), Lovecraft revised some passages. For example, in the second paragraph Lovecraft wrote in the typescript: "The great war was then at its very beginning, and the ocean forces of the Hun had not completely sunk to their later degradation . . ." In *Weird Tales* the latter part of the sentence reads: ". . . and the enemy's navy had not reached its later degree of ruthlessness . . ." It is very unlikely that this was a change instituted by *Weird Tales* (Lovecraft had previously specified that his stories must be printed strictly as written), so it must constitute a deliberate revision by Lovecraft. Since the Arkham House editions preceding mine also followed the single-spaced typescript, revisions such as the above have never been printed in any edition of the story.

The Hippocampus Press edition will first appear as a limited hardcover, followed by a paperback and ebook edition. It is hoped that scholars, critics, and interested readers will henceforth use this edition for citation purposes, and in this journal it will be regarded as the authoritative text of Lovecraft's original fiction. An extensive review of it will appear in next year's *Lovecraft Annual*.

—S. T. JOSHI

Letters to Farnsworth Wright

H. P. Lovecraft

Edited by S. T. Joshi and David E. Schultz

H. P. Lovecraft's long and tortured relationship with Farnsworth Wright (1888–1940), editor of *Weird Tales* (*WT*) from 1924 to 1940, is vividly captured in his surviving letters to Wright. The letters survive mostly in the Arkham House Transcripts (AHT); the originals apparently are lost. A few were printed, almost certainly abridged, in the letter column of *Weird Tales* ("The Eyrie"), usually commenting upon certain notable tales published in the magazine. The celebrated letter of 5 July 1927 outlines some of the central tenets of Lovecraft's cosmic philosophy. (The letter was heavily abridged in the *Weird Tales* appearance, and the version in AHT is presumably complete, or at least more nearly so.)

In mid-1927 Wright apparently asked Lovecraft to provide a prospective table of contents for a collection of his tales that the Popular Fiction Publishing Company (the parent company of *Weird Tales*) would publish. Lovecraft wrote a lengthy letter outlining a potential volume of 40,000 words, presciently titled *The Outsider and Other Stories*; but the project came to naught, as the publisher's anthology *The Moon Terror* (1927; *LL* 93) sold so poorly that no further volumes could be contemplated.

Other letters discuss anthology reprints from *Weird Tales*, a potential rival to the magazine (Carl Swanson's *Galaxy*), the deaths of Henry S. Whitehead and Robert E. Howard, radio dramatization rights for "The Dreams in the Witch House," and Lovecraft's repeated pleas that Wright publish a higher grade of story in *Weird Tales* rather than the formula work praised by readers in "The Eyrie."

Editors' Note

The letters are printed with as little alteration as possible, and the
editors have retained Lovecraft's idiosyncrasies of usage and occasional spelling errors or slips of the pen. No omission has know-
ingly been made. The non-Roman characters in letters 10 and 21
are copied from the renderings in the Arkham House transcripts,
and thus are not by Lovecraft himself.

———————

[1]   [*WT*]

[c. January 1926]

I have lately read your December issue, and believe the general
qualitative level is kept commendably high—we don't find any of
the frank crudities that marked the earlier issues. Long's "The Sea
Thing" strikes me as the best tale, with Owen's "The Fan" as a
good second.[1]

Notes

1. HPL is commenting on stories by Frank Belknap Long and Frank Ow-
en in the December 1925 issue of *WT*.

[2]   [AHT]

10 Barnes St.,
Providence, R.I.,
July 5, 1927

Dear Mr. Wright:—

Yours of the 1st. arrived this morning. Wandrei
has written me of his long and pleasant call at the *Weird Tales*
headquarters, and was very complimentary in his description of
those whom he met there. He is now in New York, and I expect
to see him here on or about the tenth. I shall try to induce him to
stay in New England long enough to imbibe some of our fascinating scenery and antiquities—including the prototypes of "Kingsport" and "Arkham", and the hellish North End district in Boston
which forms the locale of "Pickman's Model".[1]

In accordance with your suggestion I am re-submitting "The Call of Cthulhu",[2] though possibly you will still think it a trifle too bizarre for a clientele who demand their weirdness in name only, and who like to keep both feet pretty solidly on the ground of the known and the familiar. As I said some time ago, I doubt if my work—and especially my later products—would "go" very well with the sort of readers whose reactions are represented in the "Eyrie". The general trend of the yarns which seem to suit the public is that of essential normality of outlook and simplicity of point of view—with thoroughly conventional human values and motives predominating, and with brisk action of the best-seller type as an indispensable attribute. The weird element in such material does not extend far into the fabric—it is the artificial weirdness of the fireside tale and the Victorian ghost story, and remains external camouflage even in the seemingly wildest of the "interplanetary" concoctions. You can see this sort of thing at its best in Seabury Quinn, and at its worst in the general run of contributors. It is exactly what the majority want — for if they were to see a *really* weird tale they wouldn't know what it's all about. This is quite obvious from the way they object to the *reprints*, which in many cases have brought them the genuine article.

Now all my tales are based on the fundamental premise that common human laws and interests and emotions have no validity or significance in the vast cosmos-at-large. To me there is nothing but puerility in a tale in which the human form—and the local human passions and conditions and standards—are depicted as native to other worlds or other universes. To achieve the essence of real externality, whether of time or space or dimension, one must forget that such things as organic life, good and evil, love and hate, and all such local attributes of a negligible and temporary race called mankind, have any existence at all. Only the human scenes and characters must have human qualities. *These* must be handled with unsparing *realism*, (*not* catch-penny *romanticism*) but when we cross the line to the boundless and hideous unknown—the shadow-haunted *Outside*—we must remember to leave our humanity and terrestrialism at the threshold.

So much for theory. In practice, I presume that few commonplace readers would have any use for a story written on these psychological principles. They want their conventional best-seller values and motives kept paramount throughout the abysses of apocalyptic vision and extra-Einsteinian chaos, and would not deem an "interplanetary" tale in the least interesting if it did not have its Martian (or Jovian or Venerian or Saturnian) heroine fall in love with the young voyager from Earth, and thereby incur the jealousy of the inevitable Prince Kongros (or Zeelar or Hoshgosh or Norkog) who at once proceeds to usurp the throne etc.; or if it did not have its Martian (or etc.) nomenclature follow a closely terrestrial pattern, with an Indo-Germanic '*-a*' name for the Princes, and something disagreeable and Semitic for the villain. Now I couldn't grind out that sort of junk if my life depended on it. If I were writing an "interplanetary" tale it would deal with beings organised very differently from mundane mammalia, and obeying motives wholly alien to anything we know upon Earth—the exact degree of alienage depending, of course, on the scene of the tale; whether laid in the solar system, the visible galactic universe outside the solar system, or the *utterly unplumbed* gulfs still father out—nameless vortices of never-dreamed-of strangeness, where form and symmetry, light and heat, even matter and energy themselves, may be unthinkably metamorphosed or totally wanting. I have merely got at the edge of this in "Cthulhu", where I have been careful to avoid terrestrialism in the few linguistic and nomenclatural specimens from Outside which I present. All very well—but will the readers stand for it? That's all they're likely to get from me in the future—except when I deal with definitely terrestrial scenes—and I am the last one to urge the acceptance of material of doubtful value to the magazine's particular purpose. Even when I deal with the mundanely weird, moreover, I shan't be likely to stress the popular artificial values and emotions of cheap fiction.

However—you can best judge this matter from some recent samples of my scribbling; wherefore I'll enclose, purely for your personal perusal, (although gawd knows you can print 'em if you like, since nobody else is likely to do so!) two characteristic neo-Lovecraftian outbursts—"The Silver Key" and "The Strange High House in the Mist". I fancy you won't find much of professional interest in 'em—so that you may be sure your readers aren't missing much! When I do write any more things with a fairly earthly "slant", I'll certainly send them along, but my winter fiction crop consisted only of two novelettes too long for any but serial use, (and I haven't had the energy to type them yet, either!) whilst this spring and summer I've been too busy with revisory and kindred activities to write more than one tale—which, oddly enough, was accepted at once by *Amazing Stories* despite its full possession of the non-terrestrial qualities so characteristic of my recent work.[3] Toward autumn I hope to arrange for some writing leisure, and I shall then 'get off my chest' several plots which have been insistently clamouring for expression lately. Among these are at least two which I shall try on you—though they won't seem much like the recent *Weird Tales* type. Which reminds me that in the latest (July) issue I found Hugh Irish's "Mystery of Sylmare" closest to my notion of a weird tale, with R. Ernest Dupay's "Edge of the Shadow" as a not very close second. Munn's tale was good, but he seems to be getting the popular fiction 'bug'. Has he shown you his ninety-two page sequel to the story—"The Werewolf's Daughter"? And by the way let me congratulate you on your new illustrator Rankin. He's the best yet![4]

Glad to hear of the improving rates—they ought to attract new cohorts of able authors. I feel sure that scores of 'top-notchers' would be glad to write weird stories if they could find any place to market them on their own terms.

With every good wish, and hoping the enclosed won't bore you too badly,

I remain—most sincerely yrs—

H. P. Lovecraft.

P.S. My history of weird fiction[5] is all in type, and I have told Cook (whose private publication will contain it) to be sure to send you a copy. He is later going to issue my "Shunned House" as a little book uniform with Long's poems.[6]

[P.]P.S. Besides my visit from Wandrei, I'm expecting a visit from young Long and his parents on the 21st. If Wandrei can stay over until then, we'll have quite a weird conclave beneath my lowly roof-tree! Wandrei is a great boy—he has had some poignant imaginative

glimpses *Outside* which few living writers have shared, and will undoubtedly develop remarkably. In sheer, daemonic extra-
mundaneness he excels anybody I know except Clark Ashton Smith.

Notes

1. Wandrei visited HPL in Providence on 12–29 July 1927.
2. HPL surely had not yet heard the following testimony from Wandrei: "I
casually worked in a reference to a story, 'The Call of Cthulhu,' that Lovecraft was revising and finishing and which I thought was a wonderful tale.
But I added that for some reason or other, Lovecraft had talked about
submitting it to other magazines. I said I just couldn't understand why he
was apparently planning to by-pass *Weird Tales* unless he was seeking to
broaden his markets or widen his reading public. None of this was true,
but I could see that my fanciful account took effect, in the way Wright
began to fidget and show signs of agitation." Donald Wandrei, "Lovecraft in
Providence" (1959), in Peter Cannon, ed., *Lovecraft Remembered* (Sauk
City, WI: Arkham House, 1998), 315. Wandrei came to read "The Call of
Cthulhu" because Clark Ashton Smith had sub-loaned the ms. to him.
Wandrei writes as though HPL had not previously submitted the story to
WT, but HPL had told him *WT* rejected the story.
3. "The Colour out of Space." HPL's comment suggests that he had not
previously mentioned or submitted this story to *WT*, as some scholars
have maintained.
4. H. Warner Munn's tale in the July 1927 issue was "The Return of the
Master." "The Werewolf's Daughter," a sequel to "The Werewolf of Ponk-
ert" (*WT*, July 1925), appeared as a three-part serial (*WT*, Oct.–Dec. 1928).
5. "Supernatural Horror in Literature," *The Recluse* (1927).
6. HPL refers to Frank Belknap Long's *The Man from Genoa and Other
Poems* (Athol, MA: Recluse Press, 1926). Cook's edition of *The Shunned
House* (1928) was printed but not bound or distributed. FW had rejected
the story when it was submitted to him in late 1924.

[3]   [AHT]

                              10 Barnes St.,
                                 Providence, R.I.,
                                    July 16, 1927

My dear Wright:—

          I am very glad to hear that you have found
"Cthulhu" available for use, and assure you that $165.00 is entirely
adequate remuneration. I hope that Price will like "The Strange
High House",[1] and would certainly be surprised and pleased if it

found its way to ultimate publication! A third pleasure is given me by the news of "Red Hook's" anthological reprinting; and I'd like to see the book if you can get me a copy later on. I can most emphatically and advantageously use any royalties, be they ever so humble, which may chance to trickle in from Mr. Lovell.[2] I've been meaning to ask Belknap whether he obtained anything for the two stories reprinted in previous issues.

What you say of Price interests me very much—he must be a delightful companion, with his many unique accomplishments. Indeed, you seem to be building up a "gang" eclipsing even our famous aggregation of a couple of years ago—Long, Leeds, Morton, Loveman, Talman, Kirk, etc.[3] I recall Kline's work, but can't say I was ever exactly bowled over with it. His Semitic phiz must be quite a cross—but I know a man of mixed Irish and French Huguenot ancestry who is in the same boat. I imagine that in the Middle Ages many Jews mixed into the Aryan population of all European nations, so that strains may crop out in unexpected places. Then, too, the Phoenicians may have left a bit of their hook-nosed blood in sundry parts of the ancient world. I once wrote a couple of replies to that famous pair of monometer couplets during a discussion of their authorship. They were:

"De gus-	In haste
tibus—	His taste,
Why scan and	Perhaps,
His plan?	Might lapse!

This Carr certainly appears to be a phenomenal being, and I congratulate him upon a spectacular success which I—with my elderly and antiquarian indifference to the sensational—am never likely to achieve.[4] I fancy that for the next few years "flaming youth" will occupy the same place in the vulgar eye that Greenwich Village did ten years ago, studio life twenty years ago, and stage life thirty or forty years ago. Those who are informed and glib can cash in—and I trust that the Carr of today may be the Robert W. Chambers of yesterday. Chambers, by the way, used to write weird tales. Do you know his "King in Yellow"? I hope that Carr will always gratefully remember the start which you and the group have given him.

Thanks for the "Pickman's Model" sketch—which isn't at all bad. Rankin certainly has the stuff in him and cannot even be considered in the same breath with Olinick. I am anxious to see the heading for Wandrei's tale.[5] Wandrei is still with me—after Tuesday's Newport trip we spent two days in the haunted woods north of Providence, and are in Boston today—taking in the art museum and waiting for a thundershower to blow over. He's a great kid—watch his stuff grow in the years ahead! Tomorrow we hope to "do" Salem (Arkham) and Marblehead, (Kingsport) and next Thursday we shall be on hand in Providence to welcome Long. I was glad to see Long's and Talman's tales in the current issue. That "Symphony Hall" tale was very fair—we're about to pass the building now, and I'm all a-tremble![6]

    With all good wishes,
        Sincerely yrs—
           H. P. L.

P.S. I shall be interested in the book proposition when—or if—it develops.

[Addition by Wandrei:]
Dear W.—I'm very glad you found "Cthulhu acceptable—I'll look for it. Am enjoying myself with H. P. L., and trying to convince him he never should have sent "The Colour Out of Space" to *Am. St.* will drop in again on y return in two or Three weeks, with perhaps a brief case full of manuscripts.—Donald Wandrei.

Notes

1. E. Hoffmann Price (with whom HPL was not then acquainted) was apparently an informal editorial adviser to FW.
2. Charles Lovell was *WT*'s London agent.
3 I.e., the Kalem Club.
4. HPL refers to Robert Spencer Carr (1909–1994), who sold his first story to *WT* at the age of fifteen and had a best-selling novel, *The Rampant Age* (1928), published when he was nineteen.
5. "The Red Brain" (*WT*, Oct. 1927). It was illustrated by Hugh Rankin.
6. Stories in *WT*, Aug. 1927: Frank Belknap Long, "The Man with a Thousand Legs"; Wilfred B. Talman, "Two Black Bottles" (revised by HPL); George Malcolm-Smith, "Satan's Fiddle" mentioned "Symphony Hall" as the venue where the story's events take place.

[4]   [AHT]

10 Barnes St.,

Providence, R.I.,

Dec. 22, 1927

Dear Mr. Wright:—

I'm glad *The Recluse* came through safely. Cook was so uneven about mailing the copies that some haven't received it yet; and I've been quite besieged with inquiries. I hope my article won't bore you. It is abominably written, some whole sections having been thrust in at the eleventh hour when most of the type was set up; and if it were ever to be reprinted as a brochure, (as your fellow-townsman Mr. Starrett and Cook himself both suggest for the future) I would want to change whole chapters. Chamisso's stuff, for example, which I could not unearth in either Providence or New York, and which I rashly wrote up from hearsay, is not really part of the authentic horror-tradition. I got hold of "The Man Without a Shadow" this autumn, and was bored to death. So out it goes from any future edition![1] Note also the misprint of *Clarence* for *Clemence* Housman. That was a final insert on which I couldn't read proof.

I may have some more tales to send you before spring—but just now revision has me in a daemon clutch. An old fellow[2] once associated with Ambrose Bierce is having me do over a whole book full of execrable short stories—published and forgotten twenty-five years ago—for a second edition which he wants to float on the strength of some publicity gained in connexion with a new Bierce death report. And if this thing goes through, he may want me to help him on a book of Bierce reminiscences. Poor old Ambrosius—how the ghouls feed! This especial old bird, according to an anecdote recorded by George Sterling, parted from Bierce under the dramatic circumstance of having a cane broken over his head![3] When I saw his fiction I wondered why Ambrosius didn't use a crowbar.

As to that problematical volume of my tales—I'm really not very particular about the contents, since of course it would have to be formulated with the *Weird Tales* clientele in view and couldn't represent any real choice of mine. However, it appears to me that a certain group of tales can be considered as definitely better than the rest from *both* popular and artistic points of view;

and I will here record their names as I conceive them—together
with my rough estimates of their length in words:

"Outsider"	2500
"Arthur Jermyn"	3500

("White Ape")—that title concocted by Baird, gives me acute
cervical agony. The original title is "Facts Concerning the Late
Arthur Jermyn and His Family"—but I think plain "Arthur
Jermyn" is the best.

"Rats in Walls"	7500
"Picture in House"	3000
"Pickman's Model"	5500
"Erich Zann"	4000
"Dagon"	2000
"Randolph Carter"	3000
"Cats of Ulthar"	1400
	———
	32400

Here, then, is what I call the *indispensable* nucleus of any book
purporting to represent the *popular* side of my fiction. I omit all
things of any length—"Cthulhu", "Red Hook", &c.—because only
one long tale can be included in a volume of this length. As for a
title—my choice is "The Outsider and Other Stories". This is because I consider the touch of cosmic *outsideness*—of dim, shadowy
non-terrestrial hints—to be the characteristic feature of my writing.

Thus we have 32,400 words accounted for. I would advise
piecing out with one of the longish (10,000-word) tales and as
many more shorter ones as are needed to fill the space you have in
mind. Of my longer tales—exclusive of the two novelettes never
typed or seen by anyone but Wandrei[4]—I think the following
classification in order of merit is possible:

1. "The Colour Out of Space"
2. "Cthulhu"
3. "Red Hook"

"The Shunned House" won't be available, since Cook wants to
print that as a thin book uniform with Belknap's poems. Incidentally—I have my doubts about the *popular* appeal of "The

Colour". I advise choice of "Cthulhu", for in spite of what Belknap says and what the British anthologist chose, I think "Red Hook" is comparatively poor. Another alternative, though, is that thunderously melodramatic thing which I let Houtain publish in his nauseous *Home Brew** (ugh!) five years ago—"The Lurking Fear"—which of course I have the right to use again in a *book*. It is poor art, because it was written to order with certain limitations, but it ought to please the followers of Nictzin Dyalhis and his congeners. I'll enclose a manuscript of it—which please return if you don't care for it.

Now as to shorter "fillers" to round out your 45 or 6 thousand words—(32400 plus 10000 = 42400; 46000 – 42400 = 3600)—here are my suggestions:

"Festival"	3000
"Unnamable"	2500
"Terrible Old Man"	1400

These can be juggled around as you like, since the *exact* size of the volume is not a fixed quantity. Incidentally, by the way—that 32400-word essential nucleus is only my own estimate. I'm perfectly agreeable to any changes in that which you may choose to make. Cut out anything you fancy would decrease the book's profit, and insert anything you think would increase it. If you want a touch of my other and more fantastic style, try "The White Ship".[†]

But of course the thing may never take form, so just file away this letter as a possible source of suggestion in case it does. If I were more affluent I'd order a copy of the "Moon Terror"[5]—though I have the story in my complete *Weird Tales* file. I trust the volume may prove successful, and the first of a long series. A really fine book could be made of certain selections from different authors covering the entire history of the magazine.

By the way—I was flattered last Monday by receiving a letter from the anthologist Edward J. O'Brien, asking for an autobio-

---

*Don't give this damn thing credit if you use the tale. The magazine failed amidst many debts and dubieties in 1924, and Houtain can't afford to raise objections anent lack of recognition!

[†]Although of course "The Strange High House", "Doom that Came to Sarnath", etc. are vastly better.

graphical note for "The Best Short Stories of 1927". It was addressed to *Amazing Stories* and forwarded, so I suppose his mention of me will be based on "The Colour Out of Space". I don't fancy he'll go so far as to reprint it—but even a favourable allusion from so Olympian a source will be encouraging. I note from his letter that he is residing in Switzerland.

   With best wishes for a Merry Christmas and Happy New Year,

                    I remain

                         most cordially and sincerely yrs—
                              H. P. L.

P.S. I duly received the Selwyn and Blount anthology which you forwarded. Not half bad! My first appearance between cloth covers, save for prefaces to two books of other people's poetry which I've edited.[6] I note that their illiterate proofreader copied the misprinted punctuation of the Latin quotation—the comma after *tali* which so lacerated my heart in *Weird Tales*.[7] O *tempora, O mores!*

Notes

1. HPL refers to Adalbert von Chamisso (1781–1838), a German author. In the first publication of "Supernatural Horror in Literature" HPL had written: "Adalbert von Chamisso, in his famous *Peter Schlemihl*, (1814) tells of a man who lost his own shadow as the consequence of a misdeed, and of the strange developments that resulted." He removed the sentence in subsequent appearances of the essay. "The Man without a Shadow" presumably refers to *Peter Schlemihl*, although no English translation with that title can be found.

2. Adolphe de Castro.

3. Sterling's anecdote appears in his introduction to Bierce's *In the Midst of Life* (New York: Modern Library, 1927; *LL* 88).

4. *The Dream-Quest of Unknown Kadath* and *The Case of Charles Dexter Ward*, neither of which were published in HPL's lifetime.

5. By A. G. Birch et al., consisting of three stories from *WT* (*LL* 93). The book sold so poorly that plans for volumes by HPL and others were indefinitely postponed.

6. HPL refers to *The Poetical Works of Jonathan E. Hoag* (New York: Privately printed, 1927; *LL* 425) and John Ravenor Bullen's *White Fire* (Athol, MA: Recluse Press, 1927; *LL* 131).

7. HPL refers to the Latin quotation from Antoine Delrio ("*An sint un-*

quam daemones incubi et succubae, et an ex tali congressu proles nasci queat?") in "The Horror at Red Hook."

[5]   [*WT*]

[December 1927]

There's one fine story in your current issue[1]—"The Shadows", by Henry S. Whitehead. Wish you could get more of his material—it has the marks of a real brain and fancy behind it.

Notes

1. *WT*, Nov. 1927.

[6]   [*WT*]

[c. January 1928]

That[1] was what I call a *genuine weird tale*, with all the subtle atmospheric conditions adequately realised. Why in heaven's name can't the bulk of the writers catch at least some faint echo of the black, brooding whispers from unholy abysses and blasphemous dimensions which give a narrative like this its imponderable element of competence and mastery? Next best thing in the issue was Burks' "Bells of Oceana". That had the genuine thrill of Outsideness, too.

Notes

1. "The Canal" by Everil Worrell (*WT*, Dec. 1927).

[7]   [AHT]

10 Barnes St., Providence, R.I.,
Sept. 24, 1928

My dear Wright:—

Pardon my bothering you with the enclosed manuscript by Mrs. Z. B. Reed,[1] (joint revision client of Belknap and myself) but she insists that she wants you to see it despite its thoroughly non-weird nature and its consequent ineligibility for *Weird Tales*. Why she wants to send it is beyond me—unless perhaps she has read in the "Eyrie" how you helped young Robert S. Carr to fame, and imagines you can do likewise with her. I pass it up—I personally would consider it a damned imposition to load you with irrelevant manuscripts—but in this case I can only carry out orders! The tale itself I don't consider at all bad for a novice.

Another thing—Mrs. Reed would be prodigiously grateful if you could tell her the approximate date when her "Curse of Yig" will appear. You might drop a card to her address—4125 Walnut St., Kansas City, Mo.—if the time of publication is decided upon. Within a month—if other work lets me get at it—I may send you a new Reed weird story; a thing with an Oklahoma locale like "Yig", but at present in such poor shape that it will require careful retouching. If I can't get at it soon, I'll let my bright little partner Belknap tackle it with his fresh young wits.[2]

Incidentally—here's a new thing of my own,[3] which I cooked up last month by ruthlessly neglecting all the piled-up work before me. It embodies some of the rural atmosphere which I picked up during my summer wanderings, and the two people who have seen it (Belknap and Bernard Dwyer) speak so favourably of it that I've decided to let you have a look at it. I can't resist enclosing Sonny's card of criticism—though I must not be thought of as endorsing the child's ecstatic opinion. I hope the *length* won't repel you. Lately my ideal of fiction has shifted toward the longish short tale, in which there is opportunity for cumulative incident and gradually thickening atmospheric clouds. I suppose you'd call this a "novelette" in modern magazine language. Don't feel any undue hurry about reading it, and don't hesitate to shoot it back if it doesn't look right for *Weird Tales*.

Trusting that the submission of this Reed tale does not form a wholly unwarranted encroachment, (you can return it to the author unread if you like, of course)

I remain

      Yr most oblig'd obt Servt

        H. P. L.

Notes

1. I.e., Zealia Brown Reed Bishop. See Glossary of Names. The ms. HPL submitted was presumably one Bishop wrote on her own without HPL's assistance. It was presumably rejected.
2. It is unclear what story HPL is referring to. The next story HPL revised for Bishop, "The Mound," was not begun until Dec. 1929.
3. "The Dunwich Horror."

[8]   [AHT]

10 Barnes St.,

Providence, R.I.,

Nov. 8, 1928

My dear Wright:—

I hate to bother you, but I thought I'd ask what you think of the enclosed—which came in the envelope you have just forwarded to me.[1] I don't believe I would ever be likely to achieve a more profitable re-sale of "Cthulhu", so would be inclined to accept Mr. Harré's offer but for the fact that I recall your mentioning "Cthulhu" as one of the things you might like to reprint yourself some time in a collection of my stuff. Of course, that plan may have long been abandoned—but I thought I ought to ask you nevertheless before disposing of "Cthulhu" otherwise. If you *do* want it eventually, I think I'll suggest to Harré that he use my "Colour out of Space"—which, by the way, got a three-star or Roll of Honour classification in O'Brien's annual *Transcript* article last month.

I'm rather interested in the idea of a new anthology, and hope that some of my popularly unknown favourites will be included. In answering Mr. Harré I am suggesting that he use Shiel's "House of Sounds" and Robert W. Chambers' "Yellow Sign" and "Harbour-Master".[2]

Haven't had time to read the last two *Weird Tales*, but am glad to note a respite from Senf covers. In the Nov. issue I did read Hamilton's "Polar Doom" and thought it splendid in conception.[3]

With best wishes, and hoping to hear soon about "Cthulhu", I remain

Yr most oblig'd and obt

H. P. L.

Notes

1. HPL refers to T. Everett Harré's request to reprint "The Call of Cthulhu" in his anthology *Beware After Dark!* (1929).
2. Harré did not reprint Shiel's "The House of Sounds" but did reprint "Huguenin's Wife." No story by Chambers was included in the book.
3. Edmond Hamilton, "The Polar Doom" (*WT*, Nov. 1928).

[9]   [AHT]

Feb. 15, 1929

My dear Wright:—

I am indeed interested to hear of the proposed action regarding "Not at Night", and certainly hope the matter can be properly straightened out.[1] It seems rather a tangle—I never heard of this Jeffries before; but was told last September by the agent Lovell that a certain Hutchinson and Co. had bought the edition of the book containing "Red Hook", and that I would receive from them such royalties as would have been due me from the late lamented Selwyn and Blount. At that time nothing was said of any other sale of rights, British or American. I fancied that Macy-Masius might have later bought the rights from Hutchinson—and bought the rights to the earlier books from the receiver of the deceased corporation—but in any case it seemed to me that something was due the various authors represented.

As to including me on the list of plaintiffs—I suppose it's all right so long as there is positively no obligation for expense on my part in case of defeat. My financial stress is such that I am absolutely unable to incur any possible outgo or assessment beyond the barest necessities; so that, unsportsmanlike though it may seem, I cannot afford to gamble on any but a "sure thing"—sure, that is, not to involve loss. If, however, the guarantee of non-assessment on your part is to be taken literally as covering all possible expenses both principal and incidental, I suppose it would be foolish not to stand behind the action and reap whatever royalties might be due me in case of victory. I certainly need all such things that human ingenuity can collect!

Therefore—it being understood that I am in no position to share in the burthens of defeat—you may act for me if you wish; though I doubt if my profits will amount to very much in case of victory. I will pass on your letter to Little Belknap, and fancy he will extend similar authorisation.

I read the March *Weird Tales* the other day, and think it is the best issue in several months.[2] Of the new material Belknap's "Tindalos" and your British cousin's "Rat" seem to me to divide first honours, with second honours shared by "The Immortal Hand" (good idea, but with mediocre development) and "The Sea of

Horror". (splendid atmosphere and promise until it falls into the familiar Hamilton formula). Third I would place Whitehead's "People of Pan"—pretty fair, but not up to its author's usual standard. The popular-magazine formula is apparently threatening to "get" Whitehead as it "got" Quinn long ago. Speaking of Quinn—"The Phantom Farmhouse", which I well recall from 1923, is really the *lucida* of the issue. It almost makes one weep to see this fine tale and realise what the author *can* do, and then to turn and behold that endless stream of artificial rabble-catering hokum featuring the trick mechanical dolls De Grandin and "Friend Trowbridge"! *Sic transit gloria Quinni!*

With best wishes both literary and litigational, I am, Sir,

Ever yr most oblig'd obt Servt

H. P. L.

Notes

1. Herbert Asbury edited an anthology, *Not at Night!* (New York: Macy-Macius/The Vanguard Press, Nov. 1928), that included "The Horror at Red Hook." The book was assembled from various anthologies assembled by Christine Campbell Thomson and was later withdrawn by the publisher.

2. HPL refers to the following stories in *WT*, March 1929: Frank Belknap Long, "The Hounds of Tindalos"; S. Fowler Wright, "The Rat"; Arlton Eadie, "The Immortal Band"; Edmond Hamilton, "The Sea Horror"; Henry S. Whitehead, "The People of Pan"; Seabury Quinn, "The Phantom Farmhouse" (rpt. from the Oct. 1923 issue).

[10]   [AHT]

Saturday
[January? 1930]

My dear Wright:—

Well—here are your 10 hand-picked Fungi—and may they adorn with appropriate morbidity the unhallowed gardens which bloom betwixt your covers! Trust I've copied them correctly, and hope the typothetae Corneliarum will do likewise.[1]

Shall be interested to know what you think of "The Mound" when you get around to it.[2] You will learn therein—back to a certain point—where Klarkash-Ton's nighted *Tsathoggua* came from. Possibly later documents will trace Its history still farther back in-

to the hellish mists of elder entity, and across the unthinkable
voids whence It first came. It is incredibly palaeo-ouranian—even
Cthulhu and Yog-Sothoth are parvenus in comparison. In the
Necronomicon Abdul Alhazred could do little more than hint of it
under another name— ٮ ٮٮٮ in the original Arabic, (Al Azif)
and Θασσογος[3] in the Greek translation (A.D. 950) (TO NE-
KRONOMIKON) of the Byzantine monk Theodorus Philetas of
Constantinople.

Last week I went over my whole file of *Weird Tales* in an effort to check up a list of best stories prepared by young Derleth,
and came to the conclusion that, of everything published since the
first number, the following items have the greatest amount of truly cosmic horror and macabre convincingness. I don't know
whether Derleth will agree with me or not, but these are all on his
vastly longer list of superior tales. They are:

"Beyond the Door"	—	Paul Suter
"The Floor Above"	—	M. Humphreys
"The Night Wire"	—	H. F. Arnold
"The Canal"	—	Everil Worrell
"Bells of Oceana"	—	Arthur J. Burks
"In Amundsen's Tent"	—	John Martin Leahy.

I'd include Belknap's "Black Druid" if it were published—the
Child has improved steadily since the "Death Waters" period
when the impress of the artificial Kipling convention was on him.[4]
The authors producing the best and most consistent average of
high-grade material (not necessarily the most poignant in sheer
horror) are Henry S. Whitehead, Arthur J. Burks, E. Hoffmann
Price, Belknap, Munn, Frank Owen, and Clark Ashton Smith.
Quinn probably *could* make the grade if he (a) wouldn't try to
write so much, and (b) would write seriously for persons of adult
mental age (as in "The Phantom Farmhouse") instead of frankly
catering to the microcephalic rabble. Hamilton has great stuff in
him, but like Quinn has become the slave of the herd and of his
one recurrent plot formula. Robert E. Howard is on the up-grade.
If he will avoid popular catering, he will turn out important stuff
in future. Little Derleth, too, is growing—though his most marked
improvement is in his non-weird work . . . . reminiscent stuff in

the Proust vein. Klarkash-Ton's future prose work will be worth watching, and Wandrei is always splendid when he writes at all.

But pardon the rambling.

Best wishes—

Yr most obt Servt

H. P. L.

Notes

1. B. Cornelius was the creditor and printer of *Weird Tales*. The 10 poems were numbered 1 through 10 to show they were part of a series, but the numbers (and sequence) are not that of the long poem.

2. FW rejected "The Mound." It was not published until after HPL's death.

3. HPL is attempting to render "Tsathoggua" in a putative Greek version (Thassogos).

4. J. Paul Suter, "Beyond the Door" (Apr. 1923; rpt. Sept. 1930); M. L. Humphreys, "The Floor Above" (May 1923; rpt. June 1933); H. F. Arnold, "The Night Wire" (Sept. 1926; rpt. Jan. 1933); Everil Worrell, "The Canal" (Dec. 1927; rpt. Apr. 1935); Arthur J. Burks, "Bells of Oceana" (Dec. 1927; rpt. Apr. 1934); John Martin Leahy, "In Amundsen's Tent" (Jan. 1928; rpt. Aug. 1935); Frank Belknap Long, "The Black Druid" (July 1930) and "Death Waters" (Dec. 1924; rpt. Sept. 1933).

[11]   [AHT]

Feby. 18, 1932

Dear Mr. Wright:—

I'll tell Swanson that tales prior to "The Moon-Bog" are unavailable for magazine publication.[1] The commercial tangles connected with literature, near-literature, and not-so-near literature are certainly annoying enough—but I hope that the new magazine will not prove an injurious competitor to *Weird Tales*. If reprints prove to be really in demand, you could buy up the best items yourself and get ahead of other media—though perhaps, after all, only the newer readers would forego fresh material in favour of something which had appeared before. It is very possible that the new venture will not survive in a field so overcrowded. If it does, it will probably be due less to its reprints than to its admission of material which the established magazines reject because of purely conventional standards of length, style, mood, and subject-matter‡. The feeble newcomer unable to pay much to authors *has* to "take a chance"—and in so doing often prints not only some notably bad things, but many notably original and un-hackneyed things of which the vested interests are rather afraid.

Sorry to say I haven't anything new which you would be likely to care for. Latterly my tastes have run to studies in geographical atmosphere requiring greater length than the popular editorial fancy relishes—my new "Shadow over Innsmouth" is three typed pages longer than "Whisperer in Darkness", and conventional mag-azine standards would undoubtedly rate it "intolerably slow", "not conveniently divisible", or something of that sort.[2] For the present I don't think I'll submit any new material anywhere, for the con-stant pressure of arbitrary requirements—plus the psychological effect of repeated rejections—leaves me absolutely tongue-tied so far as creation goes. I think I shall write with only my own tastes—and those of disinterested critics—in mind for a consider-able period in the future; once more accumulating a stack of un-published material as I did before 1923. Later, perhaps, there will be some opportunity for placing the accumulation. But of course—if by chance I turn out anything short and apparently conventional I may try my luck with it now and then; and if I do, I shall certainly send it to *Weird Tales* first of all.

With best wishes—
     Yrs most sincerely—
         H. P. L.

Notes

1. Carl Swanson was attempting to establish a magazine, *Galaxy*, consist-ing in part of reprints from *WT*.
2. HPL is making a sarcastic reference to the reasons given by FW for his rejection of HPL's *At the Mountains of Madness* in the summer of 1931. HPL never submitted "The Shadow over Innsmouth" to FW, but August

‡The new *Strange Tales* illustrates the recent trend. Nothing but flat, juvenile nonsense aside from the Whitehead, deRezske, and Barker tales. The Clayton policy absolutely excludes anything original or sincere in the way of mood, at-mosphere, or development. [Note: HPL refers to stories in the March 1932 issue of *Strange Tales of Mystery and Terror*, published by Clayton Magazines, Inc.: Henry S. Whitehead, "The Trap" (revised by HPL); Eugene de Rezske, "The Veil of Tanit"; S. Omar Barker, "Back Before the Moon."]

Derleth did so on two occasions without HPL's knowledge; the story was rejected both times.

[12]   [AHT]

                                   10 Barnes St.,
                                   Providence, R.I.,
                                   Jan. 6, 1933

Dear Mr. Wright:—

                    Yours of 28th ult. awaited me when I returned from a holiday visit to young Belknap in N.Y. I also saw Wandrei, who is making good progress on a non-weird psychological novel.[1] Derleth wrote of his pleasant dinner with you in Chicago—too bad your cold prevented more frequent contacts.

Whitehead's passing has caused more universal regret among the group than any other event of recent years. He was almost undoubtedly the most well-rounded character contributing to the pulp magazines, and it will be long before work of the Canevin calibre can be found again. I am glad that he furnished you with biographical data by which later notices can be checked. In my own rambling account I forgot to mention that H. S. W. was a *liturgiologist* of note—performing valuable services in many churches through artistic arrangements of the rituals and sacerdotal pageantry. No doubt his own notes mentioned this point. I read "The Chadbourne Episode"[2] with extreme interest, and wish you could get hold of the other two Chadbourne stories which are in existence. One was accepted by the Clayton outfit and returned when *Strange* and *Astounding* collapsed, while the other seems not to have been submitted anywhere. Whitehead also had another story under way—his old tale "The Bruise", with a new ending (suggested and mapped out by myself) involving the fabulous lost continent of Mu 20,000 years ago; but whether this was ever put in final publishable shape I don't know. Another unpublished Whitehead manuscript—"White Wool of Lambs"—is in the possession of Bernard Austin Dwyer, Box 43, West Shokan, N.Y. This is not really a weird tale, but a delicate phantasy of rather religious cast about a Chicago gangster in a castle in his hereditary Italy. I suppose Whitehead's father will appoint some sort of literary executor to go over his papers and do what is possible toward placing unpublished manuscripts—at least, he ought to. Many tales like "Henri Menjou", hitherto rejected, certainly deserve printing.[3]

Glad to hear that a memorial notice will appear in the March "Eyrie". Readers tell me that the current issue is above the average. I've been buying the magazine right along, but have been so driven to the wall with work that I've not had time to look at any pulp magazine since September.

With every good wish for 1933—

Yrs most cordally and sincerely,

H. P. L.

Notes

1. *Invisible Sun.*
2. *WT*, Feb. 1933.
3. "The Bruise" was posthumously published in *West India Lights* (1946). "White Wool of Lambs" and "Henri Menjou" are unpublished and may not survive.

[13]   [AHT]

Tenbarnes—
Feb. 8, 1933

Dear Wright:—

I have just had a letter from Harry Bates—late editor of the defunct *Strange* and *Astounding*, and now in Clearwater, Fla., writing a play—which sheds much light on the details of good old Canevin's passing. Clearwater lies between Dunedin and St. Petersburg, and Bates has been in touch with Whitehead's father and friends. On account of your interest in H. S., and your long connexion with him, I fancy you will be eager to hear the melancholy particulars.

It seems that during the autumn of 1932 H. S.'s cousin from the north was replaced by the bright little "cracker" boy C. J. Fletcher (whom he had had before—in 1930) as secretary and general factotum. On the Sunday before his death—Nov. 20—he complained of what he termed a "general malaise"—*not* connected with his long-afflicted stomach. His friend Miss M. I. Starr (a middle-aged lady who, during my 1931 visit, lent him the use of her car) was rather worried, and told young Fletcher to watch him carefully and telephone her if anything alarming developed. Late that night the boy heard a thud—as of someone falling—in Whitehead's room, and found H. S. in a queer and disturbing condition—partly deprived of speech. He telephoned Miss Starr, and she went over—finding H. S. semi-conscious. She then telephoned Dr. Mease (prop. of the Dunedin Sanitorium, and H. S.'s regular physician), who came at once and sent for two other doctors. They diagnosed the case as concussion of the brain caused by a fall. Before morning old Mr. Whitehead was notified and rushed up from St. Petersburg. H. S. was still semi-conscious, recognised his father, raised an arm, smiled, and said "My daddy." Those were his last words. From then until the end he doctors kept himn under opiates. Fleter, Dr. Mease, Miss Starr, Mr. Whitehead, and others were on hand and awake most of the time. Death came early and imperceptibly on the morning of Wednesday the 23d. It is clear that H. S. never had a chance to read my reply to his last letter.

H. S. was feeling *unusually well* until Sunday, Nov. 20, hence I doubt if the old gastric trouble was really the *direct* cause of death. To me it looks like a malignly tragic *accident*—the fall in the night; which, though doubtless caused by the general weakness resulting from the old trouble, might easily have not occurred. It seems that shortly before his death H. S. had had all his books and household effects shipped down from the north, where for years they had been in storage. He had also just finished a new sun porch on the roof of his new home in Pasadena Drive. It is tragic that he could not have lived to enjoy these things.

Old Mr. Whitehead (now eighty-five), Bates says, is visibly failing under the shock—although he carries on with outward cheerfulness—the hereditary Canevin stamina. He is quite deaf, and of late his eyes have been developing cataracts. H. S.'s body has been placed temporarily in a St. Petersburg mausoleum, and Mr. Whitehead plans to unite all the family dust by having Mrs. Whitehead's remains brought south and arranging for three graves (including his own) side by side in St. Petersburg cemetery—father, mother, and only child. Thus good old Canevin will rest under the semi-tropical sky he loved so well, and beside the parents to whom he was so warmly and undeviatingly devoted.

With best wishes—
        Yrs most sincerely,
                H. P. L.

[14]   [AHT]

                        10 Barnes St.,
                            Providence, R.I.,
                                Feb. 16, 1933

Dear Wright:—

        Yours of the 13th arrived just after I had
dropped you a card in reply to your earlier note. So little Augie
has been shewing Grandpa's stories, eh? Quite a boy![1]

    Yes—if you want to use the "Witch House", go ahead. Surely
$140 is as much as can be expected in these times. As for radio
dramatisation rights—I really think an author ought to be able to
have at least a censorship of anything which goes out under his
name—for what a popular dialogue-arranger could do to the atmosphere and artistic integrity of a seriously written story is ap-
palling to contemplate! Indeed, it is not likely that *any* really
finely wrought weird story—where so much depends on mood,
and on nuances of description—could be changed to a drama
without irreparable cheapening and the loss of all that gave it
power. Of course, weird drama *can* be written—when the author
starts out *from the first* to utilise the dramatic form. Dunsany's
"Gods of the Mountain" and "Night at an Inn" are typical specimens. But when a thing is written *as a story*, it will fare best by
staying that way. What the public consider "weirdness" in drama is
rather pitiful or absurd—according to one's perspective. As a
thorough soporific I recommend the average popularly "horrible"
play or cinema or radio dialogue. They are all the same—flat,
hackneyed, synthetic, essentially atmosphereless jumbles of conventional shrieks and mutterings and superficial, mechanical situa-
tions. "The Bat" made me drowse back in the early 1920's—and
last year an alleged "Frankenstein" on the screen *would* have made
me drowse had not a posthumous sympathy for poor Mrs. Shelley
made me see red instead. Ugh! And the screen "Dracula" in 1931—
I saw the beginning of that in Miami, Fla.—but couldn't bear to

watch it drag to its full term of dreariness, hence walked out into the fragrant tropic moonlight![2]

Of course, as you say, the dramatisation of my "Witch House" is very unlikely; but on the whole, if it's all the same to you, I wouldn't mind seeing it protected against the dialoguer's unconscious caricaturing. You may recall that I wouldn't contribute to *Strange Tales* because Bates couldn't guarantee me immunity from the copy-slasher's shears and blue pencil.

So I fancy that, on general principles, it would be simplest to sell First N. A. serial rights only. I hope that doesn't sound too fussy—but when I reflect on how much the force of any carefully written story depends on atmospheric effects peculiar to the *original wording*, I really feel that demands for integrity of form are justified . . . even in instances of second presentation.

Price is getting me to attempt collaboration on a sequel to "The Silver Key", involving some of his dimensional theories. If I can't work up the proper synthesis, I may turn the job over to Klarkash-Ton.

Best wishes—
        Yrs most cordially,
                H. P. L.

Notes

1. August Derleth had submitted "The Dreams in the Witch House" to FW without HPL's knowledge.
2. *The Bat* (United Artists, 1926) directed and produced by Roland West; staring George Beranger, Charles Herzinger, and Louise Fazenda; *Frankenstein* (Universal, 1931), directed by James Whale, produced by Carl Laemmle, Jr.; starring Colin Clive, Mae Clarke, John Boles, and Boris Karloff; *Dracula* (Universal, 1931) directed by Tod Browning and Karl Freund; starring Bela Lugosi, Edward Van Sloan, Helen Chandler, and David Manners.

[15]   [AHT]

                        66 College St.,
                        Providence, R.I.,
                                June 18, 1933

Dear Mr. Wright:—
                Thanks for the sheets—I wish I had asked for proofs, since there are at least six slips in the text; three occurring

in the manuscript (which I ought to have gone over more thoroughly) and the balance made by the printer.[1]

ERRATA

(a)—p. 92, co. 1.—l. 11:—for *love* read *lore* (printer's error)

(b)—p. 93, co. 1.—l. 11:—for *the doctor's* read *a doctor's* (error in manuscript)

(c)—p. 93, co. 2.—l. 39:—for *his* read *its* (error in manuscript)

(d)—p. 100, co. 2.—l. 41:—for *Desrocher's* read *Desrochers'* (printer's error)

(e)—p. 101, co. 2.—l. 25:—for *human element* read *known element* (printer's error)

(f)—p. 102, co. 2.—l. 35:—for *hearty-sleeping* read *heavily-sleeping* (error in manuscript)

The worst two are (a) and (e), which make the text sound like vapid nonsense. The most damnable kind of a misprint is that which does not *look* like an error, but gives a false appearance of sense—though really misrepresenting the author's intention and sometimes making him appear responsible for unutterable vapidities. A slip like that in Klarkash-Ton's "Ubbo-Sathla"[2] (*palaegean* for *palaeogean*) hurts nobody, for it is *obviously* a mistake of the printer. But where an allusion to *magical lore* becomes, seemingly a coherent yet inanely meaningless allusion to *magical "love"*—or where the expression *known* (*chemical*) *element* seems to be the coherent but out-of-place phrase *"human" element*—the author is unjustly laid open to the suspicion of rambling feebleness and semi-illiteracy. I wish there were a way of getting these two errata indicated on the cards to be sent friends.

As for a list of names—I recall your similar experiment in 1925, when my "Erich Zann" was thus heralded. Enclosed is a list based upon the principle then followed—a membership roll of the amateur press association, with likely names marked, plus a number of additional names. I hope that this measure may prove effective in increasing the sale of the magazine—it ought to work in the case of some authors, even if not in this one.

I shall certainly send along any tales of mine which may seem to suit your ideas of length and content. Recently I have had no time for original composition, though I did perform one piece of collabo-

ration with our brilliant friend Malik Taus, the Peacock Sultan—
the results of which he will probably forward for your editorial attention before many weeks have flown. Incidentally, I hope you
will take Little Belknap's latest venture—which he calls "The Dark
Beasts", but for which I'd prefer a subtler title such as "When They
Came".[3] This thing has a brooding atmosphere of ineffable potency,
and seems to me to mark a "comeback" on Sonny's part to his very
best form. My own opinion is that seriously written stories are not
as badly resented by the illiterate contingent as is commonly supposed, and I wish that more of them could appear in magazines like
Weird Tales. These specialised magazines—since there are no publications of a parallel nature on a more fastidious literary level—
undoubtedly have a larger percentage of cultivated readers than
most observers suspect; though because of the dislike of such readers for cheap publicity, they do not write in to the "Eyrie" as the
more mediocre and inferior readers do. Thus, I maintain, readers'
letters are not always a perfect guide to a magazine's reception. If a
larger proportion of seriously written material were presented, it
would probably attract a very fair-sized fringe of readers who
would not otherwise buy the magazine—yet would not be likely to
alienate the cheap and vociferous element which thrives on conventional Hamiltonian formulae and Klinesque mechanical puppet-
tableaux. Whilst a high-grade reader can *never* stand this latter junk,
the converse is by no means true—as witness the obviously ignorant multitudes who do manage to appreciate Poe somehow, and
who like good writers of Klarkash-Ton's type even though they
don't know why. If I were editing *Weird Tales*, I'd accept virtually
all of the Klarkash-Ton items which meet disfavour because of
their allegedly too-poetic quality . . . . which reminds me, I suppose
C. A. S. has sent you a copy of the brochure printed for him by the
Auburn Journal.[4] To my mind this is a collection of extraordinary
merit—and I have an idea that its sale may belie many popular no-
tions about the unmarketability of poetic phantasy. I have offered
to enclose circulars of it to all my correspondents. It is certainly a
marvellous value for a quarter—despite the crowded format and
the typically careless typography of the *Journal's* job press. I think
C. A. S. means to advertise it in *Weird Tales*.

I have been glad to see in *Weird Tales* lately a good many

items with real atmospheric value. Howard's tales of elder worlds are growing rapidly in stature, and now and then—as in "The Scarlet Citadel" and "The Tower of the Elephant"—reach a level of really tremendous power. Jacobi's "Revelations in Black" is another high spot, and Hugh B. Cave (despite a professedly hard-boiled hack attitude) did marvellously well in "Dead Man's Belt". "The Ice-Demon" and "Genius Loci" are among Klarkash-Ton's most distinctive work. And of course I was glad to see my old favourite, "The Floor Above", again.[5]

Before I forget it—Walter J. Coates, North Montpelier, Vt., wants to know how much a small advertisement in *Weird Tales* would be. He has taken over the loose sheets of my "Shunned House" booklet—printed by W. Paul Cook five years ago—and proposes to bind and attempt to market the edition, aided in part by his editorship of *Driftwind* and his proprietorship of the semi-amateur *Driftwind Press*. If not too expensive, he would like to reach your readers.

I see you have my new address—the result of a financial pressure which made it necessary for my surviving aunt and myself to combine households in as cheap a haven as possible.[6] Oddly—and indeed quite ironically—the move has the *externals* of a rise rather than a fall in the world; since an extraordinary opportunity put us in touch with a flat in the university district which, though having a minimum rent, involves no sacrifice of either comfort or quality of neighbourhood. For me in particular there is an added advantage which outweighs all the rest—namely, the fact that the house is one of those archaic reliques of other days which have fascinated me all my life, but which I have never till now inhabited. Not that it quite parallels the "Witch-House"—but it is a Georgian edifice built about 1800, of a type abundant on Providence's ancient and fascinating central precipice. Yellow and wooden, it lies on the crest of the great hill in a quaint grassy court just off College St.—behind and next to the marble John Hay Library of Brown University, and about half a mile south of 10 Barnes st. The fine colonial doorway is like my bookplate (done by Talman—I think I sent you a copy in 1929) come to life, though of course of a slightly later period. On the western side, and at a higher level behind, is a picturesque, village-like garden;

while in front is a hedge, a row of old-fashioned posts, and a flow-er-bed or two. We plan to train up the facade a slip of ivy from the Washington plantation at Mt. Vernon. The upper flat we have taken has five rooms besides kitchenette nook and bath on the main (2nd) floor, plus two attic storerooms—one of which is so attractive that I wish I could have it for an extra den! My quar-ters—a large study and small bedroom—are on the south side, with my working desk under a west window affording a splendid view of the lower town's outspread roofs and of the mystical sun-sets that flame behind them. The interior is as fascinating as the exterior—with colonial fireplaces, mantels, and chimney-cupboards, curving Georgian staircase, wide floor-boards, old-fashioned latches, small-paned windows, six-panel doors, rear wing with floor at a different level (three steps down), quaint at-tic stairs, etc.—just like the old houses open as museums. After admiring such all my life, I find something magical and dreamlike in the experience of actually *living in one*—in coming *home* through a carved Georgian doorway and sitting beside a white co-lonial mantel gazing out through small-paned windows over a sea of ancient roofs and sun-golden foliage. The old family furniture fits the place well—and many things unseen for decades (through lack of space) have emerged from storage to give it an odd air of similarity (in miniature) to the original home broken up in 1904. Enhancing the atmosphere of quaintness is the veritable symphony of chimes which proceeds every hour from the numerous old belfries that surround the place—a retinue including the famous First Baptist (1775) and Unitarian (1816) steeples, as well as the vast clock tower on the college campus. Yet the practical side is not neglected—for steam heat and hot water are piped in from the adjacent John Hay Library; the house being owned by the university. Rent is no more than what I've been paying for my one room and alcove alone—but now the problem is how to meet even this halved obligation! But I hope I can hang on here as long as possible. Just now all is chaos because of my aunt's departure for the hospital with a broken ankle—the result of a hasty step on the stairs while answering the doorbell. Clearly, it will be a long time before the new household can boast of complete and tran-quil settledness! Still—under any old conditions it is an inspiration

to be in an ancient house of the sort around which my dreams
have always revolved.

   With every good wish, and thanking you again for the advance
sheets, I remain

              Yr most oblig'd, most obt Servt
              H. P. L.

Notes

1. The corrections are to "The Dreams in the Witch House." None was
made.

2. *WT*, July 1933.

3. The story was evidently rejected by *WT*. It appeared in *Marvel Tales*
(July–Aug. 1934).

4. Smith, Clark Ashton (1893–1961). *The Double Shadow and Other Fantasies*. Auburn, CA: Auburn Journal Press, 1933. (*LL* 810)

5. Robert E. Howard, "The Scarlet Citadel" (Jan. 1933) and "The Tower
of the Elephant" (Mar. 1933); Carl Jacobi, "Revelations in Black" (Apr.
1933); Hugh B. Cave, "Dead Man's Belt" (May 1933); Clark Ashton
Smith, "The Ice-Demon" (Apr. 1933) and "Genius Loci" (June 1933);
M. L. Humphreys, "The Floor Above" (May 1923; rpt. June 1933).

6. HPL and his aunt Annie E. P. Gamwell moved into 66 College St. on
15 May 1933.

[16]   [AHT]

                              66 College St.,
                                   Providence, R.I.,
                                        Nov. 14, 1933

Dear Wright:—

              Yrs duly received—and I sent the "Silver Key"
sequel back under separate cover yesterday.[1] Sultan Malik possibly
overstates the matter in assigning me almost full authorship of the
thing. The *language* is mine, but the whole system of mathematical concepts in the central portion is his. That kind of background
is quite alien to me—indeed, while the Peacock Sultan is primarily *intellectual* in his methods and appeal, I am basically non-
intellectual or even anti-intellectual. *My* attempts represent a
striving for emotional emancipation from rigidities and certain-
ties—a reaching toward vague suggestions of liberation and adven-
turous expectancy on far horizons, and a struggle to crystallise

certain moods too ethereal and indefinite for description. The original "Silver Key" is characteristically mine (although it has naive aspects which I would not duplicate today), but the present sequel is something I would never have thought of creating alone. Therefore don't be misled by M. de Marigny's modesty into fancying that the dual authorship is merely nominal!

You have certainly been fortunate in obtaining first-hand views of contributors this year. The Peacock Sultan dropped me a card during his Chicago sojourn, and seemed to be enjoying the conference most acutely. I enjoyed his visit here—last July— tremendously, and hope that Old Juggernaut will hold together long enough to bring him this way again in 1934.

My own programme was paralysed by the accident to my aunt—which kept me very closely chained around home. My one real vacation was a trip to Quebec in early September—a glorious affair which gave me four hot, sunny days in the ancient fortalice of the north. No other town in North America can rival Quebec in sheer beauty—and only Charleston can match its atmospheric glamour and sense of accumulated ages. My aunt is now much better—all around and out with a cane—though my liberation comes too late in the season to permit of much travelling. I did, though, improve the mild days of October by taking many long walks in ancient and unfrequented parts of the countryside, where the autumnal scenery appeared to fullest advantage. Hibernating time is near now, but in my present venerable abode an indoor regime has its compensations. My desk faces a sunset vista of the utmost charm and imaginative appeal—ancient roofs and boughs in the foreground, old church towers and a Georgian belfry in the middle distance, and beyond them all a strip of far-off violet horizon with a mystical hilltop steeple silhouetted faintly against the west. It's really almost enough to keep one's mind off one's work!

Well—the fate of the S. K. is in your hands.

> Best wishes—
>> Yrs most cordially and sincerely—
>>> H. P. L.

P.S. In recent *Weird Tales* I note some elements of promise in at least two new authors—Mearle Prout, with "The House of the

Worm", and C. L. Moore, with "Shambleau".[2] Both tales have im-
maturities and inadequacies, but they seem to indicate an originality with great possibilities unless the respective authors get
sidetracked amongst commercial formulae.

Notes

1. HPL had submitted the story c. July 1933 and it was rejected. See
Farnsworth Wright to HPL, 17 Aug. 1933 (ms., JHL):

> I have carefully read THROUGH THE GATES OF THE SILVER
> KEY and am almost overwhelmed by the colossal scope of the story.
> It is cyclopean in its daring and titanic in its execution. . . .
>
> But I am afraid to offer it to our readers. Many there would be
> . . . who would go into raptures of esthetic delight while reading the
> story; just as certainly there would be a great many—probably a
> clear majority—of our readers who would be unable to wade
> through it. These would find the descriptions and discussions of
> polydimensional space poison to their enjoyment of the tale. The
> story is so much more than a piece of fiction, and so far transcends
> not only the experiences of the readers, but even their wildest
> dreams, that they would have no point of contact with the ideas and
> thoughts presented in this opus. [. . .]
>
> It may seem strange that I reject a story which arouses my ad-
> miration as much as THROUGH THE GATES OF THE SILVER
> KEY; but with business as poor as it is now, I feel that we cannot
> risk discouraging so many readers from buying the magazine, merely
> by printing a story that is so utterly alien to even their wildest
> dreams and reveries that they are incapable of comprehending it—
> let alone appreciating it.
>
> I assure you that never have I turned down a story with more
> regret than in this case.

2. Mearle Prout, "The House of the Worm" (Oct. 1933); C. L. Moore,
"Shambleau" (Nov. 1933). The Prout story was influenced by HPL and
even uses phrases from HPL's stories.

[17]   [AHT]

> 66 College St.,
> Providence, R.I.,
> Nov. 21, 1933

My dear Wright:—

　　　　　　　I am indeed glad that the collaboration has finally proved acceptable, and hope that no epistolary alarms of out-

raged illiterati may cause you to regret the decision. For my part, as I have often said, I think that a restriction of contributions to the sort of thing the densest clods like would alienate nearly as many readers as an all-literate policy would. I know surely a dozen or more followers of the magazine who would certainly not continue to follow it if its contents uniformly represented the lifeless, mechanical, stock-figure, diagrammed type of hackwork so dearly beloved by the "Eyrie"-bombarding proletariate—and that dozen can scarcely be altogether unrepresentative. The trouble is, that the readers who do the most letter-writing—in an eagerness to publicise themselves—tend to reflect a stratum of taste distinctly lower than that of the best (and by no means negligible) part of the magazine's clientele. There seems to me little doubt but that Weird Tales is bought and read by large numbers of persons infinitely above the pulp-hound level—persons who relish Machen and Blackwood and M. R. James, and who would welcome a periodical of the Machen–Blackwood–James degree of maturity and fastidiousness if such were published. Naturally, they tolerate the hack stuff merely for the sake of the occasional real stories—Clericashtonia, Howardiana, Caneviniana, etc.—which accompany it, and would certainly drop off if not assured of at least a fair supply.

I can well imagine the regret caused by the southward clattering of Old Jug, for Sultan Malik is surely a rare tonic and banisher of ennui and lassitude. Of him it may well be said, in paraphrase of the famous Johnsonese tribute to another refreshing spirit, that *Nullum quod tangit non laetificat!*[1] I don't believe you'd find any other of the living writers as interesting, though good old Canevin was in the same piquant, inexhaustibly brilliant, and intensely vital class. I am, by the way, keenly interested in your description of young Williamson—who seems to me one of the most notably promising of the new writers. His "Wand of Doom" impressed me strongly a year ago as having a certain real originality and atmospheric richness never found in hack work; and on the strength of that I tackled "Golden Blood", though I seldom spend time on serials nowadays.[2] I was not disappointed—for despite a certain quota of conventional accessories the tale reflected the same vitality, freshness, colour, and unaffectedness as its predecessor. It had crude spots—abrupt transitions, scanted emotional values, patently melodramatic combats and

tableaux—but the vitality, imagery, and inexhaustible fertility of
the whole thing made full atonement. If Williamson will keep on in
the same vein, and refuse to make increased concessions to mass
taste, he will certainly be a consistent top-notcher. It is curious that
he has such a misleading shyness in person, but this may wear off
with the years. Judging from his stories, his inarticulateness cannot
be the result of any lack of ideas or imaginative moods! Anent his
dream-world one may only echo the tribute of the Peacock Sultan.
The various social events of the late season seem to have been quite
notable and pleasing. I had pictured Single-Plot Hamilton as decid-
edly brilliant, for his earlier tales (especially "Mamurth")[3] had a remarkably original flavour. It was a distinct loss to literature when he
discovered his facile sales-making formula!

It is odd that "The House of the Worm" did not get an ample
response from the readers—though this only goes to show the su-
perficiality of their judgments. That thing had the malign, brooding
tension and gathering menace which make a real story. Picture succeeded picture, each suggesting just a *little* more of the festering evil
that lurked at the heart of the evil wood; and some of the images
were magnificently powerful and to the point. After the first visit
there was a slight letdown or trace of cumbrousness, but the tension was soon recovered. The climatic tableau was splendid—even
though the existence of the cult was sprung a little abruptly—but
the conclusion would have been more effective without the explanatory epilogue. Altogether, it was a great story; and I'd like to
see more by the same author. It was not finished in technique, but
it had the *substance*. It would have captured my vote in spite of
parallel material by Klarkash-Ton, Sonny Belknap, and Two-Gun
Bob. "Shambleau" is great stuff, too. It begins *magnificently*, on just
the right note of terror, and with black intimations of the unknown.
The subtle evil of the Entity, as suggested by the unexplained horror of the people, is extremely powerful—and the description of
the Thing itself when unmasked is no letdown. Like "The House of
the Worm", it has real atmosphere and tension—rare things amidst
the pulp tradition of brisk, cheerful, staccato prose and lifeless stock
characters and images. The one major fault is the conventional interplanetary setting. That weakens and dilutes the effect both by
introducing a parallel or rival wonder and by removing the episode

from reality. Of course a very remote setting had to be chosen for so unknown a marvel—but some place like India, Africa, or the Amazon jungle might have been used . . . with the horror made more local. I trust your revisions may make Mrs. Moore's second story as striking and interesting as this one. Malik's "Fourth Axis", in the same issue, has a magnificent incantation scene; and "The Accursed Isle" embodies a gnawing terror close to the real thing.[4]

I am surely sorry to hear of your sister's accident, and hope it will not result in any such long siege as my aunt went through. Fortunately an arm is not quite so crucial and pivotal as an ankle.

With every good wish—

Yrs most cordially and sincerely—

H. P. L.

P.S. I am intensely glad to hear that you are letting Klarkash-Ton illustrate his "Weaver in the Vault". For ten years I have wanted to see some of his monstrous pictorial conceptions in the magazine and now comes realisation! I hope his designs may become frequent features. Couldn't you let him try his hand at the "Silver Key" sequel?[5] He could make Yaddith—or the abyss beyond the ultimate gate—stand out with malign and marvellous vividness.

Notes

1. "He cheers everything he touches." An adaptation of a line from Samuel Johnson's Latin epitaph to Oliver Goldsmith at his monument in Westminster Abbey (*Nullum quod tetigit non ornavit* ["He adorned everything he touched"]).
2. Jack Williamson, "The Wand of Doom" (Oct. 1932); "Golden Blood" (6-part serial, Apr.–Sept. 1933).
3. Edmond Hamilton, "The Monster-God of Mamurth" (*WT*, Aug. 1926; rpt. Sept. 1935).
4. E. Hoffmann Price, "Lord of the Fourth Axis"; Mary Elizabeth Counselman, "The Accursed Isle," *WT* (Nov. 1933).
5. Clark Ashton Smith, "The Weaver in the Vault" (Jan. 1934). "Through the Gates of the Silver Key" was illustrated by H. R. Hammond.

[18]   [AHT]

% Barlow,

Box 88,

De Land,Fla.,

May 21, 1934.

Dear Mr. Wright:—

I am interested to hear of your plan to reprint the "Arthur Jermyn" tale—which was always one of my favourites. So far as I can recall, Baird made no inexcusable excisions or conspicuous blunders in the text, although he did stick on an the outrageously naive and give-away title. The original title of this story was "Facts Concerning the Late Arthur Jermyn and His Family", although I have always had the plain "Arthur Jermyn" in reserve as a possible alternative title. In view of the possible awkwardness of the full title in the table of contents, it might be best for you to call the story just "Arthur Jermyn". But certainly, I'd like to avoid the inept Baird-given title if it can possibly be managed.

I have a tattered carbon of this tale somewhere; but it is either going the rounds among various correspondents, or else lost among the piled-up non-letter mail on my desk at home, where my aunt could not possibly pick it out. Accordingly I'd be vastly obliged if you could let me have a copy of some sort to look over. I'll keep you in touch with my various temporary addresses of the near future—Barlow's will be the one until further notice.

I am certainly having a great time down here—with twice the energy I have in the north, and with a complete freedom (as in Dunedin in '31) from my usual sinus trouble. I ought to live here—but with my attachment to New England's antiquities the process of transition would be a hard one. Sorry I couldn't have met Hamilton and Williamson while they were in Florida. I understand that Ray Cummings, also a practitioner of certain forms of the weird, is or was in Ft. Lauderdale—but it's some time since Barlow has been in touch with him. Barlow is a great kid—incipient writer, printer, sculptor, painter, landscape gardener, book and relique collector, and what not! You ought to see the bas-relief of "Cthulhu" which he finished some time ago! He is, however, gravely handicapped by poor eyesight. In the course of time I think he'll be importantly heard from in one way or another. Which reminds me—I hope you can find it convenient to accomodate him in the matter of *Weird Tales* manuscripts and drawings, as mentioned in a recent letter of his.

Have seen some interesting antiquities recently—including the picturesque, vine-clad ruins of a Franciscan mission built in 1696. Hopes of Havana are very dim indeed, but I shall spend a week in St. Augustine and return north by slow stages. I hate to think of facing northern weather again—but what you report of the thermometer is encouraging! I'm staying here longer than I intended, but Barlow and his family are so hospitable that all suggestions for an immediate moving-on have been vetoed.

Hope you haven't been affected by the recent fire—radio reports of which were quite alarming Saturday night.[1] I am completely ignorant of Chicago topography, hence descriptions of the burned area went quite over my head.

With every good wish, and trusting that the correction of "Arthur Jermyn" may be accomplished with a minimum of inconvenience, I remain

Yrs most sincerely,

H. P. L.

Notes

1. The Union Stock Yards Fire of 19 May 1934 was the most destructive blaze since the Great Fire of 1871.

[19]   [*WT*]

[December? 1935]

"The Way Home" is one of the most atmospherically satisfying things I have seen lately, and I was interested to note that the author is Paul Ernst under an anagrammatic alias.[1] I live in hope that the purely weird element may regain its ascendancy, as tales like that would imply. . . . Other good yarns in recent issues of WT are "The Cold Gray God", "The Mystery of the Last Guest", "Shadows in Zamboula", "The Hand of Wrath", and "The Chain of Aforgomon".[2]

Notes

1. HPL refers to a story by Paul Frederick Stern (Nov. 1935).
2. Stories by C. L. Moore (Oct. 1935), John Flanders (Oct. 1935), Robert E. Howard (Nov. 1935), E. Hoffmann Price (Nov. 1935), and Clark Ashton Smith (Dec. 1935).

[20]   [AHT]

> 66 College St.,
> Providence, R.I.,
> July 1, 1936

Dear Wright:—

Young Schwartz has persuaded me to send him a lot of manuscripts for possible placement in Great Britain, and it occurs to me that I'd better exhaust their cisatlantic possibilities before turning them over to him. Accordingly I am going through the formality of obtaining your official rejection of the enclosed—so that I won't feel I've overlooked any theoretical source of badly-needed revenue.[1] In the absence of other American markets for purely weird material, I won't need to try them elsewhere—hence, if you don't mind, you might send them on after rejection to *Julius Schwartz, 255 East 188th St., New York, N.Y.,* instead of returning them to me.

I was greatly shocked about a fortnight ago to receive a card from Miss Moore with the dire news (without details, and allegedly obtained directly from Texas) of the death of Robert E. Howard by his own hand. It sounds incredible to me—for I had a long normal letter from good old Two-Gun Bob written as recently as May 13. He was worried about his mother's health, but otherwise seemed perfectly all right. I am wondering whether there can be any hope of a mistake—either a ghastly hoax, or some strange confusion of names springing from the suicide of another southwestern writer (the young science-fictionist David R. Daniels)[2] slightly earlier in the year? If the news is indeed true, it forms weird fiction's worst blow since the passing of good old Canevin in '32. Scarcely anybody else in the pulp field had quite the driving zest and spontaneity of R. E. H. He put himself into everything he wrote—and even when he made outward concessions to pulp standards he had a wholly unique inner force and sincerity which broke through the surface and placed the stamp of his personality on the ultimate product. How he could surround primal megalithic cities with an aura of aeon-old fear and necromancy! And his recent "Black Canaan" (*Weird Tales*' best story in the last three issues)[3] is likewise magnificent in a more realistic way—reflecting a genuine regional background and giving a clutchingly powerful picture of the horror that stalks through the moss-hung, shadow-cursed, serpent-ridden swamps of the farther south. Others' efforts seem pallid by contrast. I can't understand the tragedy, for although R. E. H. had a moody side expressed in his resentment against civilisation (the basis of our perennial and voluminous epistolary debate), I always thought that this was a more or less *impersonal* sentiment—like Sonny Belknap's rage against the injustices of a capitalistic civilisation. He himself seemed to me pretty well adjusted to his beloved southwestern environment. Well—weird fiction certainly has occasion to mourn, unless the melancholy report turns out to be false. I'm telling Price (the only one of the group who ever met R. E. H. in person) that he ought to prepare an obituary for *Weird Tales*—just as I did of H. S. W. four years ago.[4] (I've written a paragraph or two for the fan magazines.) But alas that there should be occasion for such!

I've had a hell of a year—rotten health, and aunt seriously ill and at hospital—though now recovering well. Programme in chaos.

Apologising for the enclosed perfunctory inflictions—

Yrs most sincerely—

H. P. L.

Notes

1. HPL was submitting "The Thing on the Doorstep" and "The Haunter of the Dark." Both were accepted.
2. David R. Daniels (1915–1936), author of several science fiction tales in *Astounding Stories* and *Wonder Stories*. He died on 17 Apr. 1936.
3. *WT*, June 1936.
4. "In Memoriam: Henry S. Whitehead."

[21]   [AHT]

66 College St.,

Providence, R.I. ,

July 4, 1936

Dear Wright:—

Sorry to bother you again, but a letter from Schwarz makes it necessary for me to do so.

(1). He asked me to get your permission for the British reprinting (book form) of those stories (prior, I believe, to some time in 1926) to which I didn't reserve residual rights. I presume you will have no objection.

(2). He has so large an assortment of my stuff that he will not need more. Hence I'll change my former request and ask that rejected manuscripts be sent back to *me* instead of to *him*.

Incidentally—he claims that material once used in a British anthology is not available for book reprinting in England. Do you think this is so? In all the American book fiascos the publishers have never objected to tales previously appearing in American anthologies, although I have been careful to state the full history of each one.

Another matter—I've been meaning for some time to get another copy of the *March 1934 Weird Tales* if such is still obtainable. I like to keep the file complete, and this issue seems to have been lost by an irresponsible borrower.[1] Enclosed are stamps covering the presumable price. Hope you can supply the magazine—*MARCH, 1934.*

Reports of R. E. H.'s suicide all too conclusively confirmed. I have just had a letter from his father, together with some Cross Plains papers. The act was impelled by grief at his mother's approaching death—indicating that his moody, neurotic side went deeper than we ever suspected. What a blow for poor old Dr. Howard—losing at once his wife and a tremendously gifted only child!

Renewed regrets at bothering you—

    Yrs most sincerely

        H. P.L.

Notes

1. The issue contained "Winged Death," a story that HPL ghostwrote for Hazel Heald.

[22]   [AHT]

        66 College St.,

           Providence, R.I.,

             Dec. 26, 1936

Dear Wright:—

    Thanks endlessly in advance for the two Finlay originals, which will have a place of honour in my files. That second specimen—for "Doorstep"—is a memorable imaginative achievement.[1]

Regarding spelling—to my mind would-be reformers overlook two all-important principles (which in a way are connected) and

thereby lead themselves needlessly into traceless labyrinths of confusion and instability:

(1) *Logic* in orthography is not to be expected save in the va-
guest and most fragmentary degree. Spelling is primarily an arbitrary matter depending upon the association of massed eye-images
with given words. It can be fairly logical only in a very homogene-
ous language of unified tradition, and even there exceptions are
multitudinous. In a strongly heterogeneous language drawing on
three main culture-streams or verbal sources—Anglo-Saxon,
Norman-French, and the Latin and Greek of classical scholarship
(as distinguished from the Latin transmitted through Norman-
French)—even approximate logic is impossible. Every attempt to
give a unified orthographical symbol to similar verbal sounds of
different derivation is likely to violate the etymological traditions
of one or more of the verbal elements involved; and such viola-
tions do more to cut off the vitality of a word—to induce a for-
getfulness of its history and overtones, and to introduce a touch of
uncertainty and deficient authority regarding its visual rendering—
than could any amount of bad logic or inconsistency in the
spelling. In view of the varied history of the words in any living
and naturally evolved language—especially such a heterogeneous
one as ours—no real logic in orthography could ever be obtained
except through the adoption of a sort of radical symbolism or
shorthand so grotesquely unlike anything we know as "spelling"
that even the most traditionless radicals would refuse to stand for
it. As things really work out, a good part of the well-meant attempts to increase logic and consistency in various isolated instances merely create fresh breaches of logic and consistency in
sundry *other* phases of the given problems—and in addition help
to undermine the foundations of orthographical stability and associative word-values. These attempts could form only a meaningless drop in the bucket if successful—and in cold fact they are not
only largely unsuccessful (for no two reformers reform the same
way), but are hurtful in other ways even when fairly successful in
their primary objective. They all lead away from unity and stability, and toward chaos and a permanent state of irresponsible flux.
One may add that *the use of similar-sounding words and roots to
express different meanings* would always constitute a barrier to

perfect linguistic logic even if a bizarre system of absolutely perfect and consistent phonetics were devised. In such a system, the few remaining necessary illogicalities would doubtless be resented even more hotly than are the countless normal illogicalities of our present system—in which no broad student expects or demands logic. Therefore—this alphabet and orthography having been already reduced to a traditionless scheme of unfamiliar symbols looking something like Pitman's shorthand—the faddists would next begin to agitate for a series of changes in the *sound* of certain words . . . . . or more probably, for prefixes, and the substitution of new and synthetic terms in their place. Thus with *missed* and *mist* . . . . perhaps spelled *mj³st* in each case . . . the reformers would insist that the latter term be dropped in favour of a new word such as gak, zib, or thop (spelled ℉ᴄ , Ꝫᵒᵒ, or ⁰ᵐᴘ, or some similar way), or that its place be supplied through synonyms or circumlocution. To such absurd extremes does the quest for phonetic and linguistic logic lead. And the joke is that such logic is *not important enough* to warrant the frightful concomitant destruction. Of course, most reformers do not seek to attain the uttermost limits of logic—and destruction. They merely meddle around the edges of the matter—creating occasional monstrosities in an effort to remedy two or three surface inconsistencies, and wreaking only enough damage to produce a generation of increasingly bad spellers and associationless linguistic drifters.[2] The ancestral speech still lives in spite of their ministrations. But why must they nibble as they do when the whole fabric would be better off if left alone as it naturally crystallised between (say roughly) 1730 and 1830? To recapitulate Principle I—orthographical logic in our language is (a) impossible anyhow, and (b) not worth bothering about even if it *were* possible at a high cultural cost.

(2) The most important thing about spelling is *not* its appeal to the analytical abstract reason, but its appeal to the *eye* as a familiar and association-wreathed pattern or set of natural symbols. The vital thing to be demanded of spelling is that it *satisfy the expectations we have formed* from our normal reading of books printed in all periods, and from our knowledge of the sources—in our own and other languages—which lie behind the words we use. To assume that the daily reading of a generation consists only of the

editions published within its own lifetime is to adopt a curiously rootless and parvenu perspective. Actually, *the usage of the immediate past* cannot be ignored. For all truly literate persons, it exists as a constant, vital, and insistent reality—moulding habits and expectations, and standing out as a norm by which present usages must necessarily be measured. Gradual departures from it will of course occur; but unless they are to cause trouble and disgust they must be *evolutionary and spontaneous* departures—departures in which all the most cultivated users of the language quietly concur without external propaganda—rather than freakish theoretical changes cooked up for change's sake by abstract visionaries. This element of *familiar and traditional eye-appeal* is of course the more important of the two elements under discussion. Historical and etymological associations, while tremendously valuable and worthy of preservation whenever they *can* be preserved, are often lost through *natural* change, and cannot be expected to be omnipresent. What we *can* ask of modern writers is simply that they refrain from meddling artificially with any historical or etymological vestigia which *have* naturally survived. Thus, we for example, must accept the loss of the normal dip[h]thongs in *Ægypt* (although Harpers retained this form in the 1850 edition of "Anthon's Ancient Geography"), *aera*, *oeconomy*, but there is no sense in forcibly ejecting them from *aeon*, *mediaeval*, *aesthetic*, and other words where they naturally survive in the usage of the most cultivated persons and most solid books and periodicals. Let us— without trying to stifle any natural mutation which may seem justified and non-decadent—simply refrain from endorsing propaganda for the artificial disturbance of naturally settled usage. To recapitulate Principle II—the two most important things about spelling are (a) first and foremost, easy familiarity to the eye accustomed to the varied books normally encountered in study and reading in home and public libraries (including imprints from all over the Anglo-Saxon world, and of dates largely involving the nineteenth century), and (b) less vitally but nevertheless far from negligibly, preservation of as many associative elements— historical and etymological—as can naturally be preserved.

These two principles appear to me extremely sound—and indeed almost irrefutable. With their basic essence a clear majority of all with whom I have discussed them (including many who follow the more standardised and natural American provincialisms of Webster et al.) seem to agree. Naturally, different individuals interpret them differently—but those who recognise their general validity are usually as one in spurning the *thrus, esthetics, advertizes,* and *ilands* of the rootless (or else Elizabethanly flexible) extremists. I myself simply follow the majority of the books—printed on both sides of the Atlantic—which shaped my education and which form the bulk of my library today. I can't follow the local flag-waving of the *meter* (for *metre* . . . shades of the gas man!) and *theater* enthusiasts who demand something radically different from the normal usage of our ancestors and relatives in the Mother Land. As well demand that California have a different spelling from Maryland, or that Ohio studiously depart from Massachusetts usage. (In all truth, this *is* the case to some extent, since the better grade of Eastern papers and magazines—to say nothing of books—adhere as always to normal forms like *theatre, centre, programme, traveller, mediaeval,* etc., although they usually drop the u in *labour* etc., and give certain *-ise* terminations the neo-American *-ize*.) Those 250% American critics forget that most of the local departures from the general norm are of relatively recent growth—within the last century at most. That is, their rise to local predominance is as recent as that. American books from the middle eighteenth century to around 1840 are divided in their handling of words like *honour* and *labour,* with the normal *u* forms probably predominating in the better grade of books until after 1830. As one with a fair percentage of pre-1830 books in his library, I can assert this from solid evidence. However—I have no quarrel with *hono'r, favo'r,* and *civilize.* These form a truly spontaneous variant sanctioned by general usage over an enormous area. There is a distinct uniformity in the mutation producing them. I can even endure *travel'er* (ugh!) with only minor nausea. It is the *sulfur, iland, brot, criticize, thru, eon, fetor,* etc. kind of stuff that completely empties my stomach. But even here, of course, I scarcely contemplate starting a crusade. After all, I recognise that the whole subject of spelling is a comparatively minor matter, and that in the greatest age of our literature—that of Elizabeth—it was in as bad a state of chaos and multiple usage as it is now in theory-ridden America. I can take it—or most of it! And I realise also that correct spelling is no sign of *intelligence*—being perhaps even the reverse, since the supernormally alert mind holds abstract concepts which run ahead of forms. I have never held up spelling as a matter of the foremost cultural significance, or tended to regard it as in any way an art or science. To my mind, it is simply a *very useful accessory* of literature—an accomplishment to be cultivated by the high-grade printer and publisher rather than by the creative author. *As a writer* I have no views whatever on orthography. Such views as I do entertain, I entertain as an amateur critic— or as one interested in neatness in the externals of expression. A bad or commercially servile story, or a trite and inane "pome", can get me seeing much redder than even a whole page full of "eons" and "esthetes", or a whole archipelago of "ilands"!

My statement of the two general principles which I follow will undoubtedly serve as an inclusive answer to many of the specific usage-points you cite. About the render of φ-derivatives—you will perceive that I am governed wholly by considerations of historic precedent and etymological usage—or rather, by a standard of *familiar and acceptable eye-appeal* as conditioned by these things. True, in Spain and Italy the spontaneous evolution of many centuries (though in Spain's case accelerated by the quasi-official dictionary of the Academy in 1803) gradually changed to *f* the *ph* transliteration of φ which had universally existed in Latin. But the fact remains that we do not inherit the linguistic stream of Spain or of Italy. On the contrary, the classical element in our language came either through the Norman-French, where the *ph* form remained intact, or directly through Latin scholarship. For us, the natural evolutionary tendency which gave the Mediterranean nations their spontaneous f-substitution has never existed. *Ph* as a φ-equivalent is the only normal and familiar form with us except in a few special cases. But I'm no stickling purist. When *natural drift* causes a φ-derivative to acquire an f-rendering in English (generally because the transition had previously occurred in French), I accept that rendering as readily as I accept the *ph* rendering of the bulk of such derivatives. Thus I say *fantastic* and *fantasy* (as did Dr. Johnson and Walker, and most after them), though I reject "fantasm" for *phantasm*. Curiously enough, Dr. Johnson *did* accept "fantasm"— although Walker balked at it, and the nineteenth century generally refused to endorse it. *Usage*, not *abstract logic*, is the criterion. The only possible orthographical norm is that remarkable *settling-down*—a novel and unprecedented development in English spelling—which began about the Restoration period, became very manifest by 1750, and a *striking and spontaneous uniformity* (not yet disturbed in Great Britain and many of the Dominions, and only fragmentarily shaken (as in *hono'r, wag'on*, etc.) in cultivated circles in the Eastern U.S.) during the first half of the nineteenth century. To break up this valuable natural growth and deliberately re-create the irresponsible chaos of Tudor times seems to me little short of a crime.

For the American modernistic chaos in spelling is by no means universal. Great Britain and most Dominions feel only feeble echoes (in Eastern Canada the less offensive American variants predominate, but not the delirium tremens fringe. I can't answer for the prairie provinces), and the eastern U.S. (despite some wild vagaries in *N.Y. Times* and *Tribune* style sheets) as a whole has not wandered far from its spontaneous "Websterian"§ variant. Few freaks can be discerned in the columns of the *Boston Transcript, Providence Journal, Atlantic Monthly, Harper's Magazine*, etc. There is still left in the world enough of the solid fabric of naturally crystallised English spelling to form a practical and sensible anchorage for friends of the language. And on the other hand, the principles and possible rewards of chaotic agitation and propaganda are so involved in fallacy and misconception that such roiling of the waters seems pitifully futile and wantonly destructive. Logic and consistency there can never be. Uniformity and traditional acceptability there can be, have been, and to some extent continues to be. And I'm for preserving the reality instead of chasing the shadow. Lord Falkland once said "where it is not necessary to change, it is necessary not to change," and I can see what he meant. If we lose all landmarks, we lose all reasons for living, and find ourselves floating directionlessly in a meaningless chaos. I believe in changing what has to be changed, but in keeping what can be kept. We can't cling to old beliefs and values and economic systems which the progress of knowledge, technology, and social consciousness has rendered obsolete and injurious—but we *can* cling to accustomed ways of doing things when there is no reason what-

---

§I use "quotes" because N. W. himself endorsed certain forms more radical than the solid norm which worked itself out in America.

ever for doing them any differently. I don't believe in the Ptolemaic universe of the Middle Ages, the Laplacian nebular hypothesis of the nineteenth century, or the capitalism of Herbie Hoover and the cobweb-brained constitution-savers of contemporary reactiondom. But on the other hand I don't see why the hell I should spell *sulphur* with an "f" or clutter up my study with futuristic chairs which look like emergency 'bus seats or bear-traps or henroost spring guns!

I can appreciate all that you say about popular carelessness with spelling. Even Klarkash-Ton spells "cemet*a*ry" that way—or has done so until recently! And I lugubriously echo your observations anent *pronunciation*. One of the phases of my big autumn job (the English text book)[3] was to compile a list of "100 words often mispronounced"—and by the time I had given the matter a little open-eared attention I began to despair for the orthoëpical future of the race. Some of the juiciest bits came from lecturers at the college . . . "son'-o-rous", "har-ass'", etc. etc. etc.

Well—pardon the ex cathedra bull of a sour, wretchedly old geezer!

My aunt and I had a Christmas tree, as in '34 and '35. Hope your Yule was pleasant, and that your New Year will be.

Yr obt Servt H. P. L.

P.S. Had an interesting and appropriate Christmas gift from young Conover—one of the *Science-Fantasy Correspondent* boys. A mouldering human skull exhumed from an ancient and mysterious necropolis! It came from an Indian mound near Conover's home—a scene of previous ghoulish and archaeological exploits of his.

Notes

1. The other illustration was for "The Haunter of the Dark."
2. See Dolton Edwards, "Meihem in ce Klasrum" [i.e., "Mayhem in the Classroom"], *Astounding Science Fiction*, 38, No. 1 (September 1946): 94–95. The story proposes, and embodies, the gradual reform of spelling, and in the result is virtually unrecognizable as English.
3. HPL refers to his revision of Anne Tillery Renshaw's *Well Bred Speech*.

Glossary of Names

Baird, Edwin (1886–1957), first editor of *WT* (Mar. 1923–Apr. 1924), who accepted HPL's first submissions to the magazine. Also editor of *Real Detective Stories.*

Bates, Harry (1900–1981), editor of *Strange Tales* and *Astounding Stories.* HPL repeatedly submitted stories to him, but all were rejected because they did not contain sufficient "action."

Bishop, Zealia Brown (Reed) (1897–1968), HPL's revision client. HPL ghostwrote "The Curse of Yig" (1928), "The Mound" (1929–30), and "Medusa's Coil" (1930) for her based on her slim plot synopses.

Blackwood, Algernon (1869–1951), prolific British author of weird and fantasy tales whose work HPL greatly admired when he read it in 1924.

Burks, Arthur J. (1898–1974). American writer and Marine colonel, whose experience in the Caribbean and knowledge of native voodoo rituals, led him to write stories of the supernatural that he sold to *Weird Tales.*

Chambers, Robert W[illiam] (1865–1933). American author. HPL discovered his early fantastic writing—*The King in Yellow* (1895), *The Maker of Moons* (1896), *In Search of the Unknown* (1904); also the later novel *The Slayer of Souls* (1920)—in early 1927. He hastily updated "Supernatural Horror in Literature" just before publication to include a discussion of Chambers.

Coates, Walter J[ohn] (1880–1941). Amateur journalist in North Montpelier, VT, who issued the little magazine *Driftwind,* which contained much poetry by HPL, including sonnets from *Fungi from Yuggoth.*

Conover, Willis (1921–1996), weird fiction fan who edited *Science-Fantasy Correspondent* (1936–37); a late correspondent of HPL.

Cook, W. Paul (1881–1948), publisher of the *Monadnock Monthly,* the *Vagrant,* and other amateur journals; a longtime amateur journalist, printer, and lifelong friend of HPL. He first visited HPL in 1917, and it was he who urged HPL to resume writing fiction after a hiatus of nine years. In 1927 Cook published the *Recluse*, containing HPL's "Supernatural Horror in Literature."

Cummings, Ray (1887–1957). American author recognized as one of the "founding fathers" of the science fiction pulp genre.

de Castro, Adolphe (Danziger) (1859–1959), author, co-translator with Ambrose Bierce of Richard Voss's *The Monk and the Hangman's Daughter*, and correspondent of HPL. HPL revised his "The Last Test" and "The Electric Executioner."

Derleth, August W[illiam] (1909–1971), author of weird tales and also a long series of regional and historical works set in his native Wisconsin. After HPL's death, he and Donald Wandrei founded Arkham House to preserve HPL's work in book form.

Dunsany, Lord (Edward John Moreton Drax Plunkett) (1878–1957), Irish writer of fantasy tales whose work notably influenced HPL after HPL read it in 1919.

Dwyer, Bernard Austin (1897–1943), weird fiction fan and would-be writer and artist, living in West Shokan, NY; correspondent of HPL.

Dyalhis, Nictzin (1873–1942), an American chemist and short story writer who specialized in science fiction and fantasy and was a popular contributor to *Weird Tales*.

Finlay, Virgil (1914–1971), one of the great weird artists of his time and a prolific contributor of artwork to the pulps; late correspondent of HPL.

Gamwell, Annie E[meline] P[hillips] (1866–1941), HPL's younger aunt, living with him at 66 College Street (1933–37).

Hamilton, Edmond (1904–1977), prolific author of weird and science fiction tales for the pulp magazines. HPL admired his story "The Monster-God of Mamurth" (*WT*, August 1926).

Houtain, George Julian (1884–1945), amateur journalist who established the semi-professional humor magazine *Home Brew*, for which he commissioned HPL to write "Herbert West—Reanimator" (1921–22) and "The Lurking Fear" (1922).

Howard, Robert E[rvin] (1906–1936), prolific Texas author of weird and adventure tales for *Weird Tales* and other pulp magazines; creator of the adventure hero Conan the Barbarian. He and HPL corresponded voluminously from 1930 to 1936. He committed suicide when he learned of his mother's impending death.

James, M[ontague] R[hodes] (1862–1936), pioneering British writer of ghost stories whose work HPL much admired.

Kirk, George [Willard] (1898–1962), member of the Kalem Club. He published *Twenty-one Letters of Ambrose Bierce* (1922) and ran the Chelsea Bookshop in New York.

Kline, Otis Adelbert (1891–1946), prolific writer for *Weird Tales* and other pulp magazines; also a literary agent for Robert E. Howard and others.

Leeds, Arthur (1882–1952?), an associate of HPL in New York and member of the Kalem Club. He was the author (with J. Berg Esenwein) of *Writing the Photoplay* (Springfield, MA: The Home Correspondence School, 1913; rev. ed. 1919).

Long, Frank Belknap (1901–1994), fiction writer and poet and one of HPL's closest friends and correspondents. Late in life he wrote the memoir, *Howard Phillips Lovecraft: Dreamer on the Nightside* (1975).

Machen, Arthur (1863–1947), Welsh author of weird fiction. He corresponded sporadically with AWD.

Morton, James Ferdinand (1870–1941), amateur journalist, author of many tracts on race prejudice, free thought, and taxation, and long-time friend of HPL.

Munn, H[arold] Warner (1903–1981), prolific contributor to the pulp magazines, living near W. Paul Cook in Athol, MA.

Olinick, George O. (1888–1957). Early *WT* illustrator.

Owen, Frank. Pseudonym of Roswell Williams (1893–1968), author of Oriental fantasies for *Weird Tales*, *Oriental Stories*, and other magazines.

Price, E[dgar] Hoffmann (1898–1989), prolific pulp writer of weird and adventure tales. HPL met him in New Orleans in 1932 and corresponded extensively with him thereafter.

Quinn, Seabury (1889–1969), prolific author of weird and detective tales to the pulps, notably a series of tales involving the psychic detective Jules de Grandin.

Rankin, Hugh Doak (1878–1956), illustrator for *WT*.

Schwartz, Julius (1915–2004), editor of *Fantasy Magazine* who acted as HPL's agent in marketing *At the Mountains of Madness* to *Astounding Stories*.

Smith, Clark Ashton (1893–1961), prolific California poet and writer of fantasy tales. He received a "fan" letter from HPL in 1922 and corresponded with him until HPL's death.

Starrett, Vincent (1886–1974), American bookman who corresponded briefly with HPL in 1927.

Sterling, George (1869–1926), American poet and early mentor of CAS. Author of *The Testimony of the Suns* (1903) and *A Wine of Wizardry* (1909).

Swanson, Carl, a fan from North Dakota who wrote to several authors of weird and science fiction asking for contributions to a magazine he planned to publish, to be called the *Galaxy*. It was never realized.

Talman, Wilfred Blanch (1904–1986), correspondent of HPL and late member of the Kalem Club. HPL assisted Talman on his story "Two Black Bottles" (1926) and wrote "Some Dutch Footprints in New England" for Talman to publish in *De Halve Maen,* the journal of the Holland Society of New York. Late in life he wrote the memoir *The Normal Lovecraft* (1973).

Wandrei, Donald (1908–1987), poet and author of weird fiction, science fiction, and detective tales. He corresponded with HPL from 1926 to 1937, visited HPL in Providence in 1927 and 1932, and met HPL occasionally in New York during the 1930s. He helped HPL get "The Shadow out of Time" published in *Astounding Stories*. After HPL's death he and AWD founded the publishing firm Arkham House to preserve HPL's work. For their joint correspondence, see *Mysteries of Time and Spirit* (Night Shade Books, 2002).

Whitehead, Henry S[t. Clair] (1882–1932), author of weird and adventure tales, many of them set in the Virgin Islands. HPL corresponded with him and visited him in Florida in 1931. HPL wrote a brief eulogy of Whitehead for *WT*.

Bibliography

I. Works by H. P. Lovecraft

  i. Fiction

"The Call of Cthulhu." *WT* 11, No. 2 (February 1928): 159–78, 287. In *Beware After Dark! The World's Most Stupendous Tales of Mystery, Horror, Thrills and Terror,* ed. T. Everett Harré. New York: Macaulay, 1929, 223–59. In *CF* 2.

"The Cats of Ulthar." *Tryout* 6, No. 11 (November 1920): [3–9]. *WT* 7, No. 2 (February 1924): 252–54. Cassia, FL: The Dragon-Fly Press, Christmas 1935. In *CF* 1.

"The Colour out of Space." *Amazing Stories* 2, No. 6 (September 1927): 557–67. In *CF* 2.

"Dagon." *Vagrant* No. 11 (November 1919): 23–29. *WT* 2, No. 3 (October 1923): 23–25. In *CF* 1.

"The Dreams in the Witch House."" *WT* 22, No. 1 (July 1933): 86–111. In *CF* 3.

"The Dunwich Horror." *WT* 13, No. 4 (April 1929): 481–508. In *CF* 2.

"Facts concerning the Late Arthur Jermyn and His Family." *Wolverine* No. 9 (March 1921): 3–11. *WT* 3, No. 4 (April 1924): 15–18 (as "The White Ape"). *WT* 25, No. 5 (May 1935): 642–48 (as "Arthur Jermyn"). In *CF* 1.

"The Festival." *WT* 5, No. 1 (January 1925): 169–74. *WT* 22, No. 4 (October 1933): 519–20, 522–28. In *CF* 1.

"The Haunter of the Dark." *WT* 28, No. 5 (December 1936): 538–53. In *CF* 2.

"The Horror at Red Hook." *WT* 9, No. 1 (January 1927): 59–73. In *You'll Need a Night Light,* ed. Christine Campbell Thomson. London: Selwyn & Blount, 1927, 228–54. In *CF* 1.

"The Lurking Fear." *Home Brew* 2, No. 6 (January 1923): 4–10; 3, No. 1 (February 1923): 18–23; 3, No. 2 (March 1923): 31–37, 44, 48; 3, No. 3 (April 1923): 35–42. *WT* 11, No. 6 (June 1928): 791–804. In *CF* 1.

"The Moon-Bog." *WT* 7, No. 6 (June 1926): 805–10. In *CF* 1.

"The Music of Erich Zann." *National Amateur* 44, No. 4 (March 1922): 38–40. *WT* 5, No. 5 (May 1925): 219–34. In *Creeps by Night: Chills and Thrills,* ed. Dashiell Hammett. New York: John Day Co., 1931, 347–63. In *Modern Tales of Horror,* ed. Dashiell Hammett. London: Victor Gollancz, 1932, 301–17. *Evening Standard* (London) (24 October 1932): 20–21. *WT* 24, No. 5 (November 1934): 644–48, 655–56. In *CF* 2.

"The Outsider." *WT* 7, No. 4 (April 1926): 449–53. *WT* 17, No. 4 (June–July 1931): 566–71. In *CF* 1.

"Pickman's Model." *WT* 10, No. 4 (October 1927): 505–14. In *By Daylight Only,* ed. Christine Campbell Thomson. London: Selwyn & Blount, 1929, 37–52. *WT* 28, No. 4 (November 1936): 495–505. In *The "Not at Night" Omnibus,* ed. Christine Campbell Thomson. London: Selwyn & Blount, [1937], 279–307. In *CF* 2.

"The Picture in the House." *National Amateur* 41, No. 6 (July 1919 [*sic*]): 246–49. *WT* 3, No. 1 (January 1924): 40–42. *WT* 29, No. 3 (March 1937): 370–73. In *CF* 2.

"The Rats in the Walls." *WT* 3, No. 3 (March 1924): 25–31. *WT* 15, No. 6 (June 1930): 841–53. In *Switch On the Light,* ed. Christine Campbell Thomson. London: Selwyn & Blount, 1931, 141–65. In *CF* 2.

The Shadow over Innsmouth. Everett, PA: The Visionary Publishing Co., 1936. In *CF* 3.

"The Shunned House." Athol, MA: W. Paul Cook (The Recluse Press), 1928 (printed but not bound or distributed). In *CF* 3.

"The Silver Key." *WT* 13, No. 1 (January 1929): 41–49, 144. In *CF* 3.

"The Statement of Randolph Carter." *Vagrant* No. 13 (May 1920): 41–48. *WT* 5, No. 2 (February 1925): 149–53. In *CF* 1.

"Strange High House in the Mist." *WT* 18, No. 3 (October 1931): 394–400. In *CF* 1.

"The Terrible Old Man." *Tryout* 7, No. 4 (July 1921): [10–14]. *WT* 8, No. 2 (Aug. 1926): 191–92. In *CF* 1.

"The Thing on the Doorstep." *WT* 29, No. 1 (January 1937): 52–70. In *CF* 2.

"The Unnamable." *WT* 6, No. 1 (July 1925): 78–82. In *CF* 1.

"The White Ship." *United Amateur* 19, No. 2 (November 1919): 30–33. *WT* 9, No. 3 (March 1927): 386–89. In *CF* 1.

ii. Essays

"In Memoriam: Henry S. Whitehead." *Weird Tales* 21, No. 3 (March 1933): 391 (unsigned). In *CE* 2.

"Supernatural Horror in Literature." *Recluse* No. 1 (1927): 23–59. Rev. ed. in *Fantasy Fan* (October 1933–February 1935). In *CE* 2.

iii. Poetry

Fungi from Yuggoth.

IX. "The Courtyard." *Weird Tales* 16, No. 3 (September 1930): 322. Numbered 1.

XIII. "Hesperia." *Weird Tales* 16, No. 4 (October 1930): 464. Numbered 3.

XIV. "Star-Winds." *Weird Tales* 16, No. 3 (September 1930): 322. Numbered 2.

XV. "Antarktos." *Weird Tales* 16, No. 5 (November 1930): 692. Numbered 4.

XIX. "The Bells." *Weird Tales* 16, No. 6 (December 1930): 798. Numbered 5.

XXI. "Nyarlathotep." *Weird Tales* 17, No. 1 (January 1931): 12. Numbered 6.

XXII. "Azathoth." *Weird Tales* 17, No. 1 (January 1931): 12. Numbered 7.

XXIII. "Mirage." *Weird Tales* 17, No. 2 (February–March 1931): 175. Numbered 8.

XXVII. "The Elder Pharos." *Weird Tales* 17, No. 2 (February–March 1931): 175. Numbered 9.

XXXII. "Alienation." *Weird Tales* 17, No. 3 (April–May 1931): 374. Numbered 10.

"Recapture." *Weird Tales* 15, No. 5 (May 1930): 693. Not part of *Fungi from Yuggoth* until 1936.

iv. Revisions and Collaborations

Bishop, Zealia. "The Curse of Yig." *WT* 14, No. 5 (Nov. 1929): 625–36. In *Switch On the Light,* ed. Christine Campbell Thomson. London: Selwyn & Blount, 1931, 9–31. In *The "Not at Night" Omnibus,* ed. Christine Campbell Thomson. London: Selwyn & Blount, [1937], 13–29. In *CF* 4.

"The Mound" (with Zealia Bishop). *WT* 35, No. 6 (November 1940): 98–120 (abridged). In *CF* 4.

Price, E. Hoffmann. "Through the Gates of the Silver Key." *WT* 24, No. 1 (July 1934): 60–85. In *CF* 4.

II. Works by Others

Anthon, Charles. *A System of Ancient and Mediaeval Geography for the Use of Schools and Colleges.* New-York: Harper & Brothers, 1850. (*LL* 35)

Birch, A. G. *The Moon Terror*. And Stories by Anthony M. Rud, Vincent Starrett, and Farnsworth Wright. Indianapolis: Popular Fiction Publishing Co., [1927]. (*LL* 93)

Chambers, Robert W. (1865–1933). *The King in Yellow*. Chicago: F. Tennyson Neely, 1895. (*LL* 167)

Dunsany, Lord. *The Gods of the Mountain*. <1914> In *Five Plays*. Boston: Little, Brown, 1923. (*LL* 275)

———. *A Night at an Inn*. In *Plays of Gods and Men*. Boston: J. W. Luce, [1917]. (*LL* 279)

O'Brien, Edward J. ed., *The Best Short Stories of 1928, and the Yearbook of the American Short Story*. New York: Dodd, Mead, 1928. Contains HPL's "[Autobiographical Notice]," 324. (*LL* 650)

Renshaw, Anne Tillery. *Well Bred Speech: A Brief Intensive Aid for English Students*. Washington, DC: Standard Press, 1936. (*LL* 726)

Smith, Clark Ashton (1893–1961). *The Double Shadow and Other Fantasies*. Auburn, CA: Auburn Journal Press, 1933. (*LL* 810)

Wandrei, Donald (1908–1987). *Dead Titans, Waken! and Invisible Sun*. Edited by S. T. Joshi. Lakewood, CO: Centipede Press, 2011.

———————————

The Night Ocean

R. H. Barlow and H. P. Lovecraft

It has been known for some time that "The Night Ocean," one of the last stories on which Lovecraft worked, was largely written by his young colleague R. H. Barlow (1918–1951). The discovery of the original typescript of the tale, with Lovecraft's revisions written in pen, confirmed that Lovecraft's contribution probably amounted to no more than 10% to 15% of the tale, although some key sections were written or revised by him. We here present a facsimile of that typescript, along with a literal transcript.

The typescript was probably prepared sometime prior to Barlow's visit to Lovecraft in Providence (28 July–1 September 1936), and Lovecraft's revisions were no doubt made during Barlow's long visit. There is clear textual evidence that Barlow later prepared a new typescript incorporating most—but not all—of the revisions; Lovecraft himself suggests as much: "Hope your opus progresses well, & that you're preparing a new copy of 'The Night Ocean' for publication" (HPL to Barlow, 30 September 1936; *O Fortunate Floridian* [Tampa, FL: University of Tampa Press, 2007], 363). The story was published in the *Californian* (Winter 1936), an amateur journal edited by Hyman Bradofsky. There are several slight divergences from the Lovecraft-revised typescript that point to some further revisions by Barlow, so that the transcript printed here does not constitute the final version of the text. That final version will appear in a variorum edition of Lovecraft's complete revisions and collaborations, edited by S. T. Joshi and scheduled for publication in 2015 by Hippocampus Press.

The Night Ocean

I went to Ellston Beach not only for the pleasures of sun and ocean, but to rest a weary mind. Since I knew no person in the little town, which thrives on summer vacationists and presents only blank windows during most of the year, there seemed no likelihood that I might be disturbed. This pleased me, for I did not wish to see anything but the expanse of pounding surf and the beach lying before my temporary home.

My long work of the summer was completed when I left the city, and the large mural design produced by it had been entered in the contest. It had taken me the bulk of the year to finish the painting, and when the last brush was cleaned I was no longer reluctant to yield to the claims of health and find rest and seclusion for a time. Indeed, when I had been a week on the beach I recalled only now and then the work whose success had so recently seemed all-important. There was no longer the old concern with a hundred complexities of colour and ornament; no longer the fear and mistrust of my ability to render a mental image actual, and turn by my own skill alone the dim-conceived idea into the careful draught of a design. And yet that which later befell me by the lonely shore may have grown solely from the mental constitution behind such concern and fear and mistrust. For I have always been a seeker, a dreamer, and a ponderer on seeking and dreaming; and who can say that such a nature does not open latent eyes sensitive to unsuspected worlds and orders of being?

Now that I am trying to tell what I saw I am conscious of a thousand maddening limitations. Things seen by the inward sight, like those flashing visions which come as we drift into the blankness of sleep, are more vivid and meaningful to us in that form than when we have sought to weld them with reality. Set a pen to a dream, and the colour drains from it. The ink with which we write seems diluted with something holding too much of reality, and we find that after all we cannot delineate the incredible memory. It is as if our inward selves, released from the bonds of daytime and objectivity, revelled in prisoned emotions which are hastily stifled

when we would translate them. In dreams and visions lie the greatest creations of man, for on them rests no yoke of line or hue. Forgotten scenes, and lands more obscure than the golden world of
childhood, spring into the sleeping mind to reign until awakening
puts them to rout. Amid these may be attained something of the
glory and contentment for which we yearn; some adumbration of
sharp beauties suspected but not before revealed, which are to us
as the Graal to holy spirits of the mediaeval world. To shape these
things on the wheel of art, to seek to bring some faded trophy from
that intangible realm of shadow and gossamer, requires equal skill
and memory. For although dreams are in all of us, few hands may
grasp their moth-wings without tearing them.

Such skill this narrative does not have. If I might, I would reveal to you the hinted events which I perceived dimly, like one
who peers into an unlit realm and glimpses forms whose motion
is concealed. In my mural design, which then lay with a multitude
of others in the building for which they were planned, I had striv-
en equally to catch a trace of this elusive shadow-world, and had
perhaps succeeded better than I shall now succeed. My stay in
Ellston was to await the judging of that design; and when days of
unfamiliar leisure had given me perspective, I discovered that—in
spite of those weaknesses which a creator always detects most
clearly—I had indeed managed to retain in line and colour some
fragments snatched from the endless world of imagining. The difficulties of the process, and the resulting strain on all my powers,
had undermined my health and brought me to the beach during
this period of waiting. Since I wished to be wholly alone, I rented
(to the delight of the incredulous owner) a small house some distance from the village of Ellston—which, because of the waning
season, was alive with a moribund bustle of tourists, uniformly
uninteresting to me. The house, dark from the sea-wind though it
had not been painted, was not even a satellite of the village; but
swung below it on the coast like a pendulum beneath a still clock;
quite alone upon a hill of weed-grown sand. Like a solitary warm
animal it crouched facing the sea, and its inscrutable dirty windows stared upon a lonely realm of earth and sky and enormous
sea. It will not do to use too much imagining in a narrative whose
facts, could they be augmented and fitted into a mosaic, would be

strange enough in themselves; but I thought the little house was lonely when I saw it, and that like myself, it was conscious of its meaningless nature before the great sea.

I took the place in late August, arriving a day before I was expected, and encountering a van and two workingmen unloading the furniture provided by the owner. I did not know then how long I would stay, and when the truck that brought the goods had left I settled my small luggage and locked the door (feeling very proprietary at having a house after months of a rented room) to go down the weedy hill and on the beach. Since it was quite square and had but one room, the house had required little exploration. Two windows in each side provided a great quantity of light, and somehow a door had been squeezed in as an afterthought on the oceanward wall. The place had been built about ten years previously, but on account of its distance from Ellston village was difficult to rent even during the active summer season. There being no fireplace, it stood empty and alone from October until far into spring. Though actually less than a mile below Ellston, it seemed more remote; since a bend in the coast caused one to see only grassy dunes in the direction of the village.

The first day, half-gone when I was installed, I spent in the enjoyment of the sun and the restless water—things whose quiet majesty made the designing of murals seem distant and tiresome. But this was the natural reaction to a long concern with one set of habits and activities. I was through with my work and my vacation was begun. This fact, while elusive for the moment, showed in everything which surrounded me that afternoon of my arrival; and in the utter change from old scenes. There was an effect of bright sun upon a shifting sea of waves whose mysteriously-impelled curves were strewn with what appeared to be rhinestones. Perhaps a water-colour might have caught the solid masses of intolerable light which lay upon the beach where the sea mingled with the sand. Although the ocean bore her own hue, it was dominated wholly and incredibly by the enormous glare. There was no other person near me, and I enjoyed the spectacle without the annoyance of any alien object upon the stage. Each of my senses was touched in a different way, but sometimes it seemed that the roar of the sea was akin to that great brightness, or as if the waves were glaring instead of the sun, each of these being so vigorous and insistent that impressions coming from them were mingled. Curiously, I saw no one bathing near my little square house during that or succeeding afternoons, although the curving shore included a wide beach even more inviting than that at the village, where the surf was dotted with random figures. I supposed that this was because of the distance, and because there had never been other houses below the town. Why this unbuilt stretch existed, I could not imagine, since many dwellings straggled along the northward coast, facing the sea with aimless eyes.

I swam until the afternoon had gone, and later, having rested, walked into the little town. Darkness hid the sea from me as I entered, and I found in the dingy lights of the street tokens of a life which was not even conscious of the great, gloom-shrouded thing lying so close. There were painted women in tinsel adornments, and bored men who were no longer young—a throng of foolish marionettes perched on the lip of the ocean-chasm; unseeing, unwilling to see, what lay above them and about, in the multitudinous grandeur of the stars and the leagues of the night ocean. I walked along that darkened sea as I went back to the bare little house, sending the beams of my flashlight out upon the naked and impenetrable void. In the absence of the moon, this light made a solid bar athwart the walls of the uneasy tide; and I felt an indescribable emotion born of the noise of the waters and the perception of my inconceivable smallness as I cast that tiny beam upon a realm immense in itself, yet only the black border of the earthly deep. That nighted deep, upon which ships were moving alone in the darkness where I could not see them, gave off the murmur of a distant, angry rabble.

When I reached my high residence I knew that I had passed no one during the mile's walk from the village, and yet there somehow lingered the impression that I had been all the while accompanied by the spirit of the lonely sea. It was, I thought, personified in a shape which was not revealed to me, but which moved quietly about beyond my range of comprehension. It was like those actors who wait behind darkened scenery in readiness for the lines which will shortly call them before our eyes to move and speak in the sudden revelation of the footlights. At last I shook off this fancy and sought my key to enter the place, whose bare walls gave a sudden feeling of security.

My cottage was entirely free of the village, as if it had wandered down the coast and was unable to return; and there I heard nothing of the disturbing clamour when I returned each night after supper. I generally stayed but a short while upon the streets of Ellston, though sometimes I went into the place for the sake of the walk it provided. There were all the multitude of curio-shops and falsely regal theater-fronts that clutter vacation towns, but I never went into these; and the place seemed useful only for its restaurants. It was astonishing the number of useless things people found to do.

There was a succession of sun-filled days at first. I rose early, and beheld the grey sky agleam with promise of sunrise; a prophecy fulfilled as I stood witness. Those dawns were cold, and their colours faint in comparison to that uniform radiance of day which gives to every hour the quality of white noon. That great light, so apparent the first day, made each succeeding day a yellow page in the book of time. I noticed that many of the beach-people were displeased by the inordinate sun, whereas I sought it. After grey months of toil the lethargy induced by a physical existence in a region governed by the simple things—the wind and light and water—had a prompt effect upon me; and since I was anxious to continue this healing process, I spent all my time outdoors in the sunlight. This induced a state at once impassive and submissive, and gave me a feeling of security against the ravenous night. As darkness is akin to death, so is light to vitality. Through the heritage of a million years ago, when men were closer to the mother sea, and when the creatures of which we are born lay languid in the shallow, sun-pierced water, we still seek the primal things when we are tired, steeping ourselves within their lulling security like those early half-mammals which had not yet ventured upon the oozy land.

The monotony of the waves gave repose, and I had no other occupation than witnessing a myriad ocean moods. There is a ceaseless change in the waters—colours and shades pass over them like the insubstantial expressions of a well-known face; and these are at once communicated to us by half-recognized senses. When the sea is restless, remembering old ships that have gone over her chasms, there comes up silently in our hearts the longing for a vanished horizon. But when she forgets, we forget also. Though we know her a lifetime, she must always hold an alien air, as if something too vast to have shape were lurking in the universe to which she is a door. The morning ocean, glimmering with a reflected mist of blue-white cloud and expanding diamond foam, has the eyes of one who ponders on strange things, and her intricately woven webs, through which dart a myriad coloured fishes, hold the air of some great idle thing which will arise presently from the hoary immemorial chasms and stride upon the land.

I was content for many days, and glad that I had chosen the lonely house which sat like a small beast upon those rounded cliffs of sand. Among the pleasantly aimless amusements fostered by such a life, I took to following the edge of the tide, (where the waves left a damp irregular outline rimmed with evanescent foam) for long distances; and sometimes I found curious bits of shell in the chance litter of the sea. There was an astonishing lot of debris on that inward-curving coast which my bare little house overlooked, and I judged that currents whose courses diverge from the village beach must reach that spot. At any rate, my pockets—when I had any—generally held vast stores of trash; most of which I threw away an hour or two after picking it up, wondering why I had kept it. Once, however, I found a small bone whose nature I could not identify, save that it was certainly nothing out of a fish; and I kept this, along with a large metal bead whose minutely carven design was rather unusual. This latter depicted a fishy thing against a patterned background of seaweed instead of the usual floral or geometrical designs, and was still clearly traceable though worn with years of tossing in the surf. Since I had never seen anything like it, I judged that it represented some fashion, now forgotten, of a previous year at Ellston, where similar fads were common.

I had been there perhaps a week when the weather began a gradual change. Each stage of this progressive darkening was followed by another subtly intensified, so that in the end the entire atmosphere surrounding me had shifted from day to evening. This was more obvious to me in a series of mental impressions than in what I actually witnessed, for the small house was lonely under grey skies, and there was sometimes a beating wind that came out of the ocean bearing moisture. The sun was displaced by long intervals of cloudiness—layers of grey mist beyond whose unknown depth the sun lay cut off. Though it might glare with the old intensity above that enormous veil, it could not penetrate. The beach was a prisoner in a hueless vault for hours at a time, as if something of the night were welling into other hours.

Although the wind was invigorating and the ocean whipped into little churning spirals of activity by the vagrant flapping, I found the water growing chill, so that I could not stay in it as long as I had done previously, and thus I fell into the habit of long walks, which—when I was unable to swim—provided the exercise that I was so careful to obtain. These walks covered a greater range of sea-edge than my previous wanderings, and since the beach extended in a stretch of miles beyond the tawdry village, I often found myself wholly isolated upon an endless area of sand as evening drew close. When this occurred, I would stride hastily along the whispering sea-border, following its outline so that I should not wander inland and lose my way. And sometimes, when these walks were late (as they grew increasingly to be) I would come upon the crouching house that looked like a harbinger of the village. Insecure upon the wind-gnawed cliffs, a dark blot upon the morbid hues of the ocean sunset, it was more lonely than by the full light of either orb; and seemed to my imagination like a mute, questioning face turned toward me expectant of some action. That the place was isolated I have said, and this at first pleased me; but in that brief evening hour when the sun left in a gore-spattered decline and darkness lumbered on like an expanding shapeless blot, there was an alien presence about the place: a spirit, a mood, an impression that came from the surging wind, the gigantic sky, and that sea which drooled blackening waves upon a beach grown abruptly strange. At these times I felt an uneasiness which had no very definite cause, although my solitary nature had made me long accustomed to the ancient silence and the ancient voice of nature. These misgivings, to which I could have put no sure name, did not affect me long, yet I think now that all the while a gradual consciousness of the ocean's immense loneliness crept upon me, a loneliness that was made subtly horrible

by intimations—which were never more than such—of some animation or sentience preventing me from being wholly alone.

The noisy, yellow streets of the town, with their curiously unreal activity, were very far away, and when I went there for my
evening meal (mistrusting a diet entirely of my own ambiguous
cooking) I took increasing and quite unreasonable care that I
should return to the cottage before the late darkness, although I
was often abroad until ten or so.

You will say that such action is unreasonable; that if I had
feared the darkness in some childish way, I would have entirely
avoided it. You will ask me why I did not leave the place since its
loneliness was depressing me. To all this I have no reply, save that
whatever unrest I felt, whatever of remote disturbance there was
to me in brief aspects of the darkening sun or in the eager salt-
brittle wind or in the robe of the dark sea that lay crumpled like
an enormous garment so close to me, was something which had
an origin half in my own heart, which showed itself only at fleeting moments, and which had no very long effect upon me. In the
recurrent days of diamond light, with sportive waves flinging blue
peaks at the basking shore, the memory of dark moods seemed
rather incredible; yet only an hour or two afterward I might again
experience these moods once more, and descend to a dim region
of despair.

Perhaps these inward emotions were only a reflection of the
sea's own mood; for although half of what we see is coloured by
the interpretation placed upon it by our minds, many of our feelings are shaped quite distinctly by external, physical things. The
sea can bind us to her many moods, whispering to us by the subtle token of a shadow or a gleam upon the waves, and hinting in
these ways of her mournfulness or rejoicing. Always, she is remembering old things, and these memories, though we may not
grasp them, are imparted to us, so that we share her gaiety or remorse. Since I was doing no work, seeing no person that I knew, I
was perhaps susceptible to shades of her cryptic meaning which
would have been overlooked by another. The ocean ruled my life
during the whole of that late summer; demanding it as recompense for the healing she had brought me.

There were drownings at the beach that year, and while I heard of these only casually (such is our indifference to a death which does not concern us, and to which we are not witness) I knew that their details were unsavoury. The people who died—some of them swimmers of a skill beyond the average—were sometimes not found until many days had elapsed, and the hideous vengeance of the deep had scourged their rotten bodies. It was as if the sea had dragged them into a chasm-lair and had mulled them about in the darkness until, satisfied that they were no longer of any use, she had floated them ashore in a ghastly state. No one seemed to know what had caused these deaths. Their frequency excited alarm among the timid, since the undertow at Ellston was not strong, and since there were known to be no sharks at hand. Whether the bodies showed marks of any attacks I did not learn, but the dread of a death which moves among the waves and comes on lone people from a lightless, motionless place is a dread which men know and do not like. They must quickly find a reason for such a death, even if there are no sharks. Since sharks formed only a suspected cause, and one never to my knowledge confirmed, the swimmers who continued during the rest of the season were on guard against treacherous tides rather than against any possible sea-animal.

Autumn, indeed, was not a great distance off, and some people used this as an excuse for leaving the sea, where men were snared by death, and going to the security of inland fields, where one cannot even hear the ocean. So August ended, and I had been at the beach many days.

There had been a threat of storm since the fourth of the new month, and on the sixth, when I set out for a walk in the damp wind, there was a mass of formless cloud, colourless and oppressive, above the ruffled leaden sea. The motion of the wind, directed toward no especial goal but stirring uneasily, provided a sensation of coming animation—a hint of life in the elements which might be the long-expected storm. I had eaten my luncheon at Ellston, and though the heavens seemed the closing lid of a great casket, I ventured far down the beach and away from both the town and my no-longer-to-be-seen house. As the universal grey became spotted with a carrion purple—curiously brilliant despite its sombre hue—I found that I was several miles from any possible shelter. This, however, did not seem very important; for despite the dark skies with their added glow of unknown presage I was in a curious mood of detachment paralleling that glow—a mood which flashed through a body grown suddenly alert and sensitive to the outline of shapes and meanings that were previously dim. Obscurely, a memory came to me; suggested by the likeness of the scene to one I had imagined when a story was read to me in childhood. That tale—of which I had not thought for many years—concerned a woman who was loved by the dark-bearded king of an underwater realm of blurred cliffs where fish-things lived, and who was taken from the golden-haired youth of her troth by a dark being crowned with a priest-like mitre and having the features of a withered ape. What had remained in the corner of my fancy was the image of cliffs beneath the water against the hueless, dusky no-sky of such a realm; and this, though I had forgotten most of the story, was recalled quite unexpectedly by the same pattern of cliff and sky which I then beheld. The sight was similar to what I had imagined in a year now lost save for random, incomplete impressions. Suggestions of this story may have lingered behind certain irritatingly unfinished memories, and in certain values hinted to my senses by scenes whose actual significance was bafflingly small. Frequently, in flashes of momentary perception, (the conditions more than the object being significant) we feel that certain isolated scenes and arrangements—a feathery landscape, a woman's dress along the curve of a road in the afternoon, or the solidity of a century-defying tree against the pale morning sky—hold something precious, some golden virtue that we must grasp. And yet when such a scene or arrangement is viewed later, or from another point, we find that it has lost its value and meaning for us. Perhaps this is because the thing we seek does not hold that elusive quality, but only suggests to the mind some very different thing which remains unremembered. The baffled mind, not wholly sensing the cause of its flashing appreciation, seizes on the object exciting it, and is surprised when there is nothing of worth therein. Thus it was when I beheld the purpling clouds. They held the stateliness and mystery of old monastery towers at twilight, but their aspect was also that of the cliffs in the old fairy-tale. Suddenly reminded of this lost image, I half-expected to see, in the fine-spun dirty foam and among the waves which were now as if they had been poured of flawed black glass, the horrid figure of that ape-faced creature, wearing a mitre old with verdigris, advancing from its kingdom in some lost gulf to which those waves were sky.

I did not see any such creature from the realm of imagining, but as the chill wind veered, slitting the heavens like a rustling knife, there lay in the gloom of merging cloud and water only a grey object, like a piece of driftwood, tossing obscurely on the foam. This was a considerable distance out, and since it vanished shortly, may have been not wood, but a porpoise coming to the troubled surface.

I soon found that I had stayed too long contemplating the rising storm and linking my early fancies with its grandeur, for an icy rain began spotting down, bringing a more uniform gloom upon a scene already too dark for the hour. Hurrying along the grey sand, I felt the impact of cold drops upon my back, and before many moments my clothing was soaked throughout. At first I had run, put to flight by the colourless drops whose pattern hung in long linking strands from an unseen sky, but after I saw that refuge was too far to reach in anything like a dry state, I slackened my pace, and returned home as if I had walked under clear skies. There was not much reason to hurry, although I did not idle as upon previous occasions. The constraining wet garments were cold upon me; and with the gathering darkness, and the wind that rose endlessly from the ocean, I could not repress a shiver. Yet there was, beside the discomfort of the precipitous rain, an exhilaration latent in the purplish ravelled masses of cloud and the stimulated reactions of my body. In a mood half of exultant pleasure from resisting the rain (which streamed from me now, and filled my shoes and pockets) and half of strange appreciation of those morbid, dominant skies which hovered with dark wings above the shifting eternal sea, I tramped along the grey corridor of Ellston Beach. More rapidly than I had expected the crouching house showed in the oblique, flapping rain, and all the weeds of the sand cliff writhed in accompaniment to the frantic wind, as if they would uproot themselves to join the far-travelling element. Sea and sky had altered not at all, and the scene was that which had accompanied me, save that there was now painted upon it the hunching roof that seemed to bend from the assailing rain. I hurried up the insecure steps, and let myself into a dry room, where, unconsciously surprised that I was free of the nagging wind, I stood for a moment with water rilling from every inch of me.

There are two windows in the front of that house, as on each side, and these face nearly straight upon the ocean; which I saw now half obscured by the combined veils of the rain and of the imminent night. From these windows I looked as I dressed myself in a motley array of dry garments seized from convenient hangers and from a chair too laden to sit upon. I was prisoned on all sides by an unnaturally increased dusk which had filtered down at some undefined hour under cover of the storm. How long I had been on the reaches of wet grey sand, or what the real time was, I could not tell, though a moment's search produced my watch—fortunately left behind and thus avoiding the uniform wetness of my clothing. I half-guessed the hour from the dimly seen hands, which were only slightly less indecipherable than the surrounding figures. In another moment my sight penetrated the gloom (greater in the house than beyond the bleared window) and saw that it was 6:45.

There had been no one upon the beach as I came in, and naturally I expected to see no further swimmers that night. Yet when I looked again from the window there appeared surely to be figures blotting the grime of the wet evening. I counted three moving about in some incomprehensible manner, and close to the house another—which may not have been a person, but a wave-ejected log, for the surf was now pounding fiercely. I was startled to no little degree, and wondered for what purpose those hardy persons stayed out in such a storm. And then I thought that perhaps like myself they had been caught unintentionally in the rain and had surrendered to the watery gusts. In another moment, prompted by a certain civilised hospitality which overcame my love of solitude, I stepped to the door and emerged momentarily (at the cost of another wetting, for the rain promptly descended upon me in exultant fury) on the small porch, gesticulating toward the people. But whether they did not see me, or did not understand, they made no returning signal. Dim in the evening, they stood as if half-surprised, or as if they awaited some other action from me. There was in their attitude something of that cryptic blankness, signifying anything or nothing, which the house wore about itself as seen in the morbid sunset. Abruptly there came to me a feeling that a sinister quality lurked about those unmoving figures which chose to stay in the rainy night upon a beach deserted by all people, and I closed the door with a surge of annoyance which sought all too vainly to disguise a deeper emotion of fear; a consuming fright that welled up from the shadows of my consciousness. A moment later, when I had stepped to the window, there seemed to be nothing outside but the portentous night. Vaguely puzzled, and even more vaguely frightened—like one who has seen no alarming thing, but is apprehensive of what may be found in the dark street he is soon compelled to cross—I decided that I had very possibly seen no one, and that the murky air had deceived me.

The aura of isolation about the place was increased that night, though just out of sight on the northward beach a hundred houses rose in the rainy darkness, their light bleared and yellow above streets of polished glass, like goblin-eyes reflected in an oily forest pool. Yet because I could not see them, or even reach them in bad weather—since I had no car nor any way to leave the crouching house except by walking in the figure-haunted darkness—I realized quite suddenly that I was, to all intents, alone with the dreary sea that rose and subsided unseen, unkenned, in the mist. And the voice of the sea had become a hoarse groan, like that of something wounded which shifts about before trying to rise.

Fighting away the prevalent gloom with a soiled lamp—for the darkness crept in at my windows and sat peering obscurely at me from the corners like a patient animal—I prepared my food, since I had no intention of going to the village. The hour seemed incredibly advanced, though it was not yet nine o'clock when I went to bed. Darkness had come early and furtively, and throughout the remainder of my stay lingered evasively over each scene and action which I beheld. Something had settled out of the night—something forever undefined, but stirring a latent sense within me, so that I was like a beast expecting the momentary rustle of an enemy.

There were hours of wind, and sheets of the downpour flapped endlessly on the meagre walls barring it from me. Lulls came in which I heard the mumbling sea, and I could guess that large formless waves jostled one another in the pallid whine of the winds, and flung on the beach a spray bitter with salt. Yet in the very monotony of the restless elements I found a lethargic note, a sound that beguiled me, after a time, into slumber grey and colourless as the night. The sea continued its mad monologue, and the wind her nagging, but these were shut out by the walls of unconsciousness, and for a time the night ocean was banished from a sleeping mind.

Morning brought an enfeebled sun—a sun like that which men will see when the earth is old, if there are any men left: a sun more weary than the shrouded, moribund sky. Faint echo of its old image, Phoebus strove to pierce the ragged, ambiguous clouds as I awoke, at moments sending a wash of pale gold rippling across the northwestern interior of my house, at others waning till it was only a luminous ball, like some incredible plaything forgotten on the celestial lawn. After a while the failing rain—which must have continued throughout the previous night—succeeded in washing away those vestiges of purple cloud which had been like the ocean-cliffs in an old fairy tale. Cheated alike of the setting and rising sun, that day merged with the day before, as if the intervening storm had not ushered a long darkness into the world, but had swollen and subsided in one long afternoon. Gaining heart, the furtive sun exerted all his force in dispelling the old mist, streaked now like a dirty window, and cast it from his realm. The shallow blue day advanced as those grimy wisps retreated, and the loneliness which had encircled me welled back into a watchful place of retreat, whence it went no farther, but crouched and waited.

The ancient brightness was now once more upon the sun, and the old glitter on the waves, whose playful blue shapes had flocked upon that coast ere man was born, and would rejoice unseen when he was forgotten in the sepulchre of time. Influenced by these thin assurances, like one who believes the smile of friendship on an enemy's features, I opened my door, and as it swung outward, a black spot upon the inward burst of light, I saw the beach washed clean of any track, as if no foot before mine had disturbed the smooth sand. With the quick lift of spirit that follows a period of uneasy

depression, I felt—in a purely yielding fashion and without voli-
tion—that my own memory was washed clean of all the mistrust
and suspicion and disease-like fear of a lifetime, just as the filth of
the water's edge succumbs to a particularly high tide, and is carried
out of sight. There was a scent of soaked, brackish grass, like the
mouldy pages of a book, commingled with a sweet odour born of
the hot sunlight upon inland meadows, and these were borne into
me like an exhilarating drink, seeping and tingling through my
veins as if they would convey to me something of their own impalpable nature, and float me dizzily in the aimless breeze. And
conspiring with these things, the sun continued to shower upon
me, like the rain of yesterday, an incessant array of bright spears;
as if it also wished to hide that suspected background presence
which moved beyond my sight and was betrayed only by a careless rustle on the borders of my consciousness, or by the aspect of
blank figures staring out of an ocean void. That sun, a fierce ball
solitary in the whirlpool of infinity, was like a horde of golden
moths against my upturned face. A bubbling white grail of fire
divine and incomprehensible, it withheld from me a thousand
promised mirages where it granted one. For the sun did actually
seem to indicate realms, secure and fanciful, where if I but knew
the path I might wander in this curious exultation. Such things
come of our own natures, for life has never yielded for one moment her secrets, and it is only in our interpretation of their hinted images that we may find ecstasy or dullness, according to a
deliberately-induced mood. Yet ever and again we must succumb
to her deceptions, believing for the moment that we may this
time find the withheld joy. And in this way the fresh sweetness of
the wind, on a morning following the haunted darkness (whose
evil intimations had given me a greater uneasiness than any menace to my body) whispered to me of ancient mysteries only half-
linked with earth, and of pleasures that were the sharper because
I felt that I might experience only a part of them. The sun and
wind and that scent that rose upon them told me of festivals of
gods whose senses are a millionfold more poignant than man's,
and whose joys are a millionfold more subtle and prolonged.
These things, they hinted, could be mine if I gave myself wholly
into their bright deceptive power. And the sun, a crouching god

with naked celestial flesh, an unknown, too-mighty furnace upon which eye might not look, seemed almost sacred in the glow of my newly-sharpened emotions. The ethereal thunderous light it gave was something before which all things must worship astonished. The slinking leopard in his green-chasmed forest must have paused briefly to consider its leaf-scattered rays, and all things nurtured by it must have cherished its bright message on such a day. For when it is absent in the far reaches of eternity, earth will be lost and black against an illimitable void. That morning, in which I shared the fire of life, and whose brief moment of pleasure is secure against the ravenous years, was astir with the beckoning of strange things whose elusive names can never be written.

As I made my way toward the village, wondering how it might look after a long-needed scrubbing by the industrious rain, I saw, tangled in a glimmer of sunlit moisture that was poured over it like a yellow vintage, a small object like a hand, some twenty feet ahead of me, and touched by the repetitious foam. The shock and disgust born in my startled mind when I saw that it was indeed a piece of rotten flesh overcame my new contentment and engendered a shocked suspicion that it might actually be a hand. Certainly, no fish, or part of one, could assume that look, and I thought I saw mushy fingers wed in decay. I turned the thing over with my foot, not wishing to touch so foul an object, and it adhered stickily to the leather shoe, as if clutching with the grasp of corruption. The thing, whose shape was nearly lost, held too much resemblance to what I feared it might be; and I pushed it into the willing grasp of a seething wave, which took it from sight with an alacrity not often shown by those ravelled edges of the sea.

Perhaps I should have reported my find, yet its nature was too ambiguous to make action natural. Since it had been partly *eaten* by some ocean-dwelling monstrousness, I did not think it identifiable enough to form evidence of an unknown but possible tragedy. The numerous drownings, of course, came into my mind—as well as other things lacking in wholesomeness, some of which remained only as possibilities. Whatever the storm-dislodged fragment may have been, and whether it were fish or some animal akin to man, I have never spoken of it until now. After all, there was no proof that it had not merely been distorted by rottenness into that shape.

I approached the town, sickened by the presence of such an object amidst the apparent beauty of the clean beach, though it was horribly typical of the indifference of death in a nature which mingles rottenness with beauty, and perhaps loves the former more. In Ellston I heard of no recent drowning or other mishap of the sea, and found no reference to such in the columns of the local paper—the only one I read during my stay.

It is difficult to describe the mental state in which succeeding days found me. Always susceptible to morbid emotions whose dark anguish might be induced by things outside myself, or might spring from the abysses of my own spirit, I was ridden by a feeling which was not fear or despair, or anything akin to these, but was rather a perception of the brief hideousness and underlying filth of life—a feeling partly a reflection of my internal nature and partly a result of broodings induced by that gnawed rotten object which may have been a hand. In those days my mind was a place of shadowed cliffs and dark moving figures, like the ancient unsuspected realm which the fairy-tale recalled to me. I felt, in brief agonies of disillusionment, the gigantic blackness of this overwhelming universe, in which my days and the days of my race were as nothing to the shattered stars; a universe in which each action is vain and even the emotion of grief a wasted thing. The hours I had previously spent in something of regained health, contentment, and physical well-being, were given now (as if those days of the previous week were something definitely ended) to an indolence like that of a man who no longer cares to live. I was engulfed by a piteous lethargic fear of some ineluctable doom which would be, I felt, the completed hate of the peering stars and of the black enormous waves that hoped to clasp my bones within them—the vengeance of all the indifferent, horrendous majesty of the night ocean.

Something of the darkness and restlessness of the sea had penetrated my heart, so that I lived in an unreasoning, unperceiving torment, a torment none the less acute because of the subtlety of its origin and the strange, unmotivated quality of its vampiric existence. Before my eyes lay the phantasmagoria of the purpling clouds, the strange silver bauble, the recurrent stagnant foam, the loneliness of that bleak-eyed house, and the mockery of the puppet town. I no longer went to the village, for it seemed only a travesty of life. Like my own soul, it stood upon a dark enveloping sea—a sea grown slowly hateful to me. And among these images, corrupt and festering, dwelt that of an object whose human contours left ever smaller the doubt of what it once had been.

These scribbled words can never tell of the hideous loneliness (something I did not even wish assuaged, so deeply was it embedded in my heart) which had insinuated itself within me, mumbling of terrible and unknown things stealthily circling nearer. It was not a madness: rather was it a too clear and naked perception of the darkness beyond this frail existence, lit by a momentary sun no more secure than ourselves: a realization of futility that few can experience and ever again touch the life about them: a knowledge that turn as I might, battle as I might with all the remaining power of my spirit, I could neither win an inch of ground from the inimical universe, nor hold for even a moment the life entrusted to me. Fearing death as I did life, burdened with a nameless dread yet unwilling to leave the scenes evoking it, I awaited whatever consummating horror was shifting itself in the immense region beyond the walls of consciousness.

Thus autumn found me, and what I had gained from the sea was lost back into it. Autumn on the beaches—a drear time betokened by no scarlet leaf nor any other accustomed sign. A frightening sea which changes not, though man changes. There was only a chilling of the waters, in which I no longer cared to enter—a further darkening of the pall-like sky, as if eternities of snow were waiting to descend upon the ghastly waves. Once that descent began, it would never cease, but would continue beneath the white and the yellow and the crimson sun, and beneath that ultimate small ruby which shall yield only to the futilities of night. The once friendly waters babbled meaningfully at me, and eyed me with a strange regard; yet whether the darkness of the scene were a reflection of my own broodings, or whether the gloom within me were caused by what lay without, I could not have told. Upon the beach and me alike had fallen a shadow, like that of a bird which flies silently overhead—a bird whose watching eyes we do not suspect till the image on the ground repeats the image in the sky, and we look suddenlu [sic] upward to find that something has been circling above us hitherto unseen.

The day was in late September, and the town had closed the resorts where mad frivolity ruled empty, fear-haunted lives, and where raddled puppets performed their summer antics. The puppets were cast aside, smeared with the painted smiles and frowns they had last assumed, and there were not a hundred people left in the town. Again the gaudy, stucco-fronted buildings lining the shore were permitted to crumble undisturbed in the wind. As the month advanced to the day of which I speak, there grew in me the light of a grey infernal dawn, wherein I felt some dark thaumaturgy would be completed. Since I feared such a thaumaturgy less than a continuance of my horrible suspicions—less than the too-elusive hints of something monstrous lurking behind the great stage, it was with more speculation than actual fear that I waited unendingly for the day of horror which seemed to be nearing. The day, I repeat, was late in September, though whether the 22nd or 23rd I am uncertain. Such details have fled before the recollection of those uncompleted happenings—episodes with which no orderly existence should be plagued, because of the damnable suggestions (and only suggestions) they contain. I knew the time with an intuitive distress of spirit—a recognition too deep for me to explain. Throughout those daylight hours I was expectant of the night; impatient, perhaps, so that the sunlight passed like a half-glimpsed reflection in rippled water—a day of whose events I recall nothing.

It was long since that portentous storm had cast a shadow over the beach, and I had determined, after hesitations caused by nothing tangible, to leave Ellston, since the year was chilling and there was no return of my earlier contentment. When a telegram came for me (lying two days in the Western Union office before I was located, so little was my name known) saying that my design had been accepted—winning above all others in the contest—I set a date for leaving. This news, which earlier in the year would have affected me strongly, I now received with a curious apathy. It seemed as unrelated to the unreality about me, as little pertinent to me, as if it were directed to another person whom I did not know, and whose message had come to me through some accident. None the less, it was that which forced me to complete my plans and leave the cottage by the shore.

There were only four nights of my stay remaining when there occurred the last of those events whose meaning lies more in the darkly sinister impression surrounding them than in anything obviously threatening. Night had settled over Ellston and the coast, and a pile of soiled dishes attested both to my recent meal and to my lack of industry. Darkness came as I sat with a cigarette before the seaward window, and it was a liquid which gradually filled the sky, washing in a floating moon, monstrously elevated. The flat sea bordering upon the gleaming sand, the utter absence of tree or figure or life of any sort, and the regard of that high moon made the vastness of my surroundings abruptly clear. There were only a few stars pricking through as if to accentuate by their smallness the majesty of the lunar orb and of the restless shifting tide.

I had stayed indoors, fearing somehow to go out before the sea on such a night of shapeless portent, but I heard it mumbling secrets of an incredible lore. Borne to me on a wind out of nowhere was the breath of some strange and palpitant life; the embodiment of all I had felt and of all I had suspected—stirring now in the chasms of the sky or beneath the mute waves. In what place this mystery turned from an ancient, horrible slumber I could not tell, but like one who stands by a figure lost in sleep, knowing that it will awake in a moment, I crouched by the windows, holding a nearly-burnt out cigarette, and faced the rising moon.

Gradually there passed into that never-stirring landscape a brilliance intensified by the overhead glimmerings, and I seemed more and more under some compulsion to watch whatever might follow. The shadows were draining from the beach, and I felt that they took with them all which might have been a harbour for my thoughts when the hinted thing should come. Where any of them did remain they were ebon and blank: still lumps of darkness sprawling beneath the cruel brilliant rays. The endless tableau of the lunar orb—dead now, whatever her past was, and cold as the unhuman sepulchres she bears amid the ruin of dusty centuries older than man—and the sea, astir, perhaps, with some unkenned life, some forbidden sentience—confronted me with a horrible vividness. I arose and shut the window; partly because of an inward prompting, but mostly, I think, as an excuse for transferring momentarily the stream of thought. No sound came to me now as I stood before the closed panes. Minutes or eternities were alike. I was waiting, like my own fearing heart and the motionless scene beyond, for the token of some ineffable life. I had set the lamp upon a box in the western corner of the room, but the moon was brighter, and her bluish rays invaded places where the lamplight was faint. The ancient glow of the round silent orb lay upon the beach as it had lain for aeons, and I waited in a torment of expectancy made doubly acute by the delay in fulfillment, and the uncertainty of what strange completion was to come.

Outside the crouching hut a white illumination suggested vague spectral forms whose unreal, phantasmal motions seemed to taunt my blindness, just as unheard voices mocked my eager listening. For countless moments I was still, as if Time and the tolling of her great bell were hushed into nothingness. And yet there was nothing which I might fear: the moon-chiselled shadows were unnatural in no contour, and veiled nothing from my eyes. The night was silent—I knew that despite my closed window—and all the stars were fixed mournfully in a listening heaven of dark grandeur. No motion from me then, or word now, could reveal my plight, or tell of the fear-racked brain imprisoned in flesh which dared not break the silence, for all the torture it brought. As if expectant of death, and assured that nothing could serve to banish the soul-peril I confronted, I crouched with a forgotten cigarette in my hand. A silent world gleamed beyond the cheap, dirty windows, and in one corner of the room a pair of grimy oars, placed there before my arrival, shared the vigil of my spirit. The lamp burned endlessly, yielding a sick light hued like a corpse's flesh. Glancing at it now and again, for the desperate distraction it gave, I saw that many bubbles unaccountably rose and vanished in the kerosene-filled base. Curiously enough, there was no heat from the wick. And suddenly I became aware that the night as a whole was neither warm nor cold, but strangely neutral—as if all physical forces were suspended, and all the laws of a calm existence disrupted.

Then, with an unheard splash which sent from the silver water to the shore a line of ripples echoed in fear by my heart, a swimming thing emerged beyond the breakers. The figure may have been that of a dog, a human being, or something more strange. It could not have known that I watched—perhaps it did not care—but like a distorted fish it swam across the mirrored stars and dived beneath the surface. After a moment it came up again, and this time, since it was closer, I saw that it was carrying something across its shoulder. I knew, then, that it could be no animal, and that it was a man or something like a man, which came toward the land from a dark ocean. But it swam with a horrible ease.

As I watched, dread-filled and passive, with the fixed stare of one who awaits death in another yet knows he cannot avert it, the swimmer approached the shore—though too far down the southward beach for me to discern its outlines or features. Obscurely loping, with sparks of moonlit foam scattered by its quick gait, it emerged and was lost among the inland dunes.

Now I was possessed by a sudden recurrence of fear, which had died away in the previous moments. There was a tingling coldness all over me—though the room, whose window I dared not open now, was stuffy. I thought it would be very horrible if something were to enter a window which was not closed.

Now that I could no longer see the figure, I felt that it lingered somewhere in the close shadows, or peered hideously at me from whatever window I did not watch. And so I turned my gaze, eagerly and frantically, to each successive pane; dreading that I might indeed behold an intrusive regarding face, yet unable to keep myself from the terrifying inspection. But though I watched for hours, there was no longer anything upon the beach.

So the night passed, and with it began the ebbing of that strangeness—a strangeness which had surged up like an evil brew within a pot, had mounted to the very rim in a breathless moment, had paused uncertainly there, and had subsided, taking with it whatever unknown message it had borne. Like the stars that promise the revelation of terrible and glorious memories, goad us into worship by this deception, and then impart nothing, I had come frighteningly near to the capture of an old secret which ventured close to man's haunts and lurked cautiously just beyond the edge of the known. Yet in the end I had nothing. I was given only a glimpse of the furtive thing; a glimpse made obscure by the veils of ignorance. I cannot even conceive what might have shown itself had I been too close to that swimmer who went shoreward instead of into the ocean. I do not know what might have come if the brew had passed the rim of the pot and poured outward in a swift cascade of revelation. The night ocean withheld whatever it had nurtured. I shall know nothing more.

Even yet I do not know why the ocean holds such a fascination for me. But then, perhaps none of us can solve those things—they exist in defiance of all explanation. There are men, and wise men, who do not like the sea and its lapping surf on yellow shores; and they think us strange who love the mystery of the ancient and unending deep. Yet for me there is a haunting and inscrutable glamour in all the ocean's moods. It is in the melancholy silver foam beneath the moon's waxen corpse; it hovers over the silent and eternal waves that beat on naked shores; it is there when all is lifeless save for unknown shapes that glide through sombre depths. And when I behold the awesome billows surging in endless strength, there comes upon me an ecstasy akin to fear; so that I must abase myself before this mightiness, that I may not hate the clotted waters and their overwhelming beauty.

Vast and lonely is the ocean, and even as all things came from it, so shall they return thereto. In the shrouded depths of time none shall reign upon the earth, nor shall any motion be, save in the eternal waters. And these shall beat on dark shores in thunderous foam, though none shall remain in that dying world to watch the cold light of the enfeebled moon playing on the swirling tides and coarse-grained sand. On the deep's margin shall rest only a stagnant foam, gathering about the shells and bones of perished shapes that dwelt within the waters. Silent, flabby things will toss and roll along empty shores, their sluggish life extinct. Then all shall be dark, for at last even the white moon on the distant waves shall wink out. Nothing shall be left, neither above nor below the sombre waters. And until that last millennium, as after it, the sea will thunder and toss throughout the dismal night.

7000 words

R.H.Barlow
P.O.Box 88
DeLand,Fla.

                            THE NIGHT OCEAN.

    I WENT TO Ellston Beach not only for the pleasures of sun and

ocean, but to rest a weary mind. Since I knew no person in the little

town, which thrives upon summer vacationists and presents only blank

windows during most of the year, there seemed no likelihood that

I might be disturbed. This pleased me, for I did not wish to see

anything but the expanse of pounding surf and the beach lying before

my temporary home.

    My long work of the summer was completed when I left the city,

and the large mural design produced by it had been entered in the con-

test. It had taken me the bulk of the year to finish the painting, and when the

last brush was cleaned, I was no longer reluctant to yield to the

claims of health, and find rest and seclusion for a time. Indeed,

when I had been a week on the beach whose success had seemed

recently all-important. There

was no longer the old concern with a hundred complexities of colour

and ornament; no longer the fear and mistrust of my ability to render

a mental image actual, and turn by my own skill alone the dim-conceived

idea into the careful draught of a design. Things seen by the inward

sight, like those flashing visions which come as we drift into the blank-

ness of sleep, are more vivid and meaningful to us in that form than

when we have sought to weld them with reality. Set a pen to a dream,

and the colour drains from it. The ink with which we write seems di-

luted with something

(2)

luted with something *holding* ~~that holds~~ too much of reality, and we find that

after all, we cannot delineate the incredible memory. It is as if our

inward selves, released from the bonds of daytime and *objectivity* ~~reality~~, revelled

in prisoned emotions *which* ~~that~~ are hastily stifled when we would translate

them. In dreams and visions *lie* ~~are~~ the greatest creations of man, for on

them *rests* ~~is~~ no yoke of line or hue. Forgotten scenes, and lands ~~~~

more obscure than the golden world of childhood, spring into the sleep-

ing mind to reign until awakening puts them to rout. Amid these may be

attained something of the glory and contentment for which we yearn; *some*

adumbration of ~~and~~ sharp beauties suspected but not before revealed, which are to us

as the Graal to holy spirits of the mediaeval world. To shape these

things on the wheel of art, *to* ~~and~~ seek to bring some faded trophy from

that intangible realm *of shadow & gossamer,* requires equal skill and memory. For although

dreams are in all of us, few hands may grasp their moth-wings without

tearing them.

 Such *a* skill this narrative does not have. ~~~~ If I might, I

would reveal to you the hinted events which I perceived dimly, like

one who peers into an unlit realm, *glimpses* ~~sensing~~ forms whose motion is con-

cealed. ~~But somehow I had caught more of uncertainty in my design, which~~

then lay with a multitude of others in the building for which they were

planned. ~~~~

~~~~ from the endless world of imagining.

The difficulties of this process, ~~coupled with a~~ resulting strain *upon*

all my powers, had *undermined* ~~~~ my health ~~~~ *brought me to* and ~~caused my presence at~~

the beach during this period of waiting.

 Since I wished to be wholly alone, I rented (to the delight of

the incredulous owner) a small house some distance from the village

(3)

of Ellston---which, ~~the~~ season, ~~nothing an order~~ was alive with a moribund bustle of tourists, uniformly uninteresting to me. The house, dark from sea-wind though it had not been painted, was not even a satellite of the village; but swung below it on the coast ~~as~~ a pendulum beneath a still clock; quite alone upon a hill of weed-grown sand. Like a solitary warm animal it crouched facing the sea, and its inscrutable dirty windows stared upon a lonely ~~land~~ of earth and sky and enormous sea. It will not do to use too much imagining in a narrative whose facts, could they be ~~added to~~ and fitted into a mosaic, would be ~~very~~ strange in themselves; but I thought the little house was lonely when I saw it, and that like myself, it was conscious of its meaningless nature before the great sea.

I took the place in late August, arriving a day before I was expected, and encountering a van and two workingmen unloading the furniture provided by the owner . I did not know then how long I would stay, and when the truck that brought the goods had left, I settled my small luggage, and locked the door (feeling very proprietary at having a house after months of a rented room) to go down the weedy hill and upon the beach. Since it was quite square and had but one room, the house had required little exploration. Two windows in each side provided a great quantity of light, and somehow a door had been squeezed in as an afterthought on the ~~the~~ oceanward wall. The place ~~was~~ built about ten years previously, but ~~since it was out of~~ from Ellston village ~~which was~~ difficult to rent even during the active ~~three of the summer~~ (after October) There being no fireplace, it stood empty and alone until far into spring. ~~And indeed, this severance,~~ Though ~~they were~~ actually less than a mile below Ellston, ~~appeared greater~~ ~~because one could~~ see only grassy dunes in the direction of the village.

(4)

~~A bond is the coast was responsible for this~~

The first day, half-gone when I was installed, I spent in the enjoyment of the sun and the restless water--- things whose quiet majesty made the designing of murals distant and tiresome. ʙut this was
the natural reaction to a long concern with one set of habits and
activities. I was through with my work and my vacation was begun. ᴛhis
fact, while elusive for the moment, showed in everything which surrounded me that afterhoon of my arrival; and in the utter change from old
scenes. ~~what was it like in memory ?--- The first thing I would convey~~
ɪs an effect of bright sun upon a shifting sea of waves, whose mysteriously-impelled curves were strewn with what appeared to be rhinestones, since there could not have been that many diamonds even in
the coronet of the sea. ʀerhaps a water-colour might ~~catch~~ the solid
masses of intoɭerable light which lay upon the beach where the sea
mingled with the sand. ᴀlthough the ocean bore her own hue, it was
dominated wholly and incredibly by the enormous glare. ᴛhere was no
other person near me, and I enjoyed the spectacle without the annoyance of any alien object upon that stage. ᴇach of my senses was touched
in a different way, ʙut sometimes it seemed that the roar of the sea
was akin to that great brightness, or as if the waves were glaring
instead of the sun, each of these being so vigorous and insistent that
impressions coming from them were mingled. ᴜuriously, I saw no one
bathing near my little square house during that or succeeding afternoons, although a wide beach ~~lay in the curving shore,~~ even more inviting than ~~might be found~~ at the village, where the surf was dotted
with random figures. I supposed this was because of the distance, ~~which~~
~~seperated this area from one more convenient,~~ and because ~~(for an un-~~
~~known reason)~~ there had never been other houses below the town,
~~though many~~ straggled along the northward coast, facing the sea with
aimless eyes.

(5.)

I swam until the afternoon had gone, and later, having rested,
walked into the little town. Darkness hid the sea from me as I ~~accompanied
its outline~~, and I found in the dingy lights of the street tokens of a
life which was not even conscious of the great, gloom-shrouded thing
lying so close. There were painted women in tinsel adornments, and bored
men who were no longer young--- a throng of foolish marionettes perched
on the lip of the ocean-chasm; unseeing, unwilling to see, what lay above
them and about, in the multitudinous grandeur of the stars ~~which had that
stolen the jewels of the afternoon waves~~ and the leagues of the night
ocean. I walked along that darkened sea as I went back to the bare little
house, sending the beams of my flashlight out upon the naked and impenetrable void. In the absence of the moon, this light made a solid bar
athwart the walls of the uneasy tide; and ~~through me went~~ an indescribable
emotion born of the noise of the waters and the perception of my inconceivable smallness as I ~~shone a~~ tiny beam upon a realm immense in itself,
yet only the black border of the earthly deep. ~~and this region,~~ upon which
ships were moving alone in the darkness where I could not see them, gave
off the murmur of a distant, angry rabble.

When I reached my high residence, I knew that I had passed no one
during the mile's walk from the village, and yet there somehow lingered
the impression that I had been all the while accompanied by the spirit
of the lonely sea, personified in a shape which was not revealed to me,
but moved quietly about beyond my range of comprehension, actors
behind darkened scenery, in readiness for the lines that will shortly call
them before our eyes to move and speak in the sudden revelation of the
footlights. Then I shook off this fancy, and sought my key to enter the
place, whose bare walls were a sudden security.

My cottage was entirely free of the village, as if it had wandered
down the coast and was unable to return; and there I heard nothing of the
disturbing clamour when I returned each night after supper.

The Lovecraft Annual: 2014   89

(6)

I generally stayed but a short while upon the streets of Allston, though
sometimes I went into the place entirely for the sake of the walk it provided. There were all the multitude of curio-shops and falsely regal
theater-fronts that clutter vacation towns, but I never went into these;
and the place seemed useful only for its resturants, ~~t~~ It was astonishing the number of useless things people found to do.

There was a succession of sun-filled days at first. I rose early,
and beheld the grey sky agleam with promise of sunrise; a prophecy fulfilled as I stood witness. Those dawns were cold, and their colours faint
in comparison to that uniform radiance of day, which ~~dominated the hours~~ *tires to every hour The quality*
~~so that all times partook~~ of the white noon. That great light, so apparent
the first day, made each succeeding day, a yellow page in the book of time.
I noticed that many of the beach-people were displeased by the inordinate
sun, whereas I sought it. *After grey months of toil* The lethargy induced by ~~days of~~ a physical existence ~~(after grey months of toil)~~ in that region governed by the simple
things, the wind and light and water, had a prompt effect upon me; and
since I was anxious to continue this healing process, I spent all my
time outdoors in the sunlight. This induced a state at once impassive and
submissive, and gave me a feeling of security against the ravenous night.
As darkness is akin to death, so is light to vitality. *Through* The heritage of a
million years ago, when men were closer to the mother sea, and when the
creatures of which we are born lay languid in the shallow, sun-pierced
water, we *still* seek ~~today in this brief stopping point on the journey to~~ *steeping ourselves* within their lulling security
~~oblivion~~ these primal things when we are tired, ~~and steep ourselves~~ like those
the early half-mammals *which* ~~that~~ had not yet ventured upon the oozy land,

The monotony of the waves gave repose, and I had no other occupation
than witnessing a myriad ocean moods. There is a ceaseless change in the
waters--- colours and shades pass over them like the insubstantial expressions of a well-known face; and these are at once communicated to us
by half-recognized senses. ~~so that~~ When the sea is restless, remembering

(7)

old ships that have gone over her chasms, in our hearts the longing for
a vanished horizon comes up silently, like the dawn behind ships that
are now forgotten in the slime of the ocean floor but are sought out
by deep-slanting rays that wander among their sunken ribs. But when
she forgets, we forget also, save that she must always hold an alien air,
Though we know her a lifetime, as if something too vast to have any
shape were lurking in the universe to which she is a door. The morning
ocean, glimmering with a reflected mist of blue-white cloud and expanding diamond foam, has the eyes of one who ponders strangeness, and her
intricately woven webs, through which dart a myriad coloured fishes,
hold the air of some great idle thing which will arise presently from
the hoary immemorial chasms, and stride upon the land.

I was content for many days, and glad that I had chosen the lonely
house which sat like a small beast upon those rounded cliffs of sand.
Among the pleasantly aimless amusements fostered by such a life, I
took to following the edge of the tide, (where the waves left
with a damp irregular outline rimmed fur evanescent foam) for long
distances; and sometimes I found curious bits of shell in the chance
litter of the sea. There was an astonishing lot of debris on that inward curving coast which my bare little house overlooked, and I judged
that currents must reach that spot, whose courses diverge from the village
At any rate, my pockets---when I had any--- generally held
vast stores of trash; most of which I threw away an hour or two after
picking it up, wondering why I had kept it. Once, however, I found a
small bone whose nature I could not identify, save that it was certainly
nothing out of a fish; and I kept this, along with a large metal bead
whose minutely carven design was rather unusual. This latter depicted a fishy
thing against a patterned background of seaweed, instead of the usual
floral or geometrical designs, and was minutely carven, though it must
have tossed in the surf for years to become so worn. Since I had never seen
anything like it, I judged that it was some fashion, now forgotten, of

(8)

a previous year at Allston, where similar fads were common.

    Perhaps I had been there a week when the weather began a gradual
change. Each stage of this progressive darkening was followed by another
subtly intensified, so that in the end, the entire atmosphere surrounding me had shifted from day to evening. This was more obvious to me in
a series of mental impressions than what I actually witnessed, for the
small house was lonely under grey skies, and sometimes there was a
beating wind that came out of the ocean bearing moisture. The
sun was displaced by long intervals of cloudiness--- layers of grey mist
beyond whose unknown depth the sun lay cut off. Though it might glare
with the old intensity above that enormous veil, it could not penetrate.
The beach was a prisoner in a hueless vault for hours at a time, as if
something of the night were welling into other hours.

    Although the wind was invigorating and the ocean whipped into
little churning spirals of activity by the vagrant flapping, I found the
water growing chill, so that I could not stay in it as long as I had done
previously, and thus I fell into the habit of long walks, which---when
I was unable to swim--- provided the exercise that I was so careful to
obtain. These walks covered a greater range of sea-edge than my previous
wanderings, and since the beach extended in a stretch of miles beyond
the tawdry village, I often found myself wholly isolated upon an endless
area of sand as evening drew close. When this occured, I would stride
hastily along the whispering sea-border, following its outline so that
I should not wander inland and lose my way. And sometimes, when these
walks were late (as they grew increasingly to be) I would come upon the
crouching house that looked like a harbinger of the village. Insecure
upon the wind-gnawed cliffs, a dark blot upon the morbid hues of the
ocean sunset, it was more lonely than by the full light of either orb;
and seemed to my imagination like a mute, questioning face turned toward
me expectant of some action. That the place was isolated I have said,
and this at first pleased me; but in that brief evening hour when the

(9)

sun left in a gore-spattered decline and darkness lumbered on *like* an expanding shapeless blot, there was an alien presence about the place: a
spirit, a mood, an impression that came from the surging wind, the gigantic sky, and that sea which drooled blackening waves upon a beach grown
abruptly strange. At these times I felt an uneasiness which had no very
definite cause, although my solitary nature had made me long accustomed
to the ancient silence and the ancient voice of nature. These misgivings,
to which I could have put no sure name, did not affect me long, yet I
think now that all the while a gradual consciousness of the *ocean's* immense loneliness crept upon me, a loneliness that was made subtly horrible by in-
timations-- which were never more than such-- of some animation or sentience preventing *me* from being wholly alone.

The noisy, yellow streets of the town, with their curiously unreal
activity, were ~~severed from the~~ *very far away,* place I ~~lived --both by~~ sea ~~and beach,~~
and ~~while~~ *when* I went there for my evening meal (mistrusting a diet entirely
of my own ambiguous cooking) I took increasing~~ld~~ and quite unreasonable
care~~~~ that I should return to the cottage before the late darkness,
though I was often abroad until ten or so.

You will say that such action is unreasonable; that if I *had* feared the
darkness in some childish way, I would have entirely avoided it *you will* ~~and~~ ask
me why I did not leave the place since its loneliness was depressing me.
To *all* this I have no reply, save that whatever unrest I felt, whatever re-
mote~~ly~~ disturb~~ing~~ there was to me in brief aspects of the darkening sun
or *in* the eager salt-brittle wind or *in* the robe of the dark sea ~~which~~ lay crumpled like an enormous garment so close to me; *was something which* ~~~~ had an origin ~~~~
~~~~ half in my own heart, *which showed itself* ~~and showing themselves~~ only at fleeting moments,
twilight had no very long effect upon me. In the recurrent days of diamond light,
with sportive waves flinging blue peaks at the basking shore, the memory
of dark moods seemed rather incredible; *yet* ~~although~~ I might again experience
them *words once word,* ~~~~, and descend to a dim region of despair (only an hour or *two)*
~~~~ *afterward*

(10)

Perhaps these inward emotions were only a reflection of the sea's own mood; for although half of what we see is coloured by the interpretation placed upon it by our minds, quite distinctly many of our feelings are shaped by external, physical things. The sea can bind us to her many moods, whispering to us by the subtle token of a shadow or a gleam upon the waves, and hinting in these ways of her mournfulness or rejoicing. Always, she is remembering old things, and these memories, though we may not grasp them, are imparted to us, so that we share her gaiety or remorse. Since I was doing no work, seeing no person that I knew, perhaps I was susceptible to shades of her cryptic meaning which would have been naught to another. The ocean ruled my life during the whole of that late summer; demanding it as recompense for the healing sh had brought me.

There were drownings at the beach that year, and while I heard of these only casually (such is our indifference to a death which does not concern us, and to which we are not witness) details were unsavoury. The people who died---some of them swimmers of a skill beyond the average--- were sometimes not found until many days had elapsed, and the hideous vengeance of the deep had scourged their rotten bodies. It was as if the sea had dragged them into a chasm-lair, and had mulled them about in the darkness, until satisfied that they were no longer of any use, she had floated them ashore in a ghastly state. No one seemed to know what had caused these deaths. Their frequency excited alarm among the timid, since the undertow at Allston was not strong, and there were known to be ho sharks at hand. Whether the bodies showed marks of any attacks I did not learn, but the dread of a death which moves among the waves, and comes on lone people from a place lightless, motionless, is a dread that men know and do not like. They must such a death, quickly find a reason for it, even if there are no sharks. Since sharks passed only a suspected cause,

94 R. H. Barlow

(11)

of one never
~~unto~~ to my knowledge ~~were some~~ confirmed, ~~those who continued swimming~~ *The swimmers who continued*
during the rest of the season were ~~cautious more of~~ treacherous tides *on guard against*
~~then of~~ any possible sea-animal. *rather than against*

Autumn, indeed, was not a great distance off, and some people used
this an excuse for leaving the sea, where men were snared by death, and
going to the security of inland fields, where one cannot even hear the
ocean. So August ended, and I had been at the beach many days.

There had been a threat of storm since the fourth of the new month,
and on the sixth, when I set out for a walk in the damp wind, there was
a mass of formless cloud, colourless and oppressive, above the ruffled
leaden sea. The motion of the wind, directed toward no especial goal but
stirring uneasily, provided a sensation of coming animation--- a hint of
life in the elements which might be that *long* expected storm. I had eaten my
luncheon at Ellston, and though *the* heavens seemed the closing lid of a great
casket, I ventured far down the beach and away from both the town and my
no-longer-to-be-seen house. As the universal grey became spotted with a
carrion purple--- curiously brilliant despite its sombre hue--- I found that
I was several miles from any possible shelter. ~~in the event of storm.~~ This,
however, **did** not seem very important; for I was in a curious mood *despite the dark skies with their added glow of...* *paralleling that glow — a mood*
which flashed through a body grow suddenly alert and sensitive to the outline
of shapes and meanings that were previously dim ~~much as the dark skies~~
~~were now suffused with a glow than was presage of something unknown~~ obscurely, a memory came to me; suggested by the likeness of the scene to
one I had imagined when a story was read to me in childhood. That tale---
of which I had not thought for many years--- concerned a woman who was
loved by the dark-bearded king of an underwater realm *by* blurred
cliffs where fish-things lived, and who was taken from the golden-haired
youth *of her birth* ~~to whom she was plighted on the land,~~ by a dark being crowned with
a priest-like mitre, and having the features of a withered ape. What had
remained in the corner of my fancy was the image of cliffs beneath the

(12)

water, against the hueless, dusky no-sky of such a realm; and though
I had forgotten most of the story, it was recalled quite unexpectedly
by the same pattern of cliff and sky which I then beheld. these were
similar to what I had imagined in a year now lost save for random, incomplete impressions. suggestions of this story may have lingered behind certain irritatingly unfinished memories, and also in the seeming
values hinted to my senses by scenes whose actual worth was bafflingly
small. frequently, in a momentary perception, we feel that a feathery
landscape, a woman's dress along the curve of a road by the
afternoon, or the solidity of a century-defying tree against the pale
morning sky (the conditions more than the object being significant) holds
something precious, some golden virtue that we must grasp. And yet when
it be viewed later, or from another point, this scene has lost its value
and meaning for us. Perhaps this is because the thing we seek does not
hold that elusive quality, but only suggests to the mind some very
different thing which remains unremembered. The baffled mind, not wholly
sensing the cause of its flashing appreciation, seizes on the object
exciting it, and is surprised when there is nothing of worth therein.
Thus it was when I beheld the purpling clouds. They held the stateliness and mystery of old monastery towers at twilight, but their aspect was also that of the cliffs in the old fairy-tale. Suddenly
reminded of this lost image, I half-expected to see, in the fine-spun
dirty foam and among the waves which were now as if they had been poured
of flawed black glass, the avenging, horrid figure of that ape-faced
creature, wearing a mitre old with verdigris, from the kingdom in some
lost gulf to which those waves were sky.

I did not see any such creature from the realm of imagining, but as
the chill wind veered, slitting the heavens like a rustling knife, there
was in the gloom of merging cloud and water only a grey object, like a
piece of driftwood, tossing obscurely on the foam. This was a consider-

(13)

able distance out, and since it vanished shortly, may have been not wood, but a porpoise coming to the troubled surface.

I soon found that I had stayed too long contemplating the rising storm linking early fancies with its grandeur, for an icy rain began spotting down, bringing a more uniform gloom upon a scene already too dark for the hour . Hurrying along the grey sand, I felt the impact of cold drops upon my back, and my clothing was soaked throughout. At first I had run, put to flight by the colourless drops whose pattern hung in long linking strands from an unseen sky, but after I saw that refuge was too far to reach in anything like a dry state, I slackened my pace, and returned home as if I had walked under clear skies. There was not much reason to hurry, although I did not idle as upon previous occasions. The constraining wet garments were cold upon me; and with the gathering darkness, and the wind that rose endlessly from the ocean, I could not repress a shiver. Yet there was, beside the discomfort of the precipitous rain, an exhilaration latent in the purplish ravelled masses of cloud and the stimulated reactions of my body. In a mood half of exultant pleasure from resisting the rain (which streamed from me now, and filled my shoes and pockets) and half of those morbid, dominant skies which hovered with dark wings above the shifting eternal sea, I tramped along the grey corridor of Ellston Beach. More rapidly than I had expected the crouching house showed in the oblique, flapping rain, and all the weeds of the sand cliff writhed in accompaniment to the frantic wind, as if they would uproot themselves to join the far-travelling element. Sea and sky had altered not at all, and the scene was that which had accompanied me , save that There was now upon it (painted) the hunching roof that seemed to bend from the assailing rain. I hurried up, the insecure steps, and let myself into a dry room, where, unconsciously surprised that I was free of the nagging wind, I stood for a moment with water rilling from every inch of me.

(14)

There are two windows in the front of that house, as on each side,
and these face nearly straight upon the ocean; which I saw now half obscured by the combined veils of the rain and the imminent night. From
these I looked as I was dressing in a motley array of dry garments seized
from convenient hangers and from a chair (laden too full to sit upon. I
was prisoned on all sides by an dusk increased unnaturally which filtered down at an undefined hour hidden by the storm.
How long I had been upon the reaches of wet grey sand, or what the real
time was, I could not tell, though a moment's search produced my watch---
fortunately left behind and thus avoiding the uniform sponginess of my
clothing. I half-guessed the hour from the dimness of the hands, which
were only slightly less indecipherable than the surrounding figures. In
another moment my sight penetrated the gloom (greater in the house than
beyond the bleary window) and saw that it was 6: 45.

There had been no one upon the beach as I came in, and naturally
I expected to see no further swimmers that night. Yet when I looked
again from the window there appeared surely to be figures blotting the
grime of the wet evening. I counted three moving about in some incomprehensible action, and close to the house, another ---which may not have
been a person, but a wave-ejected log, for the surf was now pounding
fiercely. I was startled to no little degree, and wondered for what purpose those hardy persons stayed out in such a storm. And then I thought
(perhaps that) like myself they had been caught unintentionally in the
storm, and surrendered to the watery gusts. In another moment, prompted
by a certain civilised hospitality which overcame my love of solitude,
I stepped to the door, and emerged momentarily (at the cost of another
wetting, for the rain promptly descended upon me in exultant fury) on
the small porch, gesticulating toward the people. But whether they did
not see me, or did not understand, they made no returning signal. Dim
in the evening, they stood as if half-surprised, or as if they awaited

(15.)

some other action from me. There was in their attitude something of that
cryptic blankness, signifying ~~perhaps~~ anything, which the house wore about
itself, seen on the morbid sunset. Abruptly, there came to me a feeling
that a sinister quality lurked about those unmoving figures which chose
to stay in the rainy night upon a beach deserted by all people; and I
closed the door with a surge of annoyance ~~that~~ which sought all too vainly to
disguise a deeper emotion ~~proof~~ of fear; ~~a~~ a consuming fright that welled
up from the shadows of my consciousness. A moment later, when I had stepped to the window, there seemed to be nothing (outside) but the portentous night
vaguely puzzled, even more vaguely frightened--- like one who has seen
no alarming thing, but is apprehensive of what may be found in the dark
street he is soon compelled to cross--- I decided that I had very possibly
seen no one, and that the murky air had deceived me.

     The aura of isolation about the place was increased that night,
though a hundred houses rose in the darkness, their light bleared and
yellow ~~in the rear~~ like goblin-eyes reflected in an oily forest pool
above streets of polished glass, just out of sight on the northward beach
yet because I could not see them, or even reach them in bad weather, since
I had no car nor any ~~xxxx~~ way to leave the crouching house except by walking in the figure-haunted darkness, I realized quite suddenly that I was,
to all intents, alone with the dreary sea that rose and subsided
unseen, unkenned, in the mist. And the voice of the sea had become a hoarse
groan, like that of something wounded which shifts about ~~preparatory to~~ before trying to rise
~~crising~~

     Fighting away the prevalent gloom with a soiled lamp---for the dark-
ness crept in at my windows and sat peering obscurely at me like a patient
animal from the corners--- I prepared my food, since I had no intention of
going to the village. The hour seemed incredibly advanced, though it was

(16.)

not yet nine o'clock when I went to bed. Darkness had come ~~furtively and~~
early, and throughout the remainder of my stay lingered evasively over
each scene and action ~~that~~ which I beheld. Something had settled out of the night
---something forever undefined, but stirring a latent sense within me, so
that I was like a beast expecting the momentary rustle of an enemy.

There were hours of wind, and sheets of the downpour flapped endlessly
on the meagre walls barring it from me. Lulls came in which I heard the
mumbling sea, and I could guess that large formless waves jostled one
another in the pallid whine of the winds, and flung a spray bitter with
salt. ~~upon the~~ Yet in the very monotony of the restless elements
I found a lethargic note, a sound that beguiled me, after a time, into
slumber grey and colourless as the night. The sea continued its mad monologue, and the wind her nagging, but these were shut out by the walls of
unconsciousness, and for a time the night ocean was banished from a sleeping mind.

Morning brought an enfeebled sun--- a sun like that which men will
see when the earth is old, if there are any men left: a sun more weary
than the shrouded, moribund sky. Faint echo of its old image, Phoebus strove
to pierce the ragged, ambiguous clouds as I awoke, at moments sending a
wash of pale gold rippling across the northwestern interior of my house,
at others waning till it was only a luminous ball, like some incredible
plaything forgotten on the celestial lawn. After a while the failing rain
--- which must have continued throughout the previous night---succeeded
in washing away those vestiges of purple cloud which had been like the
ocean-cliffs in an old fairy tale. Cheated alike of the setting and rising
sun, that day merged with the day before, as if the intervening storm had
not ushered a long darkness into the world, but had swollen and subsided
in one long afternoon. Gaining heart, the furtive sun exerted all his
force in dispelling the old mist, streaked now like a dirty window , and
cast it from his realm. The shallow blue day advanced as those grimy wisps

(17.)

retreated, and the loneliness which had encircled me welled back into a
watchful place of retreat, whence it went no farther, but crouched and
waited.

The ancient brightness was now once more upon the sun, and the old
glitter on the waves, whose p ayful blue shapes had flocked upon that coast
ere man was born, and would rejoice unseen when he was forgotten in. the
sepulchre of time. Influenced by these thin assurances, like one who believes
the smile of friendship on an enemy's features, I opened my door, and as it
swung outward, a black spot upon the inward burst of light, I saw the beach
washed clean of any track, as if no foot before mine had disturbed the smooth
sand. With the quick lift of spirit that follows a period of uneasy depression, I felt --- in a purely yielding fashion and without volition--- that
my own memory was washed clean of all the mistrust and suspicion and disease-
like fear of a lifetime, just as the filth of the water's edge succumbs to
a particularly high tide, and is carried out of sight. There was a scent of
soaked, brackish grass, like the mouldy pages of a book, commingled with a
sweet odour born of the hot sunlight upon inland meadows, and these were
borne to me like an exhilarating drink , seeping and tingling through my
veins as if they would convey to me something of their own impalpable nature,
and float me dizzily in the aimless breeze. And conspiring with these things,
as if it also wished to hide that suspected background presence which moved
beyond my sight and was betrayed only by a careless rustle on the borders of
my consciousness, or the aspect of blank figures staring out of an
ocean void, the sun continued to shower upon me, like the rain of yesterday,
an incessant array of bright spears, That sun, that diamond luntern by no
lity elsewhere a fierce ball solitary in the whirlpool of infinity, was like
a horde of golden moths against my upturned face. A bubbling white grail of
fire divine and incomprehensible, it withheld from me a thousand promised
mirages where it granted one. For the sun did actually seem to indicate
realms, secure and fanciful, where if I but knew the path I might wander in

(18.)

this curious exultation. Such things come of our own natures, for life has
never yielded for one moment her secrets; and it is only in our interpretation of their hinted images we may find ecstasy or dullness, according to
a deliberately-induced mood. Yet ever and again we must succumb to her deceptions, believing for the moment that we may this time find the witheld
joy. And in this way the fresh sweetness of the wind, on a morning following
the haunted darkness (whose evil intimations had given me a greater uneasiness than any menace to my body) whispered to me of ancient mysteries only
half-linked with earth, and of pleasures that were the sharper because I
felt that I might experience only a part of them. The sun and wind and that
scent that rose upon them, told me of festivals of gods, whose senses are
a millionfold more poignant than man's, and whose joys are a millionfold more subtle and
prolonged. These things, they hinted, could be mine if I gave myself wholly
into their bright deceptive power. And the sun, a crouching god with naked
celestial flesh, an unknown, too-mighty furnace upon which eye might not look,
seemed almost sacred in the ample glow of my newly-sharpened emotions. The
ethereal thunderous light it gave was something before which all things must
worship astonished. The slinking leopard in his green-chasmed forest must
have paused briefly to consider its leaf-scattered rays, and all things
nurtured by it must have cherished the bright warmth on such a day.
For when it is absent in the far reaches of eternity, earth will be lost
and black against an illimitable void. That morning, whose brief moment of
pleasure is secure against the ravenous years, and in which I shared the privilege,
was astir with the beckoning of strange things whose elusive
names can never be written.

As I made my way toward the village, wondering how it might look after
a long-needed scrubbing by the industrious rain, I saw, tangled in a glimmer
of sunlit moisture that was poured over it like a yellow vintage, a small

(19.)

object like a hand, some twenty feet ahead of me, and touched by the repetitious foam. The ~~repulsion~~ shock and disgust born in my startled mind
when I saw that it was indeed a piece of rotten flesh, overcame my ~~new~~
~~departing~~ contentment and engendered a shocked suspicion that it might
actually be a hand. Certainly, no fish, or part of one, could assume that
look, and I thought I saw mushy fingers wed in decay. I turned the thing
                      with my foot,
over ∧ not wishing to touch so foul an object, and it adhered stickily to
the leather ~~clothing~~ shoe, as if clutching with the grasp of corruption. The
thing, whose shape was nearly lost, held too much semblance to what I fear-
ed ~~that~~ it might be; and I pushed it into the willing ~~advance~~ of a ~~new~~ ~~searching~~
                              from sight
~~ing~~ wave, which took it ∧ with an alacrity not often shown by those ravelled
edges of the sea, ~~and seething above it, carried the it from sight.~~

    Perhaps I should have reported my find, yet its nature was too am-
             to make action natural.
biguous, ~~and~~ Since it had been partly eaten by some ocean-dwelling monstrousness, I did not think it identifiable enough to form evidence of an unknown but possible tragedy. The numerous drownings, of course, came into
                                                      some
my mind ∧ as well as other things lacking in wholesomeness, ~~part~~ of which
remained only as possibilities. Whatever the storm-dislodged fragment ~~had~~ ^may have
been, and whether it were fish or some animal akin to man, I have never
                          now
spoken of it until the ~~present~~ ~~day~~ After all, there was no ~~xxix~~ proof
that it had not merely been distorted ~~into~~ by rottenness into that shape.

    I approached the town, sickened by the presence of such an object ~~and~~ ^of ^the
the apparent beauty of the clean beach, though it was horribly typical
                                          which
of the indifference of death ~~xxdxxix~~ in a nature ~~that~~ mingles rottenness
                                          of   other
with beauty, and perhaps loves the former more. ~~and there~~ In Ellston I
       recent
heard ∧ no ~~reported~~ drowning or mishap of the sea, and found no reference
to such in the columns of ^the local paper--- the only one ~~that~~ I read during
my stay.

    It is difficult to describe the mental state in which succeeding days
                      unavoid'd
found me. Always susceptible to ~~surrounding~~ emotion, whose dark anguish might

(20.)

be induced by things outside myself, or might spring from the abysses of
my own spirit, I was ridden by a feeling which was not fear or despair,
or anything akin to these, but was rather a perception of the brief hideousness and the underlying filth of life--- a feeling which partly a
reflection of my internal nature, and partly the result of broodings induced by that gnawed rotten object which may well have been a hand.
In those days my mind was a place of shadowed cliffs and dark moving. figures, like the ancient realm unsuspected which the fairy-tale
recalled to me. I felt, in brief agonies of disillusionment, the gigantic
blackness of this overwhelming universe, in which my days and the days of
my race were nothing to the shattered stars; a universe in which each
action is vain and even the emotion of grief a wasted thing. The hours
that I had previously spent in something of regained health, and contentment, rendered acute by physical well-being, were given now (as if those
days of the previous week were something definitely ended) to an indolence
like that of a man who no longer cares to live. I was hopeless a piteous xxxx lethargic
fear of some ineluctable doom that would be, I felt, the completed hate
of peering stars and the black enormous waves that hoped to clasp my bones
within them, the vengeance of all the indifferent, horrendous majesty of
the night ocean.

Something of the darkness and the restlessness of the sea had penetrated
my heart, so that I lived in an unreasoning, unperceiving torment, a torment which was none the less acute because of the subtlety of its origin
and the strange, unmotivated quality of its vampiric existence. Before my
eyes lay the phantasmagoria of the purpling clouds, the strange silver
bauble, the recurrent stagnant foam, the loneliness of that bleak-
eyed house, and the puppet town to the village, for it I no longer went, seemed
only a mockery of life. Like my own soul, it stood upon a dark enveloping sea--- a sea grown slowly hateful to me. And among these images,
corrupt and festering, dwelt that of an object whose human

(21.)

contours left ever smaller the doubt of what it once had been.

These scribbled words can never tell of the hideous loneliness (which I did not even wish assuaged, so deep was it in my heart) had insinuated itself within me, mumbling of terrible and unknown things stealthily circling nearer. It was not a madness: rather was it too clear and naked perception of the darkness beyond this frail existence, lit by a momentary sun no more secure than ourselves: a realization of futility that few can experience and ever again touch the life about them: a knowledge that turn as I might, battle with all the remaining power of my spirit, I could inch of ground from the inimical universe, hold for even a moment the life entrusted to me. fearing death as I did life, burdened with a nameless dread yet unwilling to leave the scenes evoking it, I awaited whatever consummating horror was shifting itself in the immense region beyond the walls of consciousness.

Thus autumn found me, and what I had gained from the sea was lost back into it. autumn on the beaches--- a drear time betokened by no scarlet leaf nor any accustomed sign. frightening sea changes not though man changes There was only a chilling of the waters, in which I no longer cared to enter--- a further darkening of the pall-like sky, as if eternities of snow upon the ghastly waves descent began, would cease never, but continue beneath the white and the yellow and the crimson, and beneath that ultimate small ruby which shall yield only to the futilities of night. The once friendly waters babbled meaningfully at me, and eyed me with a strange regard; yet whether the darkness of the scene were a reflection of my own broodings, or the gloom within me caused by what lay without, i could not have told. Upon the beach and me alike had fallen a shadow, like that accompanying a bird which flies silently overhead, whose watching eyes we do not suspect till the image on the ground repeats the image overhead, and we look sudden-

(22.)

lu upward to find that something has been circling above us hitherto unseen.

The day was in late September, and the town had closed those resorts
where mad frivolity ruled the lives, *empty, fear-haunted*, and where raddled puppets had performed their summer
antics. The puppets were cast aside, smeared with the painted smiles and
frowns they had last assumed, and there were not a hundred people in the
town. *Again the gaudy, stucco-fronted* buildings lining the shore were permitted to
crumble in the wind (undisturbed). As the month advanced to the day
of which I speak, there grew in me the light of a grey infernal dawn,
wherein the dark thaumaturgy would be completed. Since I feared *such a thaumaturgy*
less than a continuance of my horrible suspicions, *—less than* the too-elusive
hints that something monstrous lurked behind the great stage, *unreservedly for the day of horror which seemed to be* nearing, it was with more
speculation than actual fear that I awaited. The day, I repeat, was late in
September, though whether the 22nd or 23rd I am uncertain. Such details
have fled before the recollection of those uncompleted happenings---
episodes with which no orderly existence should be plagued, because of
the damnable suggestions (and only suggestions) they contain. I knew the
time with a recognition too deep for me to explain (an intuitive distress *of spirit*).
Throughout those daylight hours I was expectant of the night;
impatient, perhaps, so that the sunlight passed like a half-glimpsed reflection in rippled water--- a day of whose events I recall nothing.

It was long since *particular* that storm cast a shadow over the beach, and I had
determined, after hesitations caused by nothing tangible, to
leave Allston, since the year was chilling, and there was no return of my
earlier contentment. When a telegram came for me (lying two days in
the Western Union office before I was located, so little was my name known)
saying that my design had been accepted *—winning* above all others in the contest,
I set a date for leaving. This news, which earlier in the year would have

(2)

affected me strongly, I now received with a curious apathy. It seemed as
unrelated to the unreality about me, as little pertinent to me, as if
it were directed to another person whom I did not know, and whose message had come to me through some accident. None the less, it was that
which forced me to complete my plans, and leave the cottage by the shore.

There were only four nights remaining of my stay when there occured the last of those events whose meaning lies more in the darkly sinister impression surrounding them than in anything obviously threatening.
Night had settled over Ellston and the coast, and a pile of soiled dishes attested both my lack of industry my recent meal. Darkness came as I
sat with a cigarette before the seaward window, and it was a liquid which
gradually filled the sky, washing in a floating moon, monstrously elevated.
The flat sea bordering upon gleaming sand, the utter absence of tree or
figure or life of any sort, and the regard of that high moon made the
vastness of my surroundings abruptly clear. There were only a few stars
pricking through as if to accentuate by their smallness the majesty of
the lunar orb and the restless shifting tide.

I had stayed indoors, fearing somehow to go out before the sea on
such a night of shapeless portent, but I heard it mumbling secrets of
an incredible lore, Borne to me on a wind out of nowhere was the
breath of some palpitant strange life; the embodiment of all that I had
felt and all I had suspected--- stirring now in the chasms of the sky
or beneath the mute waves. In what place this mystery turned from an
ancient, horrible slumber I could not tell, but like one who stands by
a figure lost in sleep, knowing that it will awake in a moment, I crouched
by the windows, holding a nearly-burnt out cigarette , and faced the
rising moon.

Gradually there passed into that never-stirring landscape a brilliance
intensified by the overhead glimmerings, and I seemed more and more under
some compulsion to watch whatever might follow.

(24)

and I felt that they took with them, all which might have been a ~~harbour~~ harbour for my thoughts when the hinted thing should come. ~~just was~~ The shadows were draining from the beach, where any of these did remain they were ebon and blank: still lumps of darkness sprawling beneath the cruel brilliant rays. The endless tableau of the lunar orb--- dead now, whatever her past was, and cold as the unhuman sepulchres she bears amid the ruin of dusty centuries older than man--- and the sea, astir, perhaps, with some unkenned life, some forbidden sentience--- confronted me with a horrible vividness. I arose and shut the window; partly because of an inward prompting, but mostly, I think, as an excuse for ~~maxing~~ transfering momentarily the stream of thought. No sound came to me now, as I stood before the closed panes. Minutes or eternities were alike. I was waiting, like ~~myself and like the motionless scenery~~ my own fearing heart and the motionless scene beyond, for the token of ~~an ittable~~ some ineffable life. I had set the lamp upon a box in the western corner of the room, but the moon was brighter, and her bluish rays invaded places where the lamplight ~~waned.~~ was faint. The ancient glow of the ~~great~~ round silent orb lay upon the beach as it had ~~done~~ lain for aeons, and I waited in a torment of expectancy made doubly acute by the delay in fulfillment, and the uncertainty of what ~~that~~ strange completion was to come.

Outside the crouching hut a white illumination ~~seemed almost to hold~~ suggested myria spectral forms, whose unreal, phantasmal motions seemed to taunt ~~with~~ my blindness, just as unheard voices mocked my eager listening. For countless moments I was still, as if Time and the tolling of her great bell were hushed into nothingness. And yet there was not ~~anything~~ which I might fear: the moon-chiseled shadows were unnatural in no contour, and veiled nothing from my eyes. The night was silent-- I knew that despite my closed window--- and all the stars were fixed mournfully in a listening heaven of dark ~~and ineffable~~ grandeur. No motion from me then, or word now, could ~~serve as token of the feared~~ reveal my plight, or hide of the fear-racked brain imprisoned in flesh ~~which that~~ dared not break the silence, for all the torture ~~that~~ it brought.

(25.)

As if ~~fully~~ expectant~~ly~~ of death, ~~and~~ assured ~~hopelessly~~ that nothing
~~could~~ ~~availing~~ serve to ~~banish~~ the soul~~'s~~-peril I confronted, I crouched
with a forgotten cigarette in my hand. A silent world gleamed beyond the
cheap, dirty windows, and in ~~the~~ one corner of the room a pair of grimy oars,
placed there before my arrival, shared the vigil of my spirit. The lamp
burned endlessly, yielding a sick light hued like a corpse's flesh~~, and~~
~~G~~lancing at it now and again, for the desperate distraction it gave, I
saw that many bubbles unaccountably rose and vanished in the kerosene-
filled base. *Curiously enough,* ~~there was no heat from the wick,~~ *But suddenly I became aware* ~~and the light was neither~~ *the light*
warm nor cold, *but strangely neutral — as if all physical forces were suspended,* ~~could all physical art things were earned~~, and all the
laws of a calm existence disrupted.

Then, with an unheard splash *which* ~~that~~ sent ~~ripples~~ from the silver water
~~existence~~ to the shore ~~sent~~ *a line of* ripples echoed in fear by my heart, a swimming thing emerged beyond the breakers. *The* figure (that may have been) ~~of a~~
dog, ~~or~~ a human being, or something more strange. It could not have known
that I watched--- perhaps it did not care--- but like a distorted fish
it ~~merely~~ swam across the mirrored stars, and dove beneath the surface.
After a moment it came up again, and this time, since it was closer, I
saw that it was carrying something across its shoulder. I knew, then,
that it could be no animal, and that it was a man or something like a
man, which came toward the land from a dark ocean. But it swam with a
horrible ease.

As ~~When~~ I watched, *dread-filled & passive,* with the fixed stare of one ~~awaiting~~ *who awaits* ~~the convulsions~~
~~of~~ death in another, knowing ~~that~~ *yet* he cannot avert it, ~~knowing almost the~~
~~very futility of despair in his impotence, and reduced to a passive,~~
~~dreadful vigil,~~ the swimmer approached the shore, though too far down
the southward beach for me to discern its ~~movements~~ *outlines* or features. Obscurely loping, with sparks of ~~moonlight~~ moonlit foam scattered
by its quick gait, it emerged and was lost among *the* inland dunes.

Now I was possessed by a sudden recurrence of fear, which had died

(26)

away in the previous moments. There was a tingling coldness all over
me, though the room, whose window I dared not open, was stuffy. I
thought it would be very horrible if something were to enter a window
which was not closed.

Now that I could no longer see the figure, I felt that it lingered
somewhere in the close shadows, or peered hideously at me from whatever
window I did not watch. And so I turned my gaze, eagerly and frantically,
to each successive pane; dreading that I might indeed behold an intrusive
regarding face, yet unable to keep myself from the terrifying inspection.
But though I watched for hours, there was no longer anything upon the beach.

So the night passed, and with it began the ebbing of that strangeness — a
strangeness which had surged up like an evil brew within a pot, had mounted to the
very rim in a breathless moment, had paused uncertainly there, and subsided, taking
with it whatever unknown message it had borne. Like the stars that promise
the revelation of terrible and glorious memories, goad us into worship
by this deception, and then impart nothing, I had come frighteningly near
to the capture of an old secret which ventured close to man's haunts, and
lurked cautiously just beyond the edge of the known.
moved cautiously about the village on that sound. Yet in the end I had
nothing. I was given only a glimpse of the furtive thing; a glimpse made
obscure by the veils of ignorance. I cannot even conceive what might have
shown itself had I been too close to that swimmer who went shoreward instead of
into the ocean. I do
not know what might have come if the brew had passed the rim of the pot
and poured outward in a swift cascade of revelation. The night ocean
withheld whatever it had nurtured. I shall know nothing more.

Even yet I do not know why the ocean holds such
a fascination for me. But then, perhaps none of us can solve those
things--- they exist in defiance of all explanation. There are men, and
wise men, who do not like the sea and its lapping surf on yellow shores;

(27.)

and they think us strange who love the mystery of the ancient and unending
deep. Yet for me there is an inscrutable and haunting glamour in all the
ocean's moods, in the melancholy silver foam beneath the moon's waxed
corpse; when silent and eternal waves beat on naked shores; when all is
lifeless save for unknown shapes that glide through sombre depths. And
when I behold the awesome billows surging in endless strength, there comes
upon me an ecstasy akin to fear; so that I must abase myself before this
mightiness, that I may not hate the clotted waters and their overwhelming beauty.

vast and lonely is the ocean, and even as all things came from it,
so shall they return. In the shrouded depths of time none shall reign
upon the earth, nor shall any motion be, save in the eternal waters. And
these shall beat on dark shores in thunderous foam, though none shall remain
in the dying world to watch the cold light of the enfeebled
moon splash on the swirling tides coarse-grained sand. a stagnant foam, gathering the shells and bones of perished shapes that dwelt within the waters.
Silent, flabby things will toss and roll along empty shores, their sluggish
life extinct. Then all shall be dark, for at last even the white moon on the distant waves shall wink out, neither above nor
below the sombre waters until that last millennium the sea will
thunder and toss throughout the dismal night.

****

****

June, 1936

Sanity, Subjectivity, and the Supernatural: Dreams of the Devil in Existentialism and the Weird Tale

Dustin Geeraert

Some comfort it would have been, could I, like a Faust, have fancied myself tempted and tormented of the Devil . . . but in our age of Down-pulling and Disbelief, the very Devil has been pulled down, you cannot so much as believe in a Devil. To me the Universe was void of Life, Steam-engine, rolling on, in its dead indifference, to grind me from limb to limb.

—Thomas Carlyle, from *Sartor Resartus* (1834)

One of the devil's main roles has always been to serve as God's enforcer. For example, medieval morality plays reinforced strict moral norms with the threat of damnation. Inevitably, any depiction of an encounter with the devil makes assumptions about the nature and purpose of the universe. Moreover, such a scenario reflects cultural values which are often expressed by who the devil is allowed to damn and for what. From Marlowe's subversive version of the Faustus legend, *Doctor Faustus* (1604), through to the Satan's temptation of Eve in Milton's *Paradise Lost* (1667), writers have envisioned the relationship between humanity and the devil in ways driven by the conflict between authority on the one hand, and ambition on the other. While Dante's gloating at certain torture victims during his tour of hell captures the sadistic authoritarianism of much of medieval theology, Marlowe obviously sympathizes with his Faustus' rebellion against orthodoxy (Greenblatt 460). Milton, of course, famously depicted the devil himself as a sympathetic character, whose intellect, charisma, and pride are admirable qualities, though turned to a dark purpose.

Philosophically, psychologically, and even politically, Satan changes with the times. In the nineteenth century writers began to recognize this and to give the character a sort of meta-textual awareness. The nineteenth century saw the rise of evolutionary theory, which arguably did more than any scientific discovery before or since to delegitimize not just the "argument from design" but the religious worldview more generally; thus, there was a new intellectual pressure for the devil to justify his presence on stage or page. Existentialism in philosophy and the weird tale in literature each focused on epistemological issues, and as a result supernatural claims were linked to cultural conditioning (folklore and superstition) and mental illness (hallucination or insanity).

For Edgar Allan Poe, the notion of a person standing in the same room as Satan and conversing about the terms of the Faustian pact had become a subject to be treated with humor. In both of his stories of encounters with the devil (both 1832), Poe uses the banter between Satan and his intended victim to satirize humanity's vain, entitled attitudes. In "The Duc de L'Omelette," the titular aristocrat is taken aback to find himself in hell and vehemently argues that it is simply not *appropriate* to damn a man of his stature. Satan acknowledges this but notes that it is just as much trouble for him to deal with hell's bureaucratic issues (617). The devil refuses a duel for the man's soul but can't resist a game of cards, which the aristocrat's skills allow him to win; apparently hell is only for the lower orders. In the latter story, meanwhile, the titular "Bon-Bon" is both a philosopher and "a *restaurateur* of uncommon qualifications" (483), and his story is really an amusing extended analogy between philosophy and food (479). Bon-Bon is no Faustus, transgressing religious limits on intellectual ambition: rather he is a superficial creature of fashion, concerned most of all with his own reputation. When the devil appears in Bon-Bon's study, the latter notes his peculiar appearance and his quaint style of dress, reminiscent of a cleric (483). Despite the devil's "expression of the most submissive humility" (483), Poe soon casts subtlety away: Bon-Bon's visitor possesses horns (hidden beneath "an inordinately tall hat"), goat's legs (indicated by "a tremulous swelling about the hinder part of his breeches"), and even a tail ("the vibration of his coat tail was a palpable fact") (484).

Bon-Bon respects the devil for his "well-known proficiency in the science of morals," and so thinks to plagiarize from him in order to "enlighten the human race, and at the same time immortalize himself" (484). Max Beerbohm's "Enoch Soames" (1916) is like a more sophisticated rewrite of "Bon-Bon"; Beerbohm's titular character, a similarly vain and self-obsessed author, makes a deal with the devil in an effort to discover whether he will achieve canonical immortality in a century's time. If anything, the philosopher Bon-Bon and the writer Soames, each of whom spouts complex nonsense for the sake of his own ego gratification, are more entitled and ridiculous than Poe's entitled and ridiculous Duke. Of course, in both cases the goal of immortality on the printed page is never to be. Poe's devil finds Bon-Bon's eleventh-hour careerism hilarious and makes the situation clear, noting Bon-Bon's initial skepticism and complaining about his medieval image: "The ridiculous prints, eh, which are in circulation, have given you a false idea of my personal appearance?" (485). This is a devil who recognizes his relationship to literature—who, indeed, is a better philosopher than Bon-Bon himself.

The devil disparages Plato for willfully misinterpreting a truth that he himself delivered in person: that the mind is material (Kemp 583). Epicurus, he says, was more on the right track; indeed, he claims credit for Epicurus' works: "Do you mean me, sir?—*I* am Epicurus!" (Poe 486). The devil is in a position to know, since he has eaten the soul of many a philosopher, properly "shelled" of course. The comparison between the supposedly immaterial (philosophy) and the material (food) reaches its apex when Satan describes his appetite for souls: "in a climate so sultry as mine, it is frequently impossible to keep a spirit alive for more than two or three hours; and after death, unless pickled immediately, (and a pickled spirit is *not* good) they will—smell—you understand, eh?" (488). When the devil claims that Bon-Bon sold his soul at one year one month of age (in exchange for his mental gifts), Bon-Bon starts drinking heavily. While the devil, ever the gentleman, claims that he is so disgusted as to want to relent temporarily from claiming his soul, it is likely that the devil simply wants Bon-Bon to die sober for the sake of *flavor*: he is disgusted in a culinary, rather than moral, sense. The story's analogy between food and philosophy, with Satan as the eater of "shelled" and "pickled" souls, seems a clear rebuke of the idea that anything immaterial exists. In classic Poe fashion, Bon-Bon's pets laugh along with the devil at the vain and deluded philosopher. It is hard to escape the sense that the real target here, as in "The Duc de L'Omelette," is human self-aggrandizement. Morbid and eccentric as Poe's humor may be, "Bon-Bon" casts aside grand philosophical abstractions and places humanity back inside, rather than above, the food chain, with the devil as our major predator. In this story, then, Satan becomes a symbol of materialism. Poe's unprecedented portrayal of weird scenarios (i.e., "MS. Found in a Bottle") made him an innovator in horror fiction: he is the pivotal figure between the Gothic tradition and the weird tale. Perhaps this innovation made him see Satan as a quaint figure, better suited for humor than horror.

Poe's contemporary Nathaniel Hawthorne, however, took the devil much more seriously.

Hawthorne's ancestors were Puritans, and much of his fiction is concerned with the psychological effects of Puritanism upon its subscribers. "Young Goodman Brown" (1835) tells of a young man's encounter with the devil in the woods outside his village. The devil takes the form of the protagonist's deceased grandfather and insinuates a family history of demonic dealings—claiming to have helped previous Brown patriarchs persecute religious dissenters and attack native villages, and to have corrupted the highest levels of church and government (134). He tries to initiate Brown and his wife Faith into devil worship, which is at its most depraved exactly where the Puritan faith is held most fanatically. At an orgy in the woods lit by a wall of flame, he speaks to the young couple: "Depending upon one another's hearts, ye had still hoped that virtue were not all a dream. Now are ye undeceived. Evil is the nature of mankind. Evil must be your only happiness. Welcome again, my children, to the communion of your race" (140). The devil's voice is his most striking feature: "a deep and solemn tone, almost sad with its despairing awfulness, as if his once angelic nature could yet mourn" (140). Brown finds himself alone in the woods and returns to his village, never knowing whether the experience was real or not. He remains a haunted man, plagued by the thought that everyone around him is secretly monstrous. The real problem for Hawthorne is that, according to Puritanism, the devil is right that "Evil is the nature of mankind," and the effect of this belief upon its subscribers is to make them paranoid, repressed, intolerant, and masochistic. Thus, for Hawthorne the devil symbolizes not modern materialism, but the conservative Christian pessimism about human nature that one cannot escape on any continent or by any form of social control or personal resolution.

"Young Goodman Brown," with its account of secret ancestral witchcraft in New England and its ambiguous ending, likely influenced H. P. Lovecraft's "The Festival" (1923), and Hawthorne's emissary of Satan from *The Scarlet Letter*, the "Black Man" who wanders the woods and induces mortals to sign his Black Book in their own blood (91), appears in Lovecraft's "The Dreams in the Witch House" (1932). Having briefly touched on nineteenth-century reinterpretations of the devil, I now turn to one major writer in existentialism (Fyodor Dostoevsky) and one in the weird tale (Lovecraft) to compare their treatments of the matter. If, as S. T. Joshi argues (*Weird Tale* 1), the weird tale as a literary genre is a vehicle by which its practitioners convey a particular worldview through mythical symbolism and philosophical speculation, then much the same can be said of existentialist writing, which evolved in parallel to the weird tale through the late nineteenth and early twentieth centuries. Lovecraft and Dostoevsky display striking parallels in method, and yet convey opposite messages.

Both writers obsess over the idea that science, particularly Darwinian evolution, threatens to dispel previous conceptions of the human condition, particularly religious ones. For both, the result of this might be that human existence must be considered ultimately meaningless. Dostoevsky and Lovecraft would have agreed that accepting the worldview implied by evolution meant accepting materialism, atheism, reductionism, and determinism—and basically in that order. Kim Sterneley clarifies the relationship between these concepts thus:

> We are primates, mammals, animals. Animals, in turn, are nothing but very complex biochemical systems. So humans are biochemical machines, though extraordinarily complex ones. That com-

plexity ensures that it will rarely be practically possible to predict future human behavior, or explain past human behaviour, through a fine-grained molecular understanding of human bodies. But, in principle, a detailed enough understanding of the physical and chemical processes internal to an agent would suffice to predict and explain all of that agent's behaviour. A full list of the complete physical, natural facts about an agent is all the facts there are. (288)

Reductionism thus assumes materialism and implies atheism and, if not total determinism, then at least a combination of determinism and randomness, neither of which allows for the concept of free will so key to the salvation-or-damnation Satanic encounter. Reductionism leaves no room for vitalist conceptions of human life such as the soul, or for any sort of supernatural entity.

Since Western traditions of religion and philosophy have long held that such scientifically unsupportable ideas give meaning and purpose to human life, starting in the nineteenth century many intellectuals rejected reductionism as a nihilistic perspective. Dostoevsky's narrator in *Notes from Underground* (1864), for example, associates evolution and reductionism with the destruction of human values:

As soon as they prove to you, for instance, that you are descended from a monkey, then it is no use scowling, accept it for a fact. When they prove to you that in reality one drop of your own fat must be dearer to you than a hundred thousand of your fellow-creatures, and that this conclusion is the final solution of all so-called virtues and duties and all such prejudices and fancies, then you have just to accept it, there is no help for it, for twice two is a law of mathematics. Just try refuting it. (34)

Lovecraft, too, thinks that "so-called virtues and duties" are, under a scientific worldview such as that found in Darwin's *The Descent of Man* (1871), only "prejudices and fancies." He explains: "Modern science has, in the end, proved an enemy to art and pleasure; for by revealing to us the *whole* sordid and prosaic basis of our thoughts, motives, and acts, it has stripped the world of glamour, wonder, and all those illusions of heroism, nobility, and sacrifice which used to sound so impressive when romantically treated" (quoted in Joshi, *Decline of the West* 91). Joshi terms Lovecraft's "mechanistic materialism" a "denial of any form of existence other than those envisaged by physics and chemistry" (*Decline of the West* 7).

Dostoevsky, on the other hand, would not accept the "stone wall" of scientific reductionism, and his narrator exclaims: "Of course I cannot break through the wall by battering my head against it if I really have not the strength to knock it down, but I am not going to be reconciled to it simply because it is a stone wall and I have not the strength" (35). He even asserts the right to take refuge from rationality in deliberately irrational acts of evil, using language similar to Poe's "The Imp of the Perverse." Dostoevsky ultimately returned to the Christianity of his youth, and he was well aware that this entailed a denial of scientific evidence: "If someone proved to me that Christ is outside the truth and that in reality, the truth were outside Christ, then I would prefer to remain with Christ rather than with the truth" (Banerjee ix). Yet he remained haunted by the thought that reductionism was correct: "As a child of the century, a child of disbelief and doubt, I am that today and (I know it) will remain so until the grave" (Banerjee ix). Despite opposing views on theism, as interpreters of post-Darwinian science Lovecraft and Dostoevsky are on exactly the same page.

Lovecraft's acceptance of, and Dostoevsky's denial of, a worldview of scientific reductionism that both writers consider nihilistic is at the core of these two writers' opposing approaches to portraying the devil in their respective fiction. Both writers place potentially supernatural religious experiences on the borders of scientific knowledge, but take opposite stances toward what the supernatural encounter means, particularly relative to nihilism. Dostoevsky's attitude is clear from his character Fyodor Pavlovich's discussion of hell in *The Brothers Karamazov*:

> It's impossible, I think, for the devils to forget to drag me down to hell with their hooks when I die. Then I wonder—hooks? Where would they get them? What of? Iron hooks? Where do they forge them? Have they a foundry there of some sort? . . . if there are no hooks it all breaks down, which is unlikely again, for then there would be none to drag me down to hell, and if they don't drag me down what justice is there in the world? (19)

With this "physics of hell" thought experiment, we are a long way
indeed from Dante or Milton. The character, who features strong
autobiographical elements of Dostoevsky and the same first name,
considers himself worthy of damnation and yet is *still* more afraid
of a meaningless existence than of hell itself. Throughout the novel, Dostoevsky admits that the advance of naturalistic (scientific)
explanations threatens belief in supernatural (religious) ones: brain
science threatens the concept of the soul, for example (557). If
one applies rational thinking to religion, the entire enterprise
breaks down, and nihilism is the end result.

As a response to this nihilism which provokes more fear than
even hell, Dostoevsky portrays religious experience as unalterably
(or irreducibly) subjective, beyond the explanatory power of science, and thus preserves an enclave for the soul that ultimately
serves as his way out of nihilism. This becomes clear during when
the devil appears in front of the atheist Ivan Karamazov. He is
worried that all human values might be illusions; he reasons that,
since there is "no law of nature that man should love mankind," all
love and moral behavior occurs only because of belief in immortality. Thus, if this belief is unjustified, "nothing then would be
immoral, everything would be lawful" (60); chaos, cruelty and
crime would result. This pessimistic view of human nature is consistent with what one finds in Hawthorne; it is ultimately a version of the "religion is useful" argument. Ivan's encounter with the
devil reflects this anguish over truth versus utility; over whether
nihilism or damnation is worse.

As in "Bon-Bon," the devil cleverly discusses philosophy;
meanwhile the beleaguered empiricist Ivan attempts to discover
whether he is hallucinating by discerning whether the devil is giving him any "new" information (that is, information Ivan does not
know and thus could not hallucinate). Ivan insists: "Never for one
minute have I taken you for reality . . . You are a lie, you are my
illness" (604). The term illness refers to what Dostoevsky's narrator tells readers at the start of this chapter: that during this experience Ivan is "on the very eve of an attack of brain fever" (601).
This sows the seeds of doubt as to whether anything supernatural
really occurs here; a doctor even tells Ivan that "Hallucinations are
quite likely in your condition" (202). In person, the devil is only

too happy agree that he is an illusion and helpfully claims that any original information he produces comes from Ivan's subconscious: "So I don't repeat your ideas, yet I am only your nightmare, nothing more." Ivan responds, "You are lying, your aim is to convince me you exist apart and are not my nightmare, and now you are asserting you are a dream" (606). When the devil relates to Ivan an anecdote about a philosopher who arrives in heaven, states that it contradicts his principles, and is sentenced to walk a quadrillion kilometers, Ivan thinks he has finally proved him unreal, for he himself invented this anecdote at age seventeen. But the devil claims that he deliberately told Ivan the anecdote to make him not believe in him (612). Although Ivan may be either haunted or mad, a "real" devil would offer Ivan a much-needed affirmation of his sanity, a resolution to his apprehensions over nihilism and, perhaps, even a chance at immortality and salvation. Yet he resists the supernatural on scientific grounds.

The devil's "I am only your nightmare" argument creates a "chicken or egg" philosophical dilemma between madness and the supernatural. Malcolm Jones writes, "There is no way of determining whether the religious experiences of his [Dostoevsky's] characters are merely projections of their own ideals, expressed in culturally available images, or whether they reflect a reality which ultimately escapes definition but which human beings try constantly to capture and transmit through such images" (154). Dostoevsky's devil dresses in formal but outworn clothes (like Poe's devil), and he appears to be a sponger like Ivan's father Fyodor (the target of his rage) and a lackey, like his half-brother Smerdyakov (the source of his guilt). Like the liberal Miusov (whom Ivan despises), he argues that "evil" is only a predetermined product of its environment. Thus, he is not responsible for his actions and indeed is only doing his job in an oppressive world:

> Before time was, by some decree which I could never make out, I was predestined 'to deny' and yet I am genuinely good-hearted and not at all inclined to negation… I don't meddle in that, I didn't create it, I am not answerable for it. Well, they've chosen their scapegoat, they've made me write the column of criticism and so life was made possible. We understand that comedy; I, for instance, simply and directly demand that I be annihilated. (609)

Yet after claiming a liberal view on crime, in the next moment he is a principled conservative with a stern approach to justice who laments that hell has reformed its torture methods:

> In the old days we had all sorts, but now they have taken chiefly to moral punishments—"the strings of conscience" and all that nonsense. We got that, too, from you, from the "mellowing of your manners." And who's the better for it? Only those who have got no conscience, for how can they be tortured by conscience when they have none? But decent people who have conscience and a sense of honor suffer for it. Reforms, when the ground has not been prepared for them, especially if they are institutions copied from abroad, do nothing but mischief! The ancient fire was better. (611)

For Dostoevsky, the time of "ancient fire" is long past. In place of the conflict between good and evil that was the hallmark of medieval Christian conceptions of the universe, the modern believer faces doubt, uncertainty, and absurdity. The devil notes this very fact and, just like Poe's devil, mocks the man he has appeared to for expecting a medieval devil in the modern age: "You are really angry with me for not having appeared to you in a red glow, with thunder and lightning, with scorched wings. . . .You are wounded, in the first place, in your aesthetic feelings" (614).

One common feature of Dostoevsky's devil with Poe's and Hawthorne's devils is his newfound identity as a respectable but poverty-stricken gentleman behind the times; another is his discussion of human nature. But in all three depictions he seems like a bit of an old windbag; he never used to have to argue over whether he existed. Despite the similarities, Dostoevsky's version of the devil is by far the most sophisticated of the three. Although in Hawthorne's version several interpretations are possible, Dostoevsky's episode deals with the close philosophical machinery of interpretation to a much greater degree. Ivan's epistemologically undecideable experience conversing with Satan is framed in the same way as every other religious experience in the novel; indeed, Ivan's mother is said to have been "possessed by devils" (8) but also to have been suffering from a "nervous disease" (8). The eccentric Father Ferapont has visionary experiences, but another monk who is "strongly in favour of fasting" notes that it is "not strange that one who kept so rigid a fast as Father Ferapont should see marvels" (155), including devils (153). Since *The Brothers Karamazov* always interweaves mental illness and religious experiences, Dostoevsky clearly knew that his own religious experiences had neurological correlates; his epilepsy is often noted as a contributing factor to his visions (Jones 75). Nevertheless, as a Christian he does not rule out the truth of his own religious experiences, but seeks a way to allow for the legitimacy of these experiences. In *The Brothers Karamazov*, every potentially supernatural event is accompanied by a natural explanation, so that the reader's reliance on his or her own philosophical assumptions in interpreting said experiences is made central. Thus, Dostoevsky implies that nihilism results not from the facts of science themselves, but from an over-privileging of these facts over subjectivity and, ultimately, a choice not to believe in God. For Lovecraft, on the other hand, subjectivity cannot take precedence over scientific facts and thus nihilism is inescapable.

The contradiction can be made plain by contrasting Dostoevsky's view that "If there is no immortality, there is no virtue" with Lovecraft's famous explanation of his approach to fiction: "Now all my tales are based on the fundamental premise that common human laws and interests and emotions have no validity or significance in the vast cosmos-at-large. . . . one must forget that such things as organic life, good and evil, love and hate, and all such local attributes of a negligible and temporary race called mankind, have any existence at all" (Joshi, *Weird Tale* 178). Dostoevsky depicts subjective religious experiences that are intelligible in human emotional terms, and which, if they are accepted as epistemologically valid, provide a purpose-driven moral framework with which to interpret reality. Lovecraft does the very opposite: in his fiction such experiences are objectively verifiable yet utterly unintelligible (and indeed completely destructive) in human emotional terms.

S. T. Joshi counts "The Dreams in the Witch House" as one of two "surprisingly inferior tales of [Lovecraft's] late period" (*Weird Tale* 177), but as a cosmicist reinterpretation of the Satanic encounter it is brilliant. Like Ivan's encounter with the devil in *The Brothers Karmazov*, it begins with a warning about the Satanic en-

counter's epistemological validity: "Whether the dreams brought
on the fever or the fever brought on the dreams Walter Gilman
did not know" (CF 3.232). Gilman's knowledge of local (New England) history, including the puritan witch trials, influences his
mind—especially since the room he is renting once belonged to a
woman, Keziah Mason, accused of witchcraft in 1692. Gilman is
also familiar with the folklore surrounding witches and their in-
termediaries, "the quasi-animals and queer hybrids which legend
depicts as witches' familiars" (CF 3.261). Keziah's familiar, Brown
Jenkin, is said to be a tiny human-like rat that can "speak all languages" (CF 3.237). Such rumors would upset any person of delicate imagination, and Gilman, like Ivan, is a nervous, sensitive, and
eccentric student of science whose intellectual ambitions set him
apart from others.

Like Ivan Karamazov, Gilman is a rigorous rationalist who refuses to give his visionary experiences any credibility, even as he
studies the subject that explains them, astrophysics: "There was a
discussion of possible freakish curvatures in space, and of theoretical points of approach or even contact between our part of the
cosmos and various other regions as distant as the farthest stars or
the transgalactic gulfs themselves—or even as fabulously remote
as the tentatively conceivable cosmic units beyond the whole Ein-
steinian space-time continuum" (CF 3.241). Gilman speculates that
Mason, "guided by some influence past all conjecture," could have
escaped from prison in 1692 using fourth-dimensional travel (CF
3.241). Once he meets Keziah in his dreams, he theorizes that she
could have survived into his own day using this knowledge. Yet
even though Gilman's science does not discredit potentially supernatural experience but supports it, Gilman prefers, like Ivan
Karamazov, to think that he is losing his mind and thus hallucinating, rather than recognizing the reality of his visions. However, as
Joshi notes, Lovecraft asserts "the brutal, objective reality of these
sights of supra-reality: although in some instances no concrete evidence is available as proof, it is precisely because the narrators
cannot pass off their adventures as dreams or hallucinations that
their minds are shattered" (*Primal Sources* 67).

Gilman suspects that Keziah and her familiar have tried to involve him with a more powerful being, who turns out to be the

devil character in the story. While Dostoevsky and Poe portrayed Satan as talkative and clever, even sarcastic, Hawthorne achieved a stronger sense of horror through restraint—providing only hints and emphasizing the mystery of this malevolent presence. Despite his skeptical outlook and use of meta-textual themes, Lovecraft's obsession with the feeling of horror wins out and, taking Hawthorne's deliberate withholding of information to an extreme, he does not give this devil a line of dialogue, only sinister silence:

> ... beyond the table stood a figure he had never seen before—a tall, lean man of dead black coloration but without the slightest sign of negroid features; wholly devoid of either hair or beard, and wearing as his only garment a shapeless robe of some heavy black fabric. His feet were indistinguishable because of the table and bench, but he must have been shod, since there was a clicking whenever he changed position. The man did not speak, and bore no trace of expression on his small, regular features. He merely pointed to a book of prodigious size which lay open on the table, while the beldame thrust a huge grey quill into Gilman's right hand. (CF 3.255)

Like Poe, Lovecraft hints that this apparently human figure possesses physical abnormalities consistent with medieval depictions of Satan. Yet whereas the devil in both Poe's and Dostoevsky's depictions mocks the idea of appearing in a traditionally satanic guise, this devil tries to cloak any satanic implications but fails: he leaves behind not footprints but instead round marks divided in half, suggesting that he walks on hooves (346). This devil's apparent neutrality seems like a sinister trick—the truth behind which is revealed to all who sign his Black Book.

Gilman's fellow tenant, a drunken and superstitious loomfixer named Joe Mazurewicz, warns Gilman to avoid the supernatural beings that haunt Arkham at all costs. He, like many of the citizens of Arkham, interprets the abnormal occurrences near the city in religious terms imported from Hawthorne: "May-Eve was Walpurgis-Night, when hell's blackest evil roamed the earth and all the slaves of Satan gathered for nameless rites and deeds. It was always a very bad time in Arkham, even though the fine folks up in Miskatonic Avenue and the High and Saltonstall streets pretended to know nothing about it" (*CF* 3.244). Shielded by their class privilege and belief in human rationality (like Dostoevsky's Miusov), the elite of society are blind to the fact that exactly those superstitious mobs whose minds *are* more primitive than theirs are *right* about the deeply threatening nature of reality. Mazurewicz may be a contemptible figure in Lovecraft's view, but in Lovecraft's fiction some superstitions are useful as a warning against real dangers. Only the exile from the upper class, the sickly philosopher, can perceive the truth: the mythic alternate reality which Gilman experiences in dreams is actually the fourth dimension.

The beings that the townspeople call "slaves of Satan" are not connected to any petty human theology but are rather of unknown—perhaps unknowable—origin and motivation. The ceremonies that are termed by the townspeople "black magic" have some relation to the fourth dimension and communication with or summoning of entities from there and elsewhere. The "Black Man" is not seeking to corrupt the young with sex and crime, but instead is a being from worlds beyond our understanding, able to defy what we take for the laws of physics. In this context, Gilman's materialism is even more counterproductive than Ivan Karamazov's. Karamazov is never given a chance to conclude whether the devil's visits are real; his fate is unknown, as Dostoevsky died before he could write his planned sequel to *The Brothers Karamazov*. But Gilman eventually recognizes the truth of his visions: "Between the phantasms of nightmare and the realities of the objective world a monstrous and unthinkable relationship was crystallising" (*CF* 3.265). Yet despite this realization, the witch's familiar still tears him apart.

Both Gilman and Karamavoz reject claims of the supernatural because they are scientifically trained materialists. Yet while Ivan is trained in the natural sciences, what he is really concerned with is the problem of evil. Ivan is prepared to recognize that some type of logic beyond human understanding could justify human suffering, just as parallel lines could meet somewhere beyond the earth where Euclidean geometry does not apply. Yet he objects to the very fact that this would be beyond human understanding: "If it is really true that [children] must share responsibility for all their fathers' crimes, such a truth is not of this world and is beyond my comprehension" (225). To an earthbound human, both the "moral beyond" and the "mathematical beyond" will simply not make sense, since it is impossible for an earthly mind to accept unearthly logic: "I acknowledge humbly that I have no faculty for settling such questions, I have a Euclidean earthly mind, and how could I solve problems that are not of this world?" (216). It is really Ivan's intense hatred for injustice which motivates his quest for the truth: "I must have retribution, or I will destroy myself. And not retribution in some remote infinite time and space, but here on earth, and that I could see myself" (225). Combining moral and empirical arguments, Ivan uses non-Euclidean geometry as a metaphor for a higher reality, but argues that even if this reality is heaven, it still does not solve the problem of evil.

Lovecraft's vision of a higher reality similarly relies on the concept of non-Euclidean geometry, yet the problem of evil is irrelevant since good and evil are only "local attributes of a negligible and temporary race called mankind" (quoted in Joshi, *Weird Tale* 178). Ivan's late nineteenth-century positivism ("How could I solve problems that are not of this world?") has been replaced by the perception-pushing uncertainties of early twentieth-century physics, and Gilman, who studies non-Euclidean calculus, thinks that it is indeed possible to solve problems not of this world. However, the non-Euclidean plane Gilman experiences does not provide any reassuring metaphysical answers, but is instead baffling and disturbing. As Lovecraft describes it, it consists of abysses inhabited by "indescribably angled masses of alien-hued substance, some of which appeared to be organic while others seemed inorganic. . . . All the objects—organic and inorganic alike—were totally beyond description or even comprehension" (*CF* 3.238). Indeed, Gilman finds his experience terrifying: "Gilman sometimes compared the inorganic matter to prisms, labyrinths, clusters of cubes and planes, and cyclopean buildings; and the organic things struck him variously as groups of bubbles, octopi, centipedes, living Hindoo idols, and intricate arabesques roused into a kind of ophidian animation. Everything he saw was unspeakably menacing and horrible" (*CF* 3.238). Just as Christians have anthropomorphized the Black Man as Satan, Hindus have apparently anthropomorphized other fourth-dimensional beings. Indeed, in

"Envisaging the Cosmos: A Note on 'The Dreams in the Witch House,'" Scott Connors argues that Keziah Mason herself, despite her initiation and abilities, views all the fourth-dimensional events, powers, and beings in the story in anthropomorphized, supernatural terms, to the point where she, like Mazurewicz, still believes that a crucifix has supernatural powers.

Gilman also witnesses objects appearing and disappearing, which are three-dimensional beings (other humans) entering or leaving the fourth dimension in travel experienced in dreams. In other Lovecraft stories such as "The Call of Cthulhu," characters witness non-Euclidean structures and beings on earth (*CF* 2.29). The tomb of Cthulhu, R'lyeh, is described as an invasion of alien physics onto the earth; the geometry is *"all wrong"* (*CF* 2.43) and "all the rules of matter and perspective seem . . . upset" (*CF* 2.52). There are angles that are acute, but behave as if they are obtuse, and areas that alternately appear concave and convex. From such a place godlike beings communicate with humans through dreams, who perform sacrifices in vain hopes of earning Their favor: "The Great Old Ones spoke to the sensitive among them by moulding their dreams; for only thus could Their language reach the fleshly minds of mammals" (*CF* 2.39). From this anthropological, external perspective on religion (which Lovecraft indeed thought was ultimately based on dreams), any messages that humans may receive in abnormal psychological states are so disturbing that puritanical fear may be justified in Darwinian terms.

Joshi has termed "The Call of Cthulhu" a watershed in Lovecraft's fiction, marking his transition from a supernaturalism influenced by Poe to materialism, in which every abnormal element is justified through science fiction. While there is no debate that Lovecraft was a materialist, Joshi's statement that "There is never an entity in Lovecraft that is not in some fashion material" (*Weird Tale* 186) may not entirely describe "The Call of Cthulhu," since the story's narrator repeatedly states that he no longer believes that materialism describes the world: "My attitude was still one of absolute materialism, *as I wish it still were*" (*CF* 2.43). The narrator may have simply expanded or modified the version of materialism in which he believes, rather than discarding the concept of materialism entirely. Yet for what the beliefs of the cultists in Lovecraft's fiction are worth, one of them states that the "gods" he worships are "not made of matter" and "not composed altogether of flesh and blood" (*CF* 2.39). Whether this information is ultimately accurate, the most important point here is that exactly those phenomena which characterize religious experience and which the narrator previously presumed to be discredited by materialism must now be accepted as real. Indeed, the very *call* of Cthulhu is a dream-vision shared by persons worldwide which accurately reflects a physically remote reality, thus epistemologically validating in Lovecraft's fiction the notion of dream-travel. Dream-travel, in fact, is core to Lovecraft's mythos—from early pieces like "Celephaïs" through to Gilman's travels and the mind-switching of "The Thing on the Doorstep."

In one of his most important statements, Lovecraft explains the nature of his fiction: "The time has come when the normal revolt against time, space & matter must assume a form not overtly incompatible with what is known of reality—when it must be gratified by images forming *supplements* rather than *contradictions* of the visible & mensurable universe" (quoted in Joshi, *Weird Tale* 179). This statement is often taken to show that Lovecraft preferred science-fictional justifications for the abnormal events in his stories to supernatural ones, but what is more remarkable about it is that Lovecraft thinks that it is "normal" to "revolt against time, space & matter." If this is not an expression of affinity with the psychological drive away from day-to-day physical reality and into intense subjectivity that characterizes religious experience, it would be hard to say what is. Lovecraft even recognized this: "Religion itself is merely a pompous formalisation of fantastic art. Its disadvantage is that it demands an intellectual belief in the impossible, whereas fantastic art does not" (quoted in Joshi, *Decline of the West* 54). Lovecraft condemns religion exactly because of his sympathy for the desire for transcendent experience.

Lovecraft's monsters are a sort of personified nihilism, and they destroy his intellectual protagonists time and again in a sort of ritualistic self-destruction. Michel Houllebecq writes: "In his stories the role of the victim is generally played by an Anglo-Saxon university professor who is refined, reserved, and well-educated. Someone who, in fact, is rather like himself. . . . He was pierced to the core by his failures" (109). Yet this symbolic self-destruction is not driven by Lovecraft's poverty and lack of recognition (as Houllebecq argues), but instead by the clash between his psychological disposition and his intellectual understanding. Dream, myth, legend, religion; the larger intuition-confirming project of Story as a way of organizing our understanding of reality and the cosmos—all are mere projections, "illusions ... which used to sound so impressive when romantically treated." Lovecraft was shaped by an early and deep appreciation of Western cultural tradition, and while one can occasionally find nihilistic ideas in the Western canon, much of its literature treats human emotions, experience, and existence as if they ultimately matter. As Lovecraft noted, modern science contradicts this view utterly.

Scientific materialism and religious thinking were utterly opposed in Lovecraft's opinion, yet the foundational principle of Lovecraft's fiction is that major features characteristic of human religions are in some sense *true*. Consider the following list of features in his works: the supernatural significance (indeed often outright haunting) of temples and holy places; the correspondence of dreams, visions, prophecies, and omens to reality; the effective practice of spells and sacrifices; supernaturally inspired books containing information about deities; out-of-body experience, possession, and remote viewing; the effective practice of rituals, invocations, and conjurations. In designing his fiction, Lovecraft *begins* with a cosmos that science has shown not to be anthropocentric and indeed indifferent toward humanity, at best; and *then* he presents as true many features of religion. The scientific justifications come afterwards and are of secondary importance to Lovecraft's interpretation of the *meaning* of scientific knowledge as nihilism. In this he is on exactly the same page as religious writers like Dostoevsky, but it is exactly due to his sympathy (indeed, empathy) for the desire for transcendent experience that Lovecraft condemned religion. Lovecraft's stories portray events that seem to transcend the laws of space and time, and which confirm in the process bizarre, ancient, and absurd doctrines about incomprehensible deities; in this way Lovecraft's body of fiction, taken as a whole, presents a nihilistic parody of religion.

No one knew better than Lovecraft that the advent of a scientific worldview does not and cannot banish humanity's ancestral fears. Satan may have exerted maximum terror over the scientifically ignorant inhabitants of the ancient world (the Bible) and the middle ages (Dante), but he survived the Renaissance (Marlowe), the Reformation (Milton), and the Enlightenment (Goethe). By the time writers of existentialism and the weird tale approached the figure of Satan, it was clear that he would need to adapt to their new age of doubt. For Poe, the devil represented an outmoded worldview to be treated with humor; for Hawthorne he was a symbol of Puritan pessimism, perhaps not as outdated as would be preferable. For Dostoevsky, he was a sophisticated specter who tormented people privately and happily issued the contradictory threats of hell and hallucinatory madness. The philosopher always pays dearly for meddling with forces that he does not understand, and no matter what heights humanity may aspire to, the devil always cuts humanity back down to size. In Lovecraft's hands, these traditional themes were quickly turned to a cosmicist purpose: Lovecraft makes Satan a human myth based on anthropomorphized accounts of a cosmic messenger, whose very existence implies "terrifying vistas of reality" and "our frightful position therein" (*CF* 2.22). By rearranging philosophical elements in his unique way, Lovecraft characteristically reintroduces sheer terror into the scene of the Satanic encounter, a scene that was elsewhere acquiring a satirical element. Uncharacteristically, Poe's treatment of the matter is the most cheerful one: Bon-Bon and the Duke may have temporarily escaped their fates, but Walter Gilman and Ivan Karamazov discuss Euclid and Epicurus in hell—with Enoch Soames and, probably, the authors themselves.

Works Cited

Banerjee, Maria Nemcova. *Dostoevsky: The Scandal of Reason.* Great Barrington, MA: Linisfarne Books, 2006.

Beerbohm, Max. "Enoch Soames." In *Nightshade: 20th Century Ghost Stories,* ed. Robert Phillips. New York: Carroll & Graf, 1999. 17–46.

Connors, Scott. "Envisaging the Cosmos: A Note on 'The Dreams in the Witch House.'" *Lovecraft Annual* No. 6 (2012): 76–81.

Dostoevsky, Fyodor. *Notes from Underground*. Trans Constance Garnett. New York: Dell, 1960.

———. *The Brothers Karamazov*. Trans Ralph E. Matlaw. New York: Norton, 1976.

Greenblatt, Stephen, et al., ed. *The Norton Anthology of English Literature: The Major Authors*. 8h ed. New York: W. W. Norton, 2006.

Hawthorne, Nathaniel. *The Scarlet Letter: A Romance*. Charlottesville, VA: University Press of Virginia, 2000.

———. "Young Goodman Brown." In *The Dark Descent*, ed. David G. Hartwell. New York: Tor, 1987. 132–41.

Houllebecq, Michel. *H. P. Lovecraft: Against the World, Against Life*. Trans. Dorna Khazeni. San Fransisco: Believer, 2004.

Jones, Malcolm. *Dostoevsky and the Dynamics of Religious Experience*. London: Anthem, 2005.

Joshi, S. T. *H. P. Lovecraft: The Decline of the West*. 1990. Berkeley Heights, NJ: Wildside Press, 2000.

———. *Primal Sources: Essays on H. P. Lovecraft*. New York: Hippocampus Press, 2003.

———. *The Weird Tale*. 1990. Holicong, PA: Wildside Press, 2003.

Kemp, Anthony. "The Greek Joke in Poe's 'Bon-Bon.'" *American Literature* 56 (December 1984): 580–83.

Poe, Edgar Allan. *Complete Tales and Poems*. Edison, NJ: Castle Books, 2002.

Sterneley, Kim. "Darwinian Concepts in the Philosophy of Mind." In *The Cambridge Companion to Darwin*, ed. Jonathon Hodge and Gregory Radick. New York: Cambridge University Press, 2003.

Terror and Terrain: The Environmental Semantics of Lovecraft County

James O. Butler

Literary works make use of a variety of ontological modes in the creation of the settings they feature, spanning the known world (which may be termed *nonfictional geographies*) through entirely fantastic creations (*fictional geographies*). Between these two extremes, however, exists a range of hybrid ontological formations that incorporate elements of both—the entire array of which would fall within the remit of *part-fictional geographies*. These worlds are constructed in part within referentially defined contextual parameters, resulting in a setting that may be attributed with similar general characteristics of the known while still bearing a creative distance from that which exists. As these geographies are not stylistically independent from a geographic placement, the development of such a setting is necessarily tied into following stylistic patterns that fit the characteristics of the landscape, reflected in the individual elements of their formation. The creative emphasis might thus be suggested as falling upon a combination of stylistic and associative properties—generated from, and even interspersed with, the emotional associations of known nonfictional entities and locations, so as to provide a desired context ready for tailoring; an approach for which Lovecraft County provides a wonderful exemplar. The name of a place may be presented as being an instrumental and efficient component of expressing these properties, especially within the entirely textual medium of literary fiction.

The part-fictional ontological mode provides a fictional setting with a prefigured environment imbued with traits a reader might expect from such a place, be it stylistic, thematic, aesthetic, or any other artistic effect that is desired. The manner that Lovecraft evokes the superstitious folklore and history of New England is held in the terrapsychological value of its landscape, providing a pertinent precursor to the development of his own Mythos-based horror, for he explicitly suggests that:

> Searchers after horror haunt strange, far places ... The haunted wood and the desolate mountain are their shrines, and they linger around the sinister monoliths on uninhabited islands. But the true epicure in the terrible, to whom a new thrill of unutterable ghastliness is the chief end and justification of existence, esteems most of all the ancient, lonely farmhouses of backwoods New England; for there the dark elements of strength, solitude, grotesqueness, and ignorance combine to form the perfection of the hideous. (CF 1.206)

It is with these opening lines that the powerful emotional ramifications of certain types of place are called into play as being a primary asset of his writing style.

The field of terrapsychology may be broadly defined as the study of the emotional responses generated by certain types of space and terrain. This is a personal analysis of the field, formed from an amalgamation of a variety of other researchers who have contributed to the development of the field (Brady; Chalquist; Foster). The examination of how and why emotional responses to certain types of environment come to be formed and the ways in which they can be altered or subverted, be this purposeful or through unintentional means, allows for the critical investigation of the functional semantic bond between form and the intended effect provided. What has been poetically called the *genius loci*, the "spirit" of place, exploring the responsive interplay between man and environment, is a fundamental aspect of artistic interpretation, which is transferable to language study as well—and with this, onyms (names).

In regard to how this concept may be applied to literary onomastic research, it is stylistic and thematic demands that may be taken to provide an essential overarching framework against which naming strategies may be assessed. The extent to which patterns in onomastic form may be identified as being a cohesive and prominent element within both individual works and wider subgenres, and the resulting semantic ties that become associated with and create lexical fields, present a valid basis for pursuing terrapsychology as an active component for artistic interpretation.

Every textual onomasticon has to be treated as a *paracosm* containing the specific elements that make each work unique. How, and why, particular elements are featured consistently throughout a genre's corpus, the emotional response they elicit in the reader, and the names used in the text present perhaps the most efficient manner by which an author may express base information about any textual asset—but especially for landscape and place.

By initiating the development of his Mythos series of texts with reference to a defined locale, Lovecraft automatically associates any expansion with the implications of this area (New England). Lovecraft's personal history with that American state is well documented throughout his life, as explored by Evans, who argues for the role of his early folk antiquarian interest and career as travelogue writer as being an integral inspiration for his future fictional developments in this same landscape. Evans argues that Lovecraft possessed "a very strong sense of place," and that similarly it is the associative qualities attached to that land that may hold more strength in their suggestiveness than the physical environment in and of itself. The history, documented folklore, and perceived environment of the area all contributed to its emotional presence that serves as the underlying terrapsychological core shaping any representation or depiction of that area.

This essay will therefore explore Lovecraft's development and use of such places within seven of his major works—and although this is just a very small selection of his Mythos fiction, it features the significant majority of Lovecraft County features that reappear throughout his writings and showcase the variety of creative artistic effects that may be creatively worked into literary names. Lovecraft did not restrict his narratives solely to his small fictional New England territory, and although his narratives span the globe (and frequently venture beyond), this New England hub presents the most developed region within his fiction, and therefore provides an ideal source for material to showcase the ontological and terrapsychological arguments presented within this article from a single environment.

The inferential qualities of the part-fictional ontological development are therefore partially dependent upon a degree of prior
knowledge pertaining to the directed area. Even a minimal degree
of knowledge or presupposition in this regard assists in the estab-
lishment of the fictional environment, which, combined with the
subsequent related terrapsychological development of a fictional
landscape, provides scene-setting qualities that serve as a means of
comparative referencing. Smith likens this knowledge to common
"scripts" or "scenarios" (227–28), which describe appropriate se-
quences for particular contexts, and the inclusion of developmen-
tal forms within these informational chunks is a plausible
extension of their role. Unlike entirely fictional geographies, focus
upon the impressionistic qualities is removed from the semantic
lexical construction, which is instead dependent upon similar
identifiable environmental or characteristic archetypes.

The Gothic nature of Lovecraft's writings is communicated
less through the qualifying lexical construction of the place-names
(although this does play a role, as will be seen throughout the critical analysis) than through adherence to a contextual familiarity
that is used to provoke a desired response. Barnes and Duncan (5–
8) argue that this relationship is "communicative and productive
of meaning," and the critic should seek to address how those
meanings are conducive to thematic tailoring. The use of external
markers situates and provides a succinct means of transferring
such meaning to an otherwise fictional setting, with the intent for
such places to be regarded as synonymous with every quality held
by the referenced location. McHale also emphasizes that such
modeling is entirely dependent upon the desired emotional response or expectation for the individual text, as different genre
types "model the reader's engagement differently, and to different
ends" (196). Part-fictional geographies—or "mixed onomastic
[worlds]," as Grimaud (30) refers to them—are built upon such
implicative models, but it is from such a suggestive base that the
landscape may be shaped at the whim of the author into an uncanny representation whose details may be exaggerated or focused
upon certain elements so as to provide an ideal template for any
thematic and stylistic accentuation to be situated.

Lovecraft's Mythos-based fiction is set within a singularly created environment that serves as a central hub for these interrelated narratives. Framed by the **New England** context within which it is situated, this fictional area is laden with the history and aesthetic attributes possessed of that American state. This hub, nicknamed **Lovecraft County** by fans and critics, is comprised of an idealized version of New England (Robinson 129), in that these attributes are exaggerated, so as to provide an emphatic base upon which the narratives reminiscent of folklore may be freely constructed. It is at once similar and yet constructed for the singular purpose of framing the texts. The land is linguistically integrated so as to appear indistinguishable from the settlements and landscape that comprise part of that state, as a comparison of the stylistic composition of the created names against their nonfictional counterparts will attest. As the narrative traverses north central Massachusetts and the reader takes "the wrong fork at the junction of the **Aylesbury pike** just beyond **Dean's Corners**, [the reader] comes upon a lonely and curious country" (CF 2.414–15), the description of which reaffirms the terrapsychological qualities that may have already been established with its environmental placement.

This is Lovecraft's fictional land, also named internally as **Arkham county**. This divergent path leads into what Lévy terms "a zone of shadow, a zone of mystery, a *dream-zone*, which spreads little by little to the rest of the countryside" (37), but no matter how divergent this fictional land may spread, the roots are still anchored within that from which it was derived. It is from this point that the reader is drawn deeper into this land and farther from the known into a semblant, yet unique and semantically guiding, form. These features mark the point of transition from the perceivable known into the fictional likeness, and are forms common to roads within this area.

The defining feature of Arkham county may be identified as the **Miskatonic Valley**, through which its namesake the **Miskatonic River** runs. The suffix of this name closely resembles that of the Housatonic River, which runs through southern Massachusetts, forming a structural equivalent that resembles a name derived from tribal Native American language that has no fully translatable meaning. This does not preclude a poetic meaning proving discernible in the name, but its form is purposefully made so as to reflect the other hydronyms within the nonfictional part of the landscape. Linguistically, the suffix -atonic may be identified as taken from the same Mohican root as the Housatonic River, which has the translation "beyond the river." Uis– or uisa– is the lexis for "water, river," and so the suffix represents the notion of "beyond." This meaning, even if it is a chance selection, is stylistically fitting with the ontological composition of this setting that borders many different hidden worlds, as will be explored in due course.

A planned reservoir of the Miskatonic may be suggested to serve as symbolic terraneous representation of the artificial physical alteration of the environment so as to meet the needs of the modern populace, with the artificial flooding of a valley burying a historical yet tainted land reflecting a theme prevalent throughout the series of Mythos texts. The path of this river is roughly traceable from details gleaned throughout the corpus and may be followed as a brief introduction to an approximate geography of this fictional landscape; originating from springs in the hills west of Dunwich, it runs eastward, turns southeast, and flows through Arkham. The river empties into the sea two miles to the south near Kingsport, which lies just south of the promontory through which the river escapes into the Atlantic. These three fictional settlements serve prominent roles and appear consistently throughout Lovecraft's writing, and are tailored to serve as the stylistic core around which the landscape is shaped.

Arkham is identified as the principal settlement within the area, appearing in thirteen of Lovecraft's tales, and houses four distinct institutions that serve central roles within each of these texts. Miskatonic University is a place of learning and education that is irrevocably tied into the landscape around it with the taking of its name. The institution is named from the land in which it was built, and this associative connection ties the place to the land and all that it semantically holds. In addition to this seat of learning, there are three additional sources of knowledge, and one that restrains those that come to learn of tainted emotionally disturbing long-hidden lore. These are respectively: the Arkham Historical Society, the *Arkham Gazette*, the *Arkham Advertiser*, and the Arkham Sanitarium, each entity designed and named so as to be enclosed organizations, dedicated to the city and local vicinity, serving to contain the narrative within the county by providing these thematically and genre-relevant services internally.

Christchurch Cemetery within the city bears common qualifiers, both "Christ-" and "-church" and the two related elements together forming an unambiguous name for the place, along with a generic that moves the focus to the adjoined graveyard. That Christchurch also has two existing counterparts may also be of structural note, given that the name belongs to both an Oxford college, possibly furnishing another link to a renowned historic academic institution, as well as a harbor town on the south coast of England potentially continuing the terrapsychological consistency of such environments. Unnamed cemeteries and potter's fields—common grave areas for unknown bodies—are featured as a stock environmental asset within many of his stories, serving to establish a terrapsychological protocol involving the emotional attributions for such sites. There is little in the way of unique descriptive elements within Christchurch; rather, the utilitarian generic serves as the identificatory focus of both name and place.

The second major town, **Kingsport**, is described in lavish detail as comprising:

> ancient vanes and steeples, ridgepoles and chimney-pots, wharves and small bridges, willow-trees and graveyards; endless labyrinths of steep, narrow, crooked streets ... ceaseless mazes of colonial houses piled and scattered at all angles and levels like a child's disordered blocks. (CF 1.407)

This description is very much tailored to present a highly stylized Gothic aesthetic, but only two names are provided for locations within the town: **Water Street** and **Central Hill**, which are again atypical non-specific onymic formations of descriptive elements. **Dunwich**, however, is a remote village that bears a potential thematic connection to a mostly abandoned port town situated in Suffolk that shares the name. The suffix *-wich* is also a frequent onomastic root in New England and could further provide a linguistic semantic parallel with the witchcraft tradition that pervades the history and arguably the terrapsychological response to the state as a whole, even though there is no etymological link with any external instance of that generic qualifier. The stylistic and poetic at the surface linguistic level of this onomastic form is thus potentially threefold.

Two types of institution are featured prominently throughout Lovecraft's texts, corresponding with the principal named buildings located within Arkham: universities (with other repositories of information) and asylums. These institutions are thematically connected through an association with knowledge, secrets, and the consequences of learning more than the human mind may comprehend. Miskatonic University is likened to several other institutions and made to seem a prestigious New England place of learning that rivals **Princeton University** and **Harvard** entirely through the comparative use of their names. **The Widener Library** at the latter is specifically mentioned, and references further afield compare the university with **the Bibliothèque Nationale, the British Museum**, and **the University of Buenos Ayres**, which are explicitly named as potential sites that possess significant amounts of interrelated occult knowledge and artefacts, again blurring the line between existing and fictional locations. Such a setup also allows for the suggestion that the latter entity houses a collection of materials akin to those referenced alongside it, and are associative powers possessed of a name used in such a referential manner.

Other asylums that are featured within Lovecraft's world include **Sefton Asylum, St. Mary's Hospital, Danvers** (although a town name, it is used to refer to the State Hospital for the Insane situated within its bounds), and **Canton**, a sanitarium on the outskirts of **Masillion, Ohio**. These locations are not only frequently encountered within the series of novellas, but also play a significant role in the attainment or containment of the thematic unintended knowledge that is encapsulated within these two types of building. As a consequence of Lovecraft's constant connection with madness and other mental disturbances as a result of, or even a key to, contact with the eldritch beings that exist within the world of the Mythos, it is this thematic concept that has terrapsychologically charged both this fictional landscape as well as the names associated with it. This fictional uncanny landscape hides a world of terror, strange powers, unknown creatures, and madness. The names of both the author and the fictional Arkham have spread beyond the texts of its genesis, and been used throughout a variety of other texts and artistic sources as a means of conveying both the supernatural and insanity, thereby reinforcing a semantic extension with such associations.

Innsmouth is a fictional town removed from the Miskatonic River, and is described as situated between **Ipswich**, and **Newburyport**, both of which are seaports and are two of the earliest settlements founded within New England. Linguistically, the name of the town makes clear its situation upon a coastal confluence; but poetically the suffix could be read as emphasizing the narrative impact of the town as a meeting point or entrance into a submerged other world. This point of entrance to the sea allows for passage in either direction, through which a long-hidden horror could one again walk the lands, and **-mouth** encountered here may be poetically suggestive of the town fulfilling such a role. The road to Innsmouth is interlaced within several nonfictional **Essex County** features, passes the **Lower Green** of Newburyport and the **Parker River**, and continues running adjacent to **Plum Island** before continuing to the north of **Cape Ann**. As experienced on the journey into the other side of Lovecraft County, the road takes an unexpected turn, and it is at this juncture that the fictional hub is once again entered: "it was as if the bus were about to keep on in its ascent, leaving the sane earth altogether" (*CF* 3.172).

Although Innsmouth was once a fishing port, a fictional river, **the Manuxet**—whose name, like Miskatonic, is comprised of several root-words from native languages—also has no discernible linguistically relevant translation. A close approximation may be seen with the Manomet River (as noted by Joshi, *Call of Cthulhu* 411n5), named for a tribal branch that resided near Portsmouth, Massachusetts, but such a form is again atypical for the region. The streets of the town betray no superficial trace of the blight that taints it, with **Federal**, **Broad**, **Washington**, **Lafayette**, **Main**, **South**, **Church**, **Fall**, **Green**, and **Bank** all described and laid out in detail. These are complemented by two names that reference the location and primary industry of the port (**Fish** and **Water**), and a selection named to honour the influential families of the town: **Marsh**, **Babson**, **Paine**, **Waite**, **Eliot**, **Bates**, **Adams**, **Martin**. Every one of these names is a typical Americana street name, used here to indicate that the taint of the town is hidden behind a superficial façade of common construction that has been slowly corrupted.

Continuing this idea, the **Masonic Hall** is repurposed as the unofficial center of the town, as it is the site of many of the blasphemous ceremonies conducted by those whose lineage is tainted by the cursed blood that runs through all the families that are still residing in the dilapidated town. That the hall has been misappropriated into the sacred place of a new (yet unaccountably old, seemingly learned from a mysterious Polynesian sect during the travels of a member of town's most powerful family) religion named **The Esoteric Order of Dagon** is an ironic transformation from one secret religious society into another. This cult promised physical riches of golden artefacts and a rich bounty of fish summoned to their shores, in return for the worship of three ancient deities bound beneath the tide, and human sacrifices in their name. The demand in return for this wealth is that individuals from the town are partnered with mysterious "sea devils," resulting in a carefully inbred bloodline that marks those of such origin with a series of physical abnormalities, which is termed "**the Innsmouth look.**"

Given this unnatural breeding, the surname attached to the main hotel in the town, **the Gilman House**, serves as a pun on the gills that taint those afflicted with the degenerative "look"; yet as it is a common New England surname, its placement is not unusual. The names are typical so as to reinforce the perceptual formation of the town as being indistinguishable from any existing New England town. Even atypical forms that exhibit little in the way of curious development may serve a literary purpose in this manner, reflecting a nondescript standard.

Lovecraft's texts are rich in both direct and indirect references to towns and features that would border his fictional county, and are encountered freely alongside those of his own creation. Characters detail their familiarity with or passage through **Boston**, **Springfield**, and **Cambridge** to reach the area of Lovecraft county. Other places are referenced as skirting the boundaries of the fictional land. **Bolton** is described as "a factory town near Arkham" (*CF* 1.304) so as to provide a closer approximation of location the fictional site, and a trio of settlements: **Marblehead**, **Ipswich**, and

Rowley are all located within the afore-discussed neighboring **Essex County**, having been passed through by one of Lovecraft's central characters. Despite their proximity, none of these towns have any link with Innsmouth, and it is this disconnection that is believed by outsiders to be the factor responsible for its decay. It is an efficient means of literary separation and explanation of how such a site could possibly exist, increasing the seeming authenticity of the entire landscape.

Narragansett Bay serves as an additional link between Lovecraft's native Rhode Island and a mysterious resident of his part-fictional county. Although **Cape Cod** is not immediately adjacent to Lovecraft county, the feature is comprised of a bay that encircles a geographic basin, and served as the initial landing point of the Pilgrim Fathers—despite the widespread belief that Plymouth Rock served in this regard. This land represents the meeting point of two worlds, and its potential tainting with the paganistic offspring of Fiji natives reflects the outside influence behind the events of "The Shadow over Innsmouth," perhaps being not restricted to that town alone.

The infamous **Salem** is only referenced indirectly, as the settlement from which the three oldest founding families of Dunwich came, thereby connecting the latter directly with the traditions and history of the former. Each of these references serves to tie Lovecraft's fictional county closer into place alongside these nonfictional counterparts, in addition to the reinforcement of terrapsychological archetypes. Scholes, Phellan, and Kellogg suggest that "selected aspects of the actual [provide] essences referable for their meaning" (88); that the use of real geographies in this manner transfers their own semantic qualities by dint of association. A passing mention alone is enough to impart this transfer of meaning, arguably made stronger through the use of fictional names within the receptor that closely resemble those entities holding the semantic value desired. It is in this manner that themed semantics may thus be shown to serve a vital role in the artistic application of names. Part-fictional geographies are intended to be indistinguishable from the land from which they are taken and subsequently re-interleaved, so the use of known markers offers economic situational aids in this regard.

The extent to which Lovecraft uses the environment as a semantic marker is emphasized by Swift, as "everywhere we look
we encounter a pre-interpreted landscape, or a landscape made
legible" (82), an act made possible through the manipulation of
pre-formed terrapsychological placement and descriptive onomastic development. This is done through the strategic implementation of a range of archetypal thematically informed semantic ideas
held by both the qualifier and generic components of a name; Evans concurs with the heavy use of "narratives of place" to provide
authenticity to the writings, which "communicates both the sen-
sual qualities . . . and the emotional qualities . . . that are part of
the human experience of place" (122). This concept may be read
as being synonymous with terrapsychology, in that the characteristics conveyed are intended to produce a measured response in the
reader. Lovecraft's literary names are crafted so as to blend seam-
lessly within its surrounding nonfictional area, yet the semantics
incorporated into their form is simultaneously intentional in atmospheric manipulation. Such use works within a stylistically
Gothic archetype, incorporating root elements that fit the ontological context culminating in an environment particular to this
style of writing.

A pass referred to as **the printless road** (CF 1.407) leads into
Kingsport, with such a descriptor suggestive of the purposity behind such an action, leaving the willfully unnamed road open only
to those aware of its presence or who accidentally come across it,
displaying the semantic power of namelessness. In contrast, a spot
named **Hooper's Pond** (CF 2.90), comprised of standing—and
likely stagnating—water, bears a designatory name informed by a
local folk history that is not detailed within the narrative, but its
inclusion reminds the reader of hidden pasts that not only provides Lovecraft county with a greater semblance of authenticity,
but weaves semantic effect nicely into thematic intent. **Ten-Acre
Meadow** and **Meadow Hill** may seem out of place in comparison
to the hermeneutics that underlie the other onomastic entities,
but the sites for which the latter is used as a reference (featured in
"Herbert West—Reanimator" [CF 1.293]) are tucked away behind
it, hidden from view of those traveling the main routes, and per-
petually in shadow. As this is a common thematic concept within

Lovecraft's body of writing, these names could reflect the superficial semantic pleasance of the environment covering the darker reality revealed under closer examination.

Round Mountain is likewise juxtaposed by its description as ravine-dominated terrain, with a "vertical slope" (DH 156) extending in a sheer rise, as opposed to the physical form suggested by the qualifier "round." Perhaps it is indicative of the idealization suggested by onomastic form contrasted against a described physical reality, in a world where dark secrets are hidden just out of sight and glossed over with a superficial aesthetic layer—the name. As for **Sentinel Hill**, the name is suggestive of its lofty physical appearance, towering over the surrounding landscape; the qualifying element is semantically suggestive of protection and familiarity for all those being watched over. Atop the hill is a stone altar, another type of landmark encountered throughout this land, with evidence of human sacrifice buried within the hill that morphs the emotional interpretation of the qualifier so as to bear more sinister connotations. The context is vital, as these examples show, to determining semantic significance of every named location, just as the places themselves reinforce this framing stylistic structure. A Gothic style is anticipated, and such is received albeit tailored to the particulars of the Lovecraft's unique setting.

The terrapsychological formation of a setting can very much be seen to be communicated through the use of generic elements to provide additional and indirect inferences that both conform and contribute to the symbolic and thematic requirements of a fictional (or part-fictional) world, and possess as much stylized value as uniquely placed specifics. This value, as has been discussed, may then be manipulated through contextual detail, be it qualifying elements, thematic embellishment, or other named locations, so as to incorporate all these aspects into an overall onomastic composition consistent with a perceptible Gothic stylization. **Kingsport Head** possesses a generic typical of headlands with a sheer cliff dropping into the ocean, and the name **Orange Point** ("The Festival" [*CF* 1.416]) is applied to a piece of terrain that sticks prominently out of the mainland cutting into the surrounding ocean, as its lexical root suggests. The latter is suggested as having been coined as a subtle pun on Peach Point situated within Marblehead

(Joshi, *Call of Cthulhu* 388n25), mimicking the environmental and linguistic layout of the area so as to further blur the fictional divide. The terrapsychological value of both these forms of terrain may lie in such features, lying open and vulnerable to the wild ravages of nature.

Chapman's Brook serves as a means of linking the place with another of Lovecraft's texts, sharing the name and skirting the site of a remote farmhouse encountered in "Herbert West—Reanimator." Specified as a "brook," the stream may be read as being small, shallow, and likely lined with a bed of rocks, and the surrounding land as being potentially marshy with stagnating water (Gelling 7). No such type of detail is described within the text, but the archetypal terrapsychological schema that has formed around the external use of the generic qualifier serves to provide a narrative environmental shortcut to those familiar with other features that share the lexical component—providing a strong working link between terrapsychological value, onomastic interpretation, and literary styling. **Cold Spring Glen**, of deep and narrow composition, with the qualifying characteristic of this location bearing a semantically loaded physical description, is evocative of an emotional response that corresponds with the thematic frame of the Gothic. Even the names of settlements are vulnerable to poetic interpretation in this manner; **Clark's Corners** is the name of a small hamlet that is tucked away from readily traveled routes and rarely visited, with such a position reflected in the name despite the etymological root of the name likely referring to its location being upon a sharp turn in a thoroughfare. This is an example of how the generic element may significantly augment the poetic identity of a location, through such stylized representation.

Patches of superstitiously named land dot Lovecraft county and serve as a physical marker of the underlying presence of blights upon the otherwise idyllic land manifested through both their appearance and resulting name. Lévy (37) argues that that these spots are the result of contact with extra-planar entities and hint at what may be the fate of the entire planet, should these creatures be unleashed. **Devil's Reef** lies just beyond the shores of Innsmouth and, lined with shallow waters, presents a danger for vessels approaching the harbor. The folkloric origin of the name refers to a legion of devils "seen sometimes on that reef—sprawled about, or darting in and out of some kind of caves near the top" (CF 3.162). Yet the environmental type of the location is one associated with the danger of shallow waters, providing semantic impetus for such legends to take hold, purposefully propagated with a religiously accursed title so as to ward off curious investigation. The intent of this onomastic attribution is enmeshed with stylistic, thematic, and terrapsychological value.

Likewise, the Devil's Hop Yard is described as a bleak, blasted hillside where no tree, shrub, or grass-blade grows just outside of Dunwich, the onomastic generic betraying the puritanical heritage of the area with the ironic reference to that crop and serving as a poetic warning. Part of the previous description is made a qualifying element for the blasted heath. The name of this land is generated from its appearance (five acres of desolate land ringed by healthy fields), and it is said that "no other name could fit such a thing, or any other thing fit such a name," for it was "grey desolation that sprawled open to the sky like a great spot eaten by acid in the woods and fields" (CF 2.367). Both of the prior names present the idea of their respective sites as being damned, but here it is the physical propagation of unearthly creatures beneath the soil that drains the natural life from the land. Both the generics and the qualifiers of these locations converge to present a terrapsychological response emphatic of their literary purpose: as simple warning markers, which the reader comes to associate with sites damaged by contact with creatures not of this world. Witch House stands alone within Arkham as a site of curious phenomena, with the nickname derived from a supposed history involving an escapee of the Salem witch trials. The house is shunned and serves as a nexus into a dreamworld filled with unearthly peril, but it is the use of the lexis "witch" that provides semantic value as a marker of warning.

The folkloric names exhibited in this world are concise in their attribution and are poetic amalgamations of legend, history, and semantic wards perhaps intended so as to warn off the curious. These onomastic tokens would retain a semblance of these meaningful elements if encountered outside the context of the setting, but within the thematic and stylistic framework of Lovecraft county their full semantic worth is wrought through a thematically pertinent connection.

Mention may also be made of one unnamed piece of land that is a "small island in the Miskatonic where the devil held court beside a curious stone altar older than the Indians" ("The Colour out of Space" [*CF* 2.369]). This place bears many of the stylistic features typical of the places found Lovecraft county: folkloric history, heathen altar, and association with the name of evil. It also presents an environmental type that is featured heavily throughout Lovecraft's work: islands. Described by Lovecraft in the excerpt included in the second paragraph of this article as "sinister monoliths," prominent terrapsychological value may be identified in the natural isolation of these environments, cut off from a mainland and within the midst of the open ocean. Unlike the marine settlements that are situated on the coastline, serving as the point of contact between the known and the mysteries of deep unknown, the remoteness of these places serve a direct hermeneutic suggestion of long-rooted heathen association with the eldritch beings hidden from the sight of civilized man. **Fiji, Ponape, the Cape Verde Islands,** and **the South Sea Islands** are all referenced within the text as being associated with their savage, cannibalistic tribes that all worship otherwise unknown deities, and so the exotic may be argued as being brought to New England by way of semantic association. Traditional onomastic interpretation of the latter provides a translation of Ponape as "upon (*pohn*) the stone altar (*pei*)," provided by Hanlon (xxi). This is an apt choice for its comparative-role within the narrative, providing a terrapsychological transference from such sites to the ancient altars scattered throughout Lovecraft county.

The semantic implications of these islands as an environmental archetype may provide a greater degree of interpretative feedback, with the form of the place proving the dominant characteristic that serves as the primary provider of role-based identity. The appearance of seas and tides are tagged with semantic markers within their textual description that betray the emotional presence that Lovecraft is constantly seeking to tap: "And against the rotting wharves the sea pounded; the secretive, immemorial sea out of which the people had come in the elder time" ("The Festival"

[*CF* 1.407]). Punter indirectly touches upon this terrapsychological imperative, arguing that Lovecraft's "backcloth brings together a number of thinly disguised East Coast towns, chosen for their historical 'depth of field', with those other depths, of the sea and of outer space, breeding-grounds for the primitive but powerful exiled beings" (2.39). This observation may be extended to the insular terrain, for it serves as an example of an environmental set that may facilitate a link between physical form and emotional response, wrought primarily through the corresponding dominant literary themes for a work.

Even a singular reference to **Alderney** (*CF* 2.420) serving as the source of the favored cattle within "The Dunwich Horror" provides a link to this motif, in that isolation forces a restricted pattern of breeding so as to keep a breed of pure stock, in spite of any genetic abnormalities that may result. This is a theme also encountered within the stagnating fictional towns and villages throughout Lovecraft County, and the use of such an environment to reinforce this concept provides a viable argument for the implementation of terrapsychology within semantically governed appreciation of space.

Through the utilization of inferential historical characteristics associated with the area of New England, Lovecraft was able to draw upon a degree of prefiguration for specific loci within his fictional Arkham Country. Working with a framework comprised of stereotypical representation in order to induce a concentrated environmental character that conveys a sense of history, myth, and style—all especially tailored so as to evoke a functional emotional response that serves in artistic rendition—observable even in the names. By working within a fictional placement, he had the freedom to add or detail the landscape in any manner he needed to fit the requirements of the individual text, all of which has a grounding in both a physical and terrapsychological level of creation, and so each literary setting may be considered a defining aspect of characterization in its own right. Each fictional world is uniquely shaped to elicit a desired thematically appropriate response, and like any literary character, as Plank argues: "the science fiction writer enjoys a degree of onomastic and other freedoms that the realistic writer does not have" (157); but such creations are still limited by the engagement of such associative properties. In drawing upon the spirit of this particular landscape of New England, Lovecraft has the advantages of utilizing nonfictional places with relevant associative traits, in addition to the freedom to exaggerate those elements that reinforce the thematic explorations of a work.

Lovecraft county is ultimately built upon a stylistic derivation of Gothic literature, which is readily discernible through the onomastic composition of the setting and sets the scene for the type of narrative that unfolds within. Lévy ultimately describes the setting as being "strangely familiar and fabulously faraway" (41), which is arguably the intent of this ontological mode of creation. Emulation of stylistic characteristics gives the impression of authenticity within the partially prefigured constructed world, but removed in some important manner; but the purposeful likeness of their portrayal primes the reception of the reader by way of an archetypal representation, which this brief exploration has hopefully shown. In this manner "the reader is made to feel at the mercy of vast, malign forces emanating from a universe perhaps in some way parallel to our own, but intruding on ours only to confound all expectation" (Punter and Byron 143–44), typical of the Gothic, and it is through this kind of response that the part-fictional ontological mode of fictional realization functions. The names mimic and closely resemble, but do not quite align with, their existing nonfictional counterparts, and it is this semantic uncanniness that presents a characteristic foreshadowing entirely in keeping with the tales that unfold within the literary world—that which looks familiar may not be quite what it seems.

Works Cited

Barnes, Trevor J., and James S. Duncan. *Writing Worlds: Discourse, Text and Metaphor in the Representation of Landscape.* New York: Routledge, 1992.

Brady, Emily. *Aesthetics of the Natural Environment.* Edinburgh: Edinburgh University Press, 2003.

Chalquist, Craig. *Terrapsychology: Reengaging the Soul of Place— An Introduction.* New Orleans: Spring Journal Books, 2007.

Evans, Timothy H. "A Last Defense against the Dark: Folklore, Horror, and the Uses of Tradition in the Works of H. P. Lovecraft." *Journal of Folklore Research* 42 (2005): 99–135.

Foster, Cheryl. "The Narrative and the Ambient in Environmental Aesthetics." *Journal of Aesthetics and Art Criticism* 56 (1998): 127–37.

Gelling, Margaret, and Ann Cole. *The Landscape of Place-Names.* Stamford, CT: Shaun Tyas, 2000.

Grimaud, Michel. "Onomastics and the Study of Literature." *Yearbook of Comparative and General Literature* 38 (1989): 16–35.

Lévy, Maurice. *Lovecraft: A Study in the Fantastic.* Trans. S. T. Joshi. Detroit: Wayne State University Press, 1988.

Lovecraft, H. P. *The Call of Cthulhu and Other Weird Stories.* Ed. S. T. Joshi. New York: Penguin, 1999.

McHale, Brian. "En Abyme: Internal Models and Cognitive Mapping." In *A Sense of the World: Essays on Fiction, Narrative, and Knowledge,* ed. John Gibson, Wolfgang Huemer, and Luca Pocci. London: Routledge, 2007. 189–205.

Plank, Robert. "Names and Roles of Characters in Science Fiction." *Names* 9 (1961): 151–59.

Punter, David. *The Literature of Terror: The Gothic Tradition,* 2nd ed. London: Longman, 1996. 2 vols.

Punter, David, and Glennis Byron. *The Gothic.* Oxford: Blackwell, 2004.

Robinson, Christopher L. "Teratonymy: The Weird and Monstrous Names of H. P. Lovecraft." *Names* 58 (2010): 127–39.

Scholes, Robert E.; Phelan, James; and Kellogg, Robert L. *The Nature of Narrative.* Oxford: Oxford University Press, 2006.

Smith, Frank. *Writing and the Writer.* Oxford: Heinemann Educational Books, 1982.

Swift, Jonathan. "The Slightly Different Thing That is Said: Writing the Aesthetic Experience." In *Writing Worlds: Discourse, Text and Metaphor in the Representation of Landscape,* ed. Trevor J. Barnes and James S. Duncan. London: Routledge, 1992. 73–85.

Turner, Jim, ed. *Eternal Lovecraft: The Persistence of HPL in Popular Culture.* Urbana, IL: Golden Gryphon Press, 1998.

Two Poets and Beauty:
H. P. Lovecraft and James Elroy Flecker

Phillip A. Ellis

What I shall not do, in this paper, is to demonstrate that Flecker was concerned with the evocation of beauty. I do so elsewhere, in another piece, one specifically on his poetry. It is also implicit in his advocacy for Parnassianism as an antidote to the aesthetic chaos among his contemporaries' poetic thought and practice. What I will do here is to discuss two basic things. The first is the degree to which H. P. Lovecraft was familiar with and inspired by Flecker's writing. This is a difficult proposition at present. The second thing is to demonstrate that Lovecraft was also concerned with beauty, an area underexplored in Lovecraft studies. Though S. T. Joshi has explored Lovecraft's aesthetic thought elsewhere (*Decline* 46–58, 112–20), in doing so he discusses Lovecraft (in large part) in relation to Bloom's concept of the anxiety of influence, and in regard to Lovecraft's abandonment of Dunsanianism (see the later section of *Decline*). So there is more that needs to be done.

I believe Lovecraft's aesthetic thought is integral to his reaction to other authors, other artists. We cannot understand his reaction to the work of Lord Dunsany as fully as possible without understanding the importance of beauty in his worldview, and in his own work. This is why I have taken the time to discuss Flecker in relation to Lovecraft. Lovecraft's response to Flecker is creative, and we see this same creative response to the other stimuli and influences, major and minor, in his life. His response to the oral weird tales of his grandfather was to create written weird tales. His response to science and astronomy was to create scientific writings. His response to literature was to create literature. Since the concept of making is evoked in the etymology of the English term "poetry" and its cognates, the self-identification of Lovecraft as a poet implicitly evokes his nature as a creator of beauty.

In this sense, Lovecraft is close to the ideal of poetry espoused by Flecker in his advocacy of Parnassianism. This movement is both classicist and involved in the evocation and creation of beauty in its practitioners' poetry. It is also a response against Romanticism (need we remember that Lovecraft dismissed what he termed "romanticism" in certain passages of his critical writing?—e.g., *CE* 5 47–48). In a sense, Flecker is as much a poet and classicist as Lovecraft. It is not surprising that Flecker would then be attractive to Lovecraft, and that certain passages of his *Hassan* should inspire Lovecraft to create, in turn, what S. T. Joshi has labeled his "Stanzas on Samarkand" (*AT* 173).

So what are we to derive from this extended study of Flecker and the place of beauty in Lovecraft's thought? I would say this: Lovecraft was concerned in large part with the evocation of beauty, and this evocation reflects its importance for his worldview. In turn, it affects his responses to the work of others, so much so that we need to understand the much-neglected role that the beautiful and theories of the beautiful have in the greater, wider worldview that he constructed, more so than we need to understand his scientific materialism.

There is little evidence that Lovecraft read Flecker and was influenced by him. It might be conventional to say that this evidence is twofold, in his poetry and in his correspondence. This distinction does not hold. There is evidence in his correspondence apart from considerations of his poetry, and evidence in his correspondence that concerns poetry. Let us first consider the evidence apart from his poetry.

Of the correspondence available to me, the references to Flecker follow the same basic pattern. A quotation from Lovecraft's letter to Donald Wandrei of 13 March 1927 illustrates this. The relevant passage reads: "Is there any line more haunting than that repeated burden spoken under the 'burning moonlight' in the last act of James Elroy Flecker's 'Hassan'—'We take the golden road to Samarkand'?" (*MTS* 52). The basic elements of this passage appear at least twice more in later passages.

In a letter to August Derleth (21 October 1929), Lovecraft writes: "Last Wednesday & Friday I took long walks under the mystical Hunter's Moon—it was especially fine Friday, when one might clearly understand what Flecker was thinking of in describing 'burning moonlight' in his 'Hassan'" (*ES* 226). Lovecraft writes to James F. Morton (8 November 1929): "Now I know what Jim Flecker meant when he pulled that one about 'burning moonlight' in the last act of 'Hassan'!" (*LJM* 178).

In all three passages, we see two basic elements: Lovecraft quotes the same phrase, "burning moonlight," and he ascribes it to the same play, *Hassan*. We know also that in quoting *Hassan* Lovecraft was less than exact. S. T. Joshi, in notes to two of these three letters, informs us of this; I quote the fuller note: "The phrase 'burning moonlight' does not occur in James Elroy Flecker's *Hassan*, but the phrase 'blazing moonlight' is found in a scene description in Act V, Scene II. See *Hassan* (London: William Heinemann, 1922), p. 179" (*ES* 226n4). The two phrases are close enough to render Lovecraft's misprision understandable.

I have mentioned Lovecraft's poetry earlier. In the same letter to James F. Morton, Lovecraft immediately follows the quoted passage with a quatrain; it runs:

> Each distant mountain glows with faery grace,
> The flame-lit lakelet laps the level strand;
> Lur'd by dim vistas beck'ning out of space,
> We take the golden road to Samarkand! (*LJM* 178; *AT* 173)

These are not the only quatrains that Lovecraft wrote on the same basic pattern. There are three others, as follows:

> Too long the jangling of the Muse run mad
> Hath vext the air of our decaying land—
> Turned to the golden past, we quit Baghdad,
> And take the Golden Road to Samarkand.
>> (letter to Frank Belknap Long,
>> 25 February 1924; *AT* 173)

> Frantick with rumours of eternal night,
>> And bury'd lore that none may understand,

We leave behind the realms of pitch and fright,
    And take the Golden Road to Samarkand.
            (letter to Frank Belknap Long,
            c. late February 1924; *AT* 173)

Reality, the King of Idiot Gods,
    Fumbles his puppets with a palsy'd hand:
Come leave him as he paws his wining clods,
    And take the Golden Road to Samarkand.
            (letter to Frank Belknap Long,
            21 March 1924; *AT* 173)

The stanzas' appearance together, under a joint title, in *The Ancient Track* implies a continuity in the four that I am not certain is there. First, I lack transcripts of the three letters to Frank Belknap Long, so can neither confirm nor deny such a continuity among those three. I lack, also, the immediate contexts of those three quatrains' appearance. Second, looking at the four, there is no continuity evident among them. They are immiscible, in sense, content, style, and tone. Third, the stanza in the letter to Morton is anomalous compared to the other three. It is later than the others, by five years; it was sent to a different correspondent; and it was given an immediate context and a degree of cosmicism that is only dimly apparent in the second of the other three quatrains.

It is probable and reasonable to consider the four as isolated instances of poetry, rather than a single poem. This is implied in Joshi's note to the stanzas in *The Ancient Track:* "The stanzas are all pastiches or parodies of James Elroy Flecker's Hassan (1922): toward the end of that play various characters recite quatrains, all ending with the line '. . . take the Golden Road to Samarkand'" (544).

This distinction between pastiche and parody is a tricky one. It may be said that the author's intent is as important as the ludic or satirical elements associated with parody as a genre. Joshi does not offer a third option, that of inspiration. It is possible to write a poem that contains elements not focusing on parody's or pastiche's emphasis on stylistic mimesis. So a poet may take that refrain and quatrain form and use stylistic and other elements to create a poem that references the original at the same time as it departs from

it. The refrain becomes more allusive, using the original to enrich
the new poem rather than embrace it, as it were.

I do not sense the ludic or satiric qualities in these stanzas, as
stanzas devoid of their immediate context (except that Morton's
has a context that I can read). The stanza to Morton, as it has a
context missing from the three others, suggests neither parody nor
pastiche. The context is the discussion of the moonlight, echoed
in the quatrain's images of sunset and the onset of night. It is not
mimetic in style or substance to Flecker's poetry, but develops its
own concerns. It is inspired by Flecker, but not imitative of Flecker.

I mentioned earlier that Lovecraft's correspondence reveals a
familiarity with Flecker's writings. We see such a familiarity
among some of Lovecraft's correspondents. Donald Wandrei, in a
passage to Lovecraft, writes:

> You are more of a poet than you let me believe in one of your
> letters. Your own prose fantasies and tales would indicate this,
> without the additional help of your appreciation of "Hassan". I
> read the refrain in his "Collected Poems", a couple of years ago,
> and was simply carried away by its haunting beauty. I looked up
> the play immediately then and read the lines in their proper set-
> ting; they brought a sigh of regret from me when I had finished.
> There are some good things in his "Collected Poems", also, though
> I don't remember any titles except the two "Sonnets of Bathro-
> laire". (21 March 1927; *MTS* 58–59)

Robert E. Howard writes to Lovecraft, noting that:

> By the way, I recently sold Weird Tales a short story, "The Children
> of the Night" in which I deal with Mongoloid-aboriginal legendry
> . . . as well as quoting likes from Flecker's "Gates of Damascus" and
> lending them a cryptic meaning which I'm sure would have
> astounded the poet remarkably! (c. October 1930; *MF* 95)

Howard, in a later letter, lists Flecker among the poets he likes
(December 1932; *MF* 510). In all three instances, the context
shows that Lovecraft was familiar enough with Flecker that he
need not query about the poet, the poetry cited, or the poetry involved. So it is very likely that, despite the absence of Flecker
from *Lovecraft's Library*, Lovecraft was familiar with more than

just the single work (*Hassan*) that he cites. Such is plausible but, at this stage, not yet provable.

So there is some evidence that Lovecraft was familiar with Flecker, even though this evidence is largely confined to a repeated misquotation from one play and imitations of one element of that play's verse. There are implications that Lovecraft would have been familiar with more than just this play, but such implications are possible rather than plausible, and currently unable to be either proved or disproved. What interests me now are questions of whether there is anything that would attract Lovecraft to Flecker, and whether there were shared elements of their creative life or worldview that would in a sense account for what we know of Lovecraft's interest in Flecker.

James Elroy Flecker was not a weird versifier; so why was Lovecraft interested enough in his work to attempt to quote it and to imitate it in part? I have noted above that I am not demonstrating that Flecker was interested in the evocation of beauty; I have also stated why. What I am interested here is in showing that Lovecraft, too, was interested in the nature and question of beauty, and extending from this to consider that the beautiful is one of the reasons for Lovecraft's interest in Flecker. In essence it implies some degree of Lovecraft's familiarity with the identification of Flecker as a Parnassian, and the resultant importance of beauty for Flecker.

The keynote for Lovecraft's prose poems, many of his poems, and a number of his fantasies, is not terror, but beauty. Certain sonnets of *Fungi from Yuggoth* explore the beautiful, such as "Mirage," "Expectancy," and "The Gardens of Yin." He also explores the beautiful more fully in certain of his short stories.

With "The Quest of Iranon," we see Iranon as almost an allegory of the artist. The chief burden of the story is that art and beauty are founded upon dreams and illusion, and, breaking these, "something of youth and beauty" (*D* 117) will die. Iranon says, for instance: "I am a singer of songs that I learned in the far city [of Aira], and my calling is to make beauty with the things remembered of childhood" (*CF* 1.255). He elaborates on this when told by the archon of Teloth to be apprenticed to a cobbler: "Ye toil to live, but is not life made of beauty and song? And if ye suffer no singers among you, where shall be the fruits of your toil? Toil without song is like a weary journey without an end" (CF 1.250). Further, Lovecraft returns to beauty in his description of the childhood land of Aira:

> "I remember the sun of morning bright above the many-coloured hills in summer, and the sweetness of flowers borne on the south wind that made the trees sing.
>
> "O Aira, city of marble and beryl, how many are thy beauties! How loved I the warm and fragrant groves across the hyaline Nithra, and the falls of the tiny Kra that flowed through the verdant valley! In those groves and in that vale the children wove wreaths for one another, and at dusk I dreamed strange dreams under the yath-trees on the mountain as I saw below me the lights of the city, and the curving Nithra reflecting a ribbon of stars.
>
> "And in the city were palaces of veined and tinted marble, with golden domes and painted walls, and green gardens with cerulean pools and crystal fountains. . . . And sometimes at sunset I would climb the long hilly street to the citadel and the open place, and look down upon Aira, the magic city of marble and beryl, splendid in a robe of golden flame." (CF 1.249)

In "Celephaïs" we read of how

> Beyond that wall in the grey dawn he came to a land of quaint gardens and cherry trees, and when the sun rose he beheld such a beauty of red and white flowers, green foliage and lawns, white paths, diamond brooks, blue lakelets, carven bridges, and red-roofed pagodas, that he for a moment forgot Celephaïs in sheer delight. (CF 1.189)

"The White Ship" contains the following passage: "when the day dawned, rosy and effulgent, I beheld the green shore of far lands, bright and beautiful, and to me unknown. Up from the sea rose lordly terraces of verdure, tree-studded, and shewing here and there the gleaming white roofs and colonnades of strange temples" (CF 1.108). This is "the Land of Zar," in which "dwell all the dreams and thoughts of beauty that come to men once and are forgotten" (CF 1.108. This imagery relates to the sunset terrace imagery catalogued by Peter Cannon in his essay "Sunset Terrace Imagery in Lovecraft." The terrace is a motif that appears elsewhere in the same story; Lovecraft writes: "Green are the groves and pastures, bright and fragrant the flowers, blue and musical the streams, clear and cool the fountains, and stately and gorgeous the temples, castles, and cities of Sona-Nyl. Of that land there is no bound, for beyond each vista of beauty rises another more beautiful" (D 39). Slightly further on, we read of "gardens where quaint pagodas peep from pleasing clumps of bushes, and where the white walks are bordered with delicate blossoms" (CF 1.110). All this confirms a vision deeply held by Lovecraft, of the garden as a locus for beauty: he speaks elsewhere of two "supreme incarnations or adumbrations" of "utter, perfect beauty" (HPL to Alfred Galpin, 15 May 1930; LG 155). The first is where

> The vistas I relish most are those in which the sunset plays a transfiguring & glorifying part. . . . Absolutely nothing else in life now has the power to move me so much; for in these momentary vistas there seem to open before me bewildering avenues to all the wonders & lovelinesses I have ever sought. . . . All that I live for is to capture some fragment of this hidden & just unreachable beauty. (HPL to Donald Wandrei, 21 April 1927; MTS 89)

Lovecraft writes elsewhere of "a mass of mystical city towers & roofs & spires outlined against a sunset & glimpsed from a fairly distant balustraded terrace" (HPL to Alfred Galpin, 15 May 1930; LG 155). The second of these two refers to the garden as the locus of beauty; Lovecraft writes of

> the experience of walking (or, as in most of my dreams, aërially floating) thro' ethereal & enchanted gardens of exotick delicacy & opulence, with carved stone bridges, labyrinthine paths, marble fountains, terraces, & staircases, strange pagodas, hillside grottos, curious statues, termini, sundials, benches, basins, & lanthorns, lily'd pools of swans & streams with tiers of waterfalls, spreading ginkgo-trees & dropping, feathery willows, & sun-touch'd flowers of a bizarre, Klarkash-Tonick pattern never beheld on land or beneath the sea . . . (HPL to Alfed Galpin, 15 May 1930; LG 155–56)

We can see, in the passages above, that Lovecraft sought beauty; I have not quoted the poetry, though, because Lovecraft notes that "Poetry is simply a reflection of beauty—not a panacea for social disorders" (HPL to Elizabeth Toldridge, 28 August 1933, SL 4.238). That is, Lovecraft attempts to evoke beauty so much that

there is wealth enough in many if not most of his poems, wealth
enough to resist easy quotation. "The East India Brick Row" is a
case in point: it intersects with both the sunset terrace imagery
and the topographical basis for much of what Lovecraft considered beautiful. Lovecraft, we must remember, says elsewhere that
"art deals with beauty rather than fact" (HPL to August Derleth, 2
January 1927; *SL* 2.96).

There is much more that can be said about the nature of beauty for Lovecraft. Before I wrap up this paper, I want to emphasize
that Lovecraft saw the arbitrariness in our conceptions of beauty,
expressing these in two extended passages in his correspondence.
The first passage runs as follows:

> To me it seems glaringly clear that there is no intrinsic value or
> meaning in anything which stands by itself. Value is wholly rela-
> tive, and the very idea of such a thing as meaning postulates a
> symmetrical relation to something else. No one thing, cosmically
> speaking, can be either good or evil, beautiful and unbeautiful; for
> entity is simply entity. The qualities of goodness and beauty are
> altogether local and temporary things, measurable only as the
> mental-physical-imaginative responses of organic beings of a given
> type and training to certain forms of relationship with given back-
> grounds made familiar through structure and experience. (HPL to
> Frank Belknap Long, April 1928; *SL* 2.234)

The second is as follows:

> It is because I ... [recognise] no such qualities as good or evil,
> beauty or ugliness, in the ultimate structure of the universe, that I
> insist on the artificial & traditional values of each particular cul-
> tural stream—proximate values which grew out of the special in-
> stincts, associations, environment, & experiences of the race in
> question, & which are the sole available criteria for the members
> of that race & culture, though of course having no validity outside
> it. These backgrounds of tradition against which to scale the ob-
> jects & events of experience are all that lend such objects &
> events the illusion of meaning, value, or dramatic interest in an ul-
> timately purposeless cosmos—hence I preach & practice an ex-
> treme conservatism in art forms, society, & politics, as the only
> means of averting the ennui, despair, & confusion of a guideless &

standardless struggle with unveiled chaos. (HPL to Donald Wandrei, 21 April 1927; *SL* 2.125)

The basic response to this proximate nature of beauty, and other aspects of our existence, is the importance of tradition for Lovecraft, and a species of classicism. The role of the artist is to create in the traditions in which that artist is familiar, so for Lovecraft this meant the evocation of the Age of Reason in the measured writing of his prose and poetry. Where this classicism works, Lovecraft succeeds, and where it intersects with his contemporary world, using his contemporaries' language, it tends to succeed admirably.

I have spoken enough about Lovecraft's conception of beauty and the beautiful. It is true that Lovecraft was concerned in evoking beauty in his work. It is also true that this evocation mirrors the importance of beauty for his wider worldview. I hold that beauty affects his responses both to other people and to the work that those same people created. We need to understand this, just as we need to understand the place that both the beautiful and theories of the beautiful have in his far greater, far wider worldview. We already understand the importance of his scientific materialism; we need to understand that of his aesthetic thought.

This paper also concerns itself with the degree to which Lovecraft was familiar with the works of Flecker. There is far less evidence, here, of this familiarity than there is of the importance of beauty for Lovecraft. It has applications for Lovecraft studies, though, that extend beyond the narrower enumeration of Lovecraft's influences and inspirations, for his poetry and otherwise. In this conclusion, I wish briefly to note why.

By taking the figure of Flecker as the creator of a certain type of beauty (in this case, poetic), it is possible to see that Lovecraft was influenced in many instances by other creators of beauty. This is why I feel that his friendships with such figures as Samuel Loveman, Frank Belknap Long, Donald Wandrei, and, as regards his serious work more than his weird fiction, August Derleth were so conducive to his creativity. These (and other) figures were so important to Lovecraft in large part because he responded to their evocations of beauty as well as of awe and terror. So much so that his early identification of himself as a poet influences his response to weird literature and underlies his later identification of himself as a weird realist.

Lovecraft himself signals the importance of beauty for himself and for his reaction to life. He does so in his letters and, more indirectly, in his fiction and poetry. And he does so more allusively in his literary criticism. This is why I am in part interested in Lovecraft's aesthetic thought, not just because I am drawn to the rhythmic creation of beauty in my own poetry, or because it is an undervalued component for his worldview. There is an importance for creative artists for consideration about what is true, what is beautiful. We may find, as Kenneth Slessor did, that the urban is beautiful; we may find, with Lovecraft, that it is the sunset terrace; we may find otherwise. But what we should find here is that the influence of Flecker on Lovecraft illustrates something greater than the transmission of a motif or a form; it illustrates, for Lovecraft, the importance of tradition, of the classical in art and poetry, and its importance as an equally valid response to the world as is the Romanticism that others have espoused.

Works Cited

Flecker, James Elroy. *The Collected Poems of James Elroy Flecker.* Edited by J. C. Squire. New York: Knopf, 1921.

———. *Hassan: The Story of Hassan of Baghdad and How He Came to Make the Golden Journey to Samarkand: A Play in Five Acts.* London: William Heinemann, 1922.

Joshi, S. T. *H. P. Lovecraft: The Decline of the West.* 1990. Mercer Island, WA: Starmont House, 1990.

———. *Lovecraft's Library: A Catalogue.* 3rd. rev. & enl. ed. New York: Hippocampus Press, 2012.

Lovecraft, H. P. *Essential Solitude: The Letters of H. P. Lovecraft and August Derleth.* Edited by David E. Schultz and S. T. Joshi. New York: Hippocampus Press, 2008. [Abbreviated in the text as *ES.*]

———. *Letters to Alfred Galpin.* Edited by S. T. Joshi and David E. Schultz. New York: Hippocampus Press, 2003. [Abbreviated in the text as *LG.*]

———. *Letters to James F. Morton.* Edited by David E. Schultz and S. T. Joshi. New York: Hippocampus Press, 2011. [Abbreviated in the text as *LJM.*]

———. *A Means to Freedom: The Letters of H. P. Lovecraft and Robert E. Howard.* Edited by S. T. Joshi, David E. Schultz, and

Rusty Burke. New York: Hippocampus Press, 2009. 2 vols. [Abbreviated in the text as *MF*.]

———. *Mysteries of Time and Spirit: The Letters of H. P. Lovecraft and Donald Wandrei*. Edited by S. T. Joshi and David E. Schultz. San Francisco: Night Shade Books, 2002. [Abbreviated in the text as *MTS*.]

IF YOU WANT
TO BE RICH
DAVID V. BUSH
DAVID V BUSH'S PSYCHOLOGICAL CAMPAIGN

Lovecraft's Third Meeting with David V. Bush

Kenneth W. Faig, Jr.

Dedicated to the EOD and its Acolytes
in Memory of Forty Years of Association

We have an ample account of Lovecraft's first two meetings with David V. Bush (1882–1959), in Boston in June 1922, in his letter to Anne Tillery Renshaw dated 14 June 1922 (*ATR* 370–74). Their first meeting apparently transpired in Bush's suite at Boston's Copley Plaza Hotel; Lovecraft provides a character sketch of his revision client and states that their first meeting lasted "little more than an hour," since he had to catch a train to Haverhill at North Station. A few days later, Lovecraft attended one of Bush's evening lectures at Convention Hall on St. Botolph Street in Boston. Lovecraft's second meeting with Bush was also cut short:

> After the show Dave wanted to dine with me at a café, but I had to beat it for the train, hence bade a cordial good-bye. After all, he's a harmless, likeable chap, & I fancy it will be a bit less impossible to do his work in the future. He enjoys life—as do all who are spared the curse of intelligence. (*ATR* 374)

At about the same time, Lovecraft's essay "East and West Harvard Conservatism," concerning the Bush campaign in Boston and Worcester (*CE* 5.72–74), was published in Bush's magazine *Mind Power Plus*; the text survives as a clipping at the John Hay Library. When they met for the first and second time in June 1922, Bush had already been Lovecraft's revision client for five years; in his *New York Times* advertisement of 10 August 1924, Lovecraft asserted that he had "for seven years handled all the prose and verse of a leading American public speaker and editor" (*CE* 5.283–84). Joshi and

Schultz state that Bush joined the Hoffman–Daas United faction in
1916 and first came into correspondence with Lovecraft in 1917
through the Symphony Literary Service (operated by Lovecraft,
Anne Tillery Renshaw, and others) (*Lovecraft Encyclopedia* 26).

Of Lovecraft's third (and apparently final) in-person meeting
with Bush, we have hitherto known only that the two met in
New York City on Sunday, 25 May 1924. This information is based
on a postcard to Lovecraft's aunt Lillian D. Clark dated 28 May
1924, owned by the John Hay Library and cited by S. T. Joshi (*IAP*
506). We can develop a little more information concerning this
meeting. The *New York Evening Post* for Saturday, 24 May 1924,
reported that Bush would lecture at Carnegie Hall for seventeen
days commencing Monday, 26 May. If Bush lectured daily, that
would mean that his final lecture at Carnegie Hall would have occurred on Wednesday, 11 June 1924. The jacket flap copy for
Bush's book *If You Want to Be Rich* (Mehoopany, PA: David V.
Bush, 1954), however, indicates that the engagement may have
been extended to meet the demand:

> It was he [Bush] in 1924 who broke all records of attendance at
> Carnegie Hall, New York City, the most famous of all concert
> and lecture platforms in America.
>
> The crowds attending his lectures were so great that the first
> time in the history of Carnegie Hall, to prevent congestion on the
> sidewalks, the doors were opened at 7:15 instead of 7:30.
>
> It was established that there were two thousand more people
> than the auditorium could seat milling up and down the ramps
> and aisles and lining the side walls. The Fire Department held up
> his lecture until those standing were ejected from the hall.
>
> The amazing feature of his tremendous crowds lies in the fact
> that he did not appear for just one night as most concert artists
> and speakers do, but for twenty-six nights thousands filled Carne-
> gie Hall and thousands were turned away. The New York Fire
> Department had to be called to control the crowds; people
> blocked the sidewalks and jammed the aisles to hear this thrilling
> and inspiring man with a message.

If Bush lectured at Carnegie Hall on twenty-six consecutive
nights, his engagement was apparently extended through Friday,
20 June 1924. We do not know exactly where Lovecraft's third

meeting with Bush on Sunday, 25 May 1924, transpired; Bush's hotel suite would be a logical guess, but the two might also have met for dinner or even have met at Carnegie Hall. The wraparound dust jacket of *If You Want to Be Rich* is a panoramic photograph of one of Bush's 1924 lectures at Carnegie Hall and is labeled "David V. Bush Psychological Campaign, Carnegie Hall, New York City." (If the photograph is dated, I have been unable to decipher the date.) The main floor (parquet) of the hall, two levels of "box seats" (called Tier 1 and Tier 2 in modern plans of Carnegie Hall), a dress circle, and a balcony are depicted. As is common in panoramic photography, the images of individuals on either side of the hall are blurred; in the relatively poor reproduction of the photograph used for the dust jacket, no individual images can be distinguished in the dress circle and the balcony; detail is poor for individuals in the two tiers of "box seats" and for individuals along the side walls of the parquet. If taken on the first night of Bush's Carnegie Hall lectures, the photograph was evidently taken after the Fire Department had cleared the aisles; on the main floor, there are only a few persons standing in the rear near the doors.

Was this photograph taken on the occasion of Bush's first Carnegie Hall lecture on Monday, 26 May 1924, or at another time? Were H. P. and Sonia Lovecraft included in the photograph? A balding David V. Bush[1] is himself pictured in the foreground on the jacket spine. The milliner Sonia Lovecraft would presumably be distinguished by a prominent hat if present. My identification of H. P. Lovecraft in the Hub Club "round-up" group photograph taken on Deer Island in Boston

David Van Bush c. 1924

1. One can trace the progression of Bush's baldness from the author's portraits included in *Peace Poems and Sausages* (2nd ed. 1916), *Inspirational Poems* (1921), *Poems of Mastery and Love Verse* (1922), and the dust jacket photograph of *If You Want to Be Rich* (taken 1924). The first of these photographs can be found on Library Thing; the second and third on archive.org. The first (1915) edition of *Peace Poems and Sausages* reproduced on archive.org does not contain the frontispiece depicting the author.

Harbor on 4 July 1923,[2] has been challenged by Donovan K. Loucks and other experts, so I am hesitant to make any identifications based on the poor-quality images in the Carnegie Hall group photograph as reproduced (*IYW* jacket). Depicted on the spine, near the doors of the main floor, is a lady in a large hat with a gentleman to her right; but there is not enough detail to make any identifications. There are other possible candidates depicted in the two tiers of "box seats," but the detail for these individuals is even poorer. It seems only natural to suppose that Lovecraft (and perhaps his wife) would have received an invitation to attend one of Bush's Carnegie Hall lectures; but whether either or both are present in the dust jacket photograph of *If You Want to Be Rich* probably cannot be resolved at this point in time.

Joshi remarks that Lovecraft was again doing "Bush work" in July 1924 (*IAP* 506). During this period, the economic prospects of Lovecraft and his wife were worsening and by the end of July Lovecraft had to write the Homestead Company that he was unable to maintain payments on the home lot in Yonkers which he and his wife had purchased in May. Whether Bush was able to provide any employment prospects to Lovecraft beyond contract revisory work (even temporary; e.g., selling literature to the audience at Carnegie Hall) during this period remains unknown. During the 1921–25 period, Bush's business headquarters were in Chicago; one may ask whether Bush might have offered a Chicago-based job opportunity to Lovecraft[3] even before Jacob Henneberger offered the editorship of *Weird Tales* to him later in the year.

According to Lovecraft (*ATR* 370), Bush was born to a poor farmer's family and came to Philadelphia at the age of six. He worked various jobs, including circus cyclist, comedian, and actor.

---

2. This photograph was first published in Charles W. Heins's amateur magazine, the *Phoenix* (9, no. 3) for January 1950 and reproduced in the *Fossil* (105 no. 4, whole no. 341) for July 2009 as the centerfold with an enlargement of the section of the photograph containing Lovecraft's alleged image on the back cover. This illustrative material is included only in the paper edition, not in the electronic edition of the Fossil at www.thefossils.org on the Internet, which is text only.

3. Throughout most of the 1920s, Bush's business activities were headquartered in Chicago. Lovecraft's well-known dislike for Chicago may help to explain why he apparently did not encounter Bush in person again after their meeting(s) in 1924.

He subsequently studied for the ministry at Temple University in Philadelphia.[4] Bush was pastor of a "mission church" located in South Dakota when he joined UAPA in 1916; *Peace Poems and Sausages* (Webster, SD: Reporter and Farmer Print, 1915 [1st ed.]; Sioux Falls, SD: Argus-Leader Job Printing, 1916 [2nd ed.]), *Pike's Peak or Bust; or, The Possibilities of the Will* (Webster, SD: Reporter and Farmer Print, 1916), *Soul Poems and Other Verse* (Madison, SD: Sentinel Press, 1916), and *Humorous Verse on Current Events and Other Topics* (1916)[5] were all published from South Dakota. From 1917 until 1921, Bush was based in St. Louis, Missouri, where he served as pastor of Memorial Congregational Church. Six folders relating to his pastorship of this church are held by the State Historical Society of Missouri.[6] Bush's twenty-six record-setting lectures at Carnegie Hall in New York City in 1924 may have marked the apogee of his career. However, Bush was not one to rest upon his past achievements. He was back on the east coast again in October–November 1924; the *Bridgeport Telegram* (30 October 1924) reported that he would lecture at the Park Theater in Bridgeport, Connecticut from 30 October through 12 November (excluding 4 November) 1924. In *Spunk* (Chicago: David V. Bush, 1924), the author advertised "Bush Chateau Rest Camp" on the banks of the Susquehanna River in Meshoppen, Wyoming County, Pennsylvania ("in the heart of the Allegeheny Mountains"), on the verso of the title page. He offered "comfortable beds in cozy cottages," "the

---

4. This information derives from the online description of the David V. Bush collection at the State Historical Society of Missouri. See shs.umsystem.edu/stlouis/manuscripts/S0782.pdf.

5. *Humorous Verse on Current Events and Other Topics* was a serial issued by Bush from Lake Preston, South Dakota. At least four numbers were apparently published: 1, no. 1 (August 1916); 1, no. 2 (September 1916); 1, no. 3 (October 1916 [filed for copyright 23 September 1916]); and 1, no. 4 (November 1916 [filed for copyright 16 October 1916]). The August 1916 number is available online at archive.org. Some references show the publisher of this serial title as "The Peace Poet and Bard of Lake Preston." The complete run of this serial might make an interesting reprint item.

6. This collection also includes one additional folder of material from 1957 relating to Bush's support of World Poetry Day. Clearly, poetry was one of Bush's principal interests both at the beginning and at the end of his literary career. See note 4 for the Internet reference for this collection.

finest food available," "cool restful nights," "no mosquitos," and "scenery that is unsurpassed in any part of the Eastern States."[7] The camp offered swimming, boating, hiking, fishing, mountain climbing, dancing, "camp stunts," and sunbathing, as well as "daily lectures given by eminent psychologists, philosophers, teachers and leaders in advanced thought on inspirational, psychological and health subjects." The camp operated from June to September and a descriptive catalog was available upon request. Bush never succeeded in turning "Bush Chateau Rest Camp" in Meshoppen into another Chautauqua, but he eventually retired to the area after his career as a lecturer waned. His final home was in Mehoopany, also in Wyoming County, Pennsylvania, on the opposite bank of the Susquehanna River, about three miles south of Meshoppen.

Lovecraft found the revision of Bush's poetry and prose generally uncongenial; he worked as Bush's revisionist for remuneration. Didacticism, combined with deficiency of poetic expression, weakens many of Bush's poems. One can sometimes see Lovecraft's hand in the development of Bush's verse as published over his career. The heartfelt nature of the feelings expressed is evident from the first publication of his poem "My Daughter, My Little Maxine" in *Peace Poems and Sausages* (1915):

> There are days that are dark and gloomy;
> There are times when the sun is not seen;
> But there's one who can always inspire me,
> And that's my daughter Maxine.
>
> Should I think life's work is a failure
> And results are not what I ween,
> There comes to my rescue a smiler,
> And that's my daughter, Maxine.
>
> Have things gone wrong and all twisted;
> Are times out of joint—not a beam
> Of sunshine to light the dark roadway,
> Then I hear my daughter, Maxine
>
> Creep up to my chair—O the darling!—

7. In his advertisement, Bush did not mention that Meshoppen meant "vomit place" in the Native American language of the locale.

And put her sweet face close to mine
And whisper, "just never mind, papa,
You're the best; you're simply just fine."

If it's preacher, writer or father,
It's the same to my daughter so keen;
No troubles, no sorrow, nor worries
Shake the faith of my daughter Maxine

Do friends misunderstand and then shun me;
She has faith and pride in her father;
She has love and caresses, all seen;
She has confidence strong as Gibraltar—
My daughter, my little Maxine.

Though all earth should endeavor to down me;
Though all foes my character screen;
I know there is one believes in me,
And that's my darling, Maxine. (79–80)

Note how this poem has been transformed when reprinted in 1954 as the dedication ("Lovingly and Gratefully Dedicated To My Daughter Maxine") of *If You Want to Be Rich:*

There are days that are dreary and gloomy,
There are times when the north-wind is keen,
But there's one who can banish all troubles,
And that is my daughter Maxine!

In the hours when I think life a failure,
With fruits that I never can glean,
There is always a smiler to cheer me—
My dear little daughter Maxine!

When my plans have all slipped and miscarried,
And the times are disjointed and lean,
There is one ray of light never failing—
The glance of my daughter Maxine!

She will creep to my chair in the twilight,
And kiss me with tenderest mien,
While she whispers, "Just never mind, papa"—
My own loving daughter Maxine!

No matter what kind of a menace
Besets me with malice unclean,
Not a thing can o'erbalance or weaken
The faith of my daughter Maxine!

Do my friends all misjudge me and shun me;
Do my critics denounce me with spleen;
Does the world in its error condemn me?
It's naught to my daughter Maxine!

For she holds a true faith in her parent,
And a pride that no darkness can screen;
She has confidence strong as Gibraltar—
My daughter, my little Maxine!

So though foes may move mountains to down me,
And ills at my doorstep convene,
There's one who can always inspire me
And that is my daughter Maxine!

Now years have sped by in their swiftness
With speed of sound that's unseen,
But she still has the power to inspire me,
That little-grown woman—Maxine! (iii–iv)

Although the final publication of this poem occurred seventeen years after Lovecraft died, it is easy to see the revisionist's
hand in the improved word choice and meter of the final version.
Perhaps the final stanza was added by Bush himself; it is not quite
as felicitous as the preceding stanzas.[8] The final version of the po-

---

8. The poem "My Daughter Maxine" is also printed in Bush's collection *Soul Poems and Love Lyrics* (103–4), which was issued by Bush from 4224 Harris Avenue
in St. Louis, Missouri, and displays a 1916 copyright on the verso of its title page.
As printed in *SPLL*, "My Daughter Maxine" exactly replicates the text printed in
IFW in 1954, except that the final stanza, apparently added by the author for the
publication of the poem in *IFW*, is omitted. Bush gave this poem its own section
in *SPLL* (which is divided into sections titled "Love Lyrics," "Home Poems," "My
Daughter Maxine," "Child Verse," "Peace Poems," and "Inspirational Verse"). The
fact that "My Daughter Maxine" has its own dedicated section in *SPLL* may provide some indication of the poem's importance to its author. It is possible that
the 1916 copyright date displayed in *SPLL* may reflect the original publication

em as published in *If You Want to Be Rich* has meter and rhythm redolent of Poe's "Ulalume." The charm of this poem surely resides in the love felt by the poet for his daughter and his admission of his own moments of doubt and discouragement. Lovecraft has faithfully preserved these central themes while vastly improving the poem's word choices and structure.

I did not find any earlier version of the poem "Darkness Before Dawn" (*Spunk*, 1924, 42–43), but the elegance and superior word choice of this poem, despite its evident didactic character, seem to bespeak a reviser's hand. Consider the final stanza:

> No grief e'er so gruesome, no night e'er so black,
> But that rosy Aurora will push the clouds back;
> So when troubles seem thickest, like gusts of foul smoke,
> And with fast-ebbing spirits in darkness we choke;
> When we think that our efforts have all been in vain,
> And our souls groan aloud in their terror and pain;
> When before us but gulfs of black space seem to yawn,
> Then remember the lesson of dusk before dawn!

Despite his client's lofty literary pretensions, Lovecraft actually liked David V. Bush quite well. He wrote to Anne Tillery Renshaw on 14 June 1922:

> David V. Bush is a short, plump fellow of about forty-five, with a bland face, bald head, & very fair taste in attire. He is actually an immensely good sort—kindly, affable, winning, & smiling. Probably he has to be in order to induce people to let him live after they have read his verse. His keynote is hearty good-fellowship, & I almost think he is rather sincere about it. (*ATR* 370)

Bush's poetry is perhaps at its best when the poet strives for humor and feeling rather than for a moral. His poem "The High

---

dates of some of its contents. Bush published a similarly titled earlier collection, *Soul Poems and Other Verse* (Madison, SD: Sentinel Press, 1916). The marked changes noted in "My Daughter Maxine" between its first publication in *Peace Poems and Sausages* and its publication in *Soul Poems and Love Lyrics* make me believe that Lovecraft had a hand in the revised version. It is possible that *SPLL* was not published until Bush's main period in St. Louis in 1917–21, after he had begun to work with Lovecraft as his revisionist.

Cost of Living; As the Optimist Sees It" (*Inspirational Poems*, 1921, 195–96) makes incidental reference to his wife Marian, a former schoolteacher:

When salt went up I cut it out,
I really didn't need it;
If Indians did not use the stuff,
Why I could supersede it!

When beef went up I smiled and said,
"I'll be a vegetarian,"
I picked right up and found a belle,
And then I married Marian!

Now spuds have gone way out of sight,
But life seems little blacker;
For rice can take their place with me,
With now and then a cracker!

The price of shoes can't bother me,
I never did like leather;
I'd rather wear a fibre shoe—
They're fit for any weather!

When prunes went on the rich man's list
(Of course that's common knowledge)
I had no kick—I tired of them
When I attended college!

I'd gladly ban and boycott eggs,
Or let them lie forgotten,
For oftentimes I have been fooled—
I often found them rotten!

No matter how food prices soar,
I always shall be able
To find a substitute somehow
To put upon my table!

Perhaps the hand of Lovecraft, who wrote such marvelous humorous poetry as "A Year Off," can already be seen in "The High Cost of Living." But Bush's politically inspired poem "Roosevelt"

(*Humorous Verse on Current Events and Other Topics* 1, no. 1 [August 1916]: 2–3) probably antedates Lovecraft's association with him:

It's reported Roosevelt will not plead his case at the Chicago convention he thinks his views are known—News item

If every hamlet town and dell
Don't know our Teddy's views,
Say Citizen, I'm here to tell
It's not because of news.

If we don't know the hunter's views
It's no wit fault of his,
For well he knows the use of news,
He's used it in his biz.

If we don't know where Teddy stands
We haven't read the press;
At home, abroad in foreign lands—
In the headlines he has dressed.

If a bear is killed, a squirrel drops dead
Or a skunk should cross his trail,
We see his wonders flared in red,
Should the game be moose or quail.

If a prize fight's on, or a divorce,
If Susie elopes with Jim,
He sees a golden chance perforce
To advertise just him.

Oh yes, we know his views, we do,
And what he'd do, and think,
Should some not know (only a few)
It's not because of ink.

Bookseller Rick Grunder[9] of Lafayette, New York, offering a copy of Bush's *The Psychology of Sex* for sale in 2010, found the

---

9. Rick Grunder, *Onan Eschewed* (Lafayette, NY, 2010). Bush's work *The Psychology of Sex: How to Make Love and Marry* (Chicago: David V. Bush, c. 1924) is listed as item 9 on pp. 11–13 of this catalogue, which can be found at www.rickgrunder.com/Catalogs/OnanCatalog.pdf.

book full of practical advice and liberally minded for its time. Grunder calls Bush's work "a highly colloquial, pragmatic approach badly needed at the time" and opines that "the author's suggestions are frequently intelligent and always encouraging." Grunder states further: "Allowing for the times, Bush handles his subject in a manner intended to enlighten rather than to suppress, and he is highly critical of 'religionists' and 'purity' authors who would prefer to keep people in miserable ignorance of their own sex potential and needs." Grunder also notes Bush's gentle, practical advice to husbands for introducing their wives to sexual relations on their wedding nights. Regrettably, a 2006 Kessinger reprint of *The Psychology of Sex* is currently unavailable and there is at present no electronic edition. The "Student Edition" of Bush's more extensive *Practical Psychology and Sex Life* —over 800 pages—sold for $25.00 from Bush from the 1920s through the 1950s; today one can have it for less in a 2006 Kessinger reprint.

In *Character Analysis: How to Read People at Sight* (Chicago: David V. Bush, 1923, 1925), Bush and co-author W. Waugh[10] classified human beings into five basic body types (although all the illustrations depicted males): alimentive, thoracic, muscular, osseous, and cerebral (70–71), and proceeded to describe qualities, aptitudes, strengths, and weaknesses for each type. The book concludes with a portrait gallery of famous individuals, including Bush's supporter, "plant wizard" Luther Burbank (588), and Edgar Allan Poe (596–97).[11] Bush was right about localized functionality in the brain (450), but seems not to have picked up on the left-right asymmetry of brain functionality and leaned in the direction of the pseudo-science phrenology. He would doubtless have classified his revisionist Lovecraft as the "cerebral" or "mental" type and the illustrations on p. 34 ("student/thinker/philosopher"), 461 ("high head"), and 467 ("narrow head") may possibly have drawn

---

10. I speculate that W. Waugh may have been the artist for this work, which at $7.50 was the second most expensive of Bush's works, after *Practical Psychology and Sex Life* at $25.00.

11. Bush's later work *If You Want to Be Rich* contains a more extended discussion of Poe (13–17). Unfortunately, like Lovecraft's first biographer L. Sprague de Camp, Bush concentrates more on Poe's lack of economic success than on his artistic achievement.

with Lovecraft in mind. In his discussion of the "cerebral" type, Bush writes under the heading "Dreamer":

> This type makes the typical dreamer, and if there is no other ele-ment in his character, will probably never put over his ideals. He lives in his head to plan and imagine and day-dream, but he has not the ambition, practicality, nor strength to materialize the things which he plans. The big, high head, especially if narrow, is the impractical head. (261)

Bush is somewhat more complimentary in his remarks con-cerning the "cerebral" type under the heading "Ahead of His Time":

> He is always ahead of his time in reforms as in everything else. While he has not the money materially to support reform measures, yet whenever there is a group of men gathered togeth-er, be it in the interest of art, science, politics or religion, discuss-ing new methods, ways and means to get out of the rut of yesterday, you will always find the Mental there and listened to with respectful attention. (263)

The heading "Not a Money Getter" (266–67) presents some of Bush's least complimentary analysis of the "cerebral" type:

> Because of his impracticality and his frail body he seldom makes money in business (unless combined with some other type), nor can he work hard enough to make money by manual effort.
> In many respects the Cerebral is the most pitiful (psychologi-cally speaking) of all the types. Not being able to cash in on his high ideals because of his unworldliness, and not being able to work because of his frail body, his next attempt to make a living is by his wits. (267)

Of course, no individual fits all the characteristics of Bush's "types." Lovecraft was not a weakling (as a mature adult) ("What He Should Do," 258), absent-minded, neglectful of social obliga-tions ("Absent-Minded," 259; "Time," 275), or indifferent about his dress ("Clothes," 265). Bush's analysis of the "cerebral" type is more "on target" for Lovecraft when he writes of his indifference to-ward eating ("Not Much on Eating," 260); his loyalty toward a

small circle of friends ("Not Cold," 261); his dedication to progress
and reform ("Gives," 263–64; "Visionary," 275); his preference for
intellectual discussion ("Friends," 265–66); his retiring ("Peaceable,"
268), modest ("Modest," 269), and chaste nature ("Not a Dissipa-
tor—Sex," 269–70); his impersonality ("Impersonal," 270); his love
of reading ("Reader," 273); and his indifference toward sports
("Sports," 274). Bush's analysis of the "cerebral" type is perhaps
most predictive of Lovecraft's posthumous trajectory when he
comments ("Talking"):

> He writes better than he talks. He wants to think over and weigh
> every word. To do this a man has to give more time to written
> composition than he does in speaking.
>   More than any other type he keeps a diary and it is always
> written well. He wants something to do in a mental way. The dia-
> ry gives him mental relaxation. Many a man has after his death
> been discovered to be great by virtue of what he wrote to his
> friends either in a diary or letters which they did not think worth
> while publishing. (274)

David Van Bush and George Julian Houtain (1884–1945) were
surely among the strongest "Type A" personalities to encounter
Lovecraft in the flesh. Yet Lovecraft liked both of them and they
in turn liked him. (I am not aware that Bush and Houtain ever
met.) Perhaps they helped Lovecraft to "open up," both as a professional revisionist and as a member of the amateur journalism
hobby. Bush paid Lovecraft faithfully and thereby helped him to
maintain an acceptable standard of living, as opposed to the outright poverty of Kalem Club associates like Everett McNeil and
Arthur Leeds. Today both Bush and Houtain are largely forgotten;
one finds Houtain mentioned only in in histories of amateur journalism, although like Bush he spent part of his career as a pastor.
Bush's work is still accorded the occasional reprint in both paper
and electronic formats, and still receives occasional mention in
treatments of popular psychology and "New Thought." Lovecraft
wrote of Bush's talents in his letter to Anne Tillery Renshaw:
"What the fellow really can do is to fascinate people by sheer
force of a pleasing manner. He is a natural orator—of that there is

no doubt—a very fair actor, & an undeniably efficient organizer & business-man" (ATR 371).

The crudity and didacticism of the great majority of Bush's verse will repel most modern readers of poetry. If he manages to turn the occasional polished phrase, as in "Darkness Before Dawn" or the final version of "My Daughter Maxine," it is probably attributable to Lovecraft's revisory skills. Bush's poems are best when they display personal emotion as in "My Daughter Maxine" (filial) or "The High Cost of Living" (spousal). A few early humorous efforts, like "The High Cost of Living" and "Roosevelt," may point toward a more congenial poetic mode that the poet unfortunately abandoned for didacticism in his later work. One presumes that Bush made effective use of humor in his lectures; Lovecraft attests to the vividness and dramatic qualities of Bush's presentations (ATR 374). A well-developed sense of humor on both sides probably helped Lovecraft get along with, and profit from his relationships with, both Houtain and Bush.

Works Cited

Bush, David V. *If You Want to Be Rich.* Mehoopany, PA: [David V. Bush], 1954. [Abbreviated in the text as *IYW.*]

———— *Soul Poems and Love Lyrics.* St. Louis: D. V. Bush, [1916?].

Bush, David V., and W. Waugh. *Character Analysis: How to Read People at Sight.* Chicago: The Huron Press, 1923, 1925.

Joshi, S. T. *I Am Providence: The Life and Times of H. P. Lovecraft.* New York: Hippocampus Press, 2010. [Abbreviated in the text as *IAP.*]

Joshi, S. T., and David E. Schultz. *An H. P. Lovecraft Encyclopedia.* 2nd ed. New York: Hippocampus Press, 2004.

Lovecraft, H. P. *Letters to Elizabeth Toldridge and Anne Tillery Renshaw.* Edited by David E. Schultz and S. T. Joshi. New York: Hippocampus Press, 2014. [Abbreviated in the text as *ATR.*]

Echoes of a Warrior Poet: The Influence of Alan Seeger on Lovecraft

J. D. Worthington

Various commentators over the years have made the observation that H. P. Lovecraft did not always show good judgment in his choices of literary models. Such statements have come not only from negative critics such as Edmund Wilson, but even from Lovecraftian correspondents such as J. Vernon Shea, as well as his biographer S. T. Joshi. Wilson criticized him for lack of taste in his admiration for the work of Lord Dunsany and Arthur Machen (48), while Shea berated him for his enthusiasm for Robert W. Chambers (126, 138), among others. Joshi has remarked that he sometimes showed at least an odd preference for science popularizers, such as Hugh Elliot and John Fiske, rather than the writings of actual scientists and philosophers of science (*I Am Providence* 1.316).

Yet perhaps the most peculiar example of this aspect of Lovecraft's personality may lie in his penchant for minor or second-rate poets, especially those who nevertheless had enjoyed at least a brief popularity. The two which come immediately to mind are the Irish bard Thomas Moore (1779–1852), whose renditions from Anacreon, as well as his Irish lyrics and ballads, retained a fair degree of popularity for most of the nineteenth century; and the now almost forgotten American poet of the First World War, Alan Seeger (1888–1916), whom Joshi has described as "almost as bad a poet as HPL" (*AT* 513). Yet in each of these cases, there are interesting points to consider, particularly similarities between Lovecraft and each of these figures in one or another philosophical or aesthetic trait. In the case of Alan Seeger, we may gather some of this information through his tribute to the young soldier-poet who was killed in the course of a military engagement in the

Great War; especially as regards their approaches to classicism and militarism. Further, combined with other comments by Lovecraft, and certain statements made in the biographical introduction to Seeger's *Poems*, an examination of this connection between the two poets may perhaps give us a different perspective on one of Lovecraft's very few recurring characters: the New England "traveller in the world of dreams," Randolph Carter.

It is sometimes rather surprising how much Lovecraft made of various minor literary figures while at the same time either overlooking or undervaluing some who were much more important or talented. Such figures would not only include poets such as Alan Seeger and Thomas Moore, whom he tended to favor over their contemporaries Rupert Brooke and Lord Byron, but also such prose writers as Robert W. Chambers who, despite having some notoriety in the fields of horror and fantasy, remains a rather negligible writer of his time, and certainly one of less artistic finish than such authors as Edith Wharton, Sarah Orne Jewett, Charlotte Perkins Gilman, or Mary E. Wilkins Freeman, each of whom not only made lasting contributions to the weird tale but also produced work one would expect to have strongly appealed to Lovecraft, given his concern with capturing the essence of his beloved New England and its people.

Yet these seeming oddities may not be quite the anomalies they initially appear. Rather, they may well be seen as examples of how acutely sensitive Lovecraft was to writers who presented similar ideas and perspectives (in some areas) to his own, but also how strongly even the work of minor figures could stimulate his imagination and aesthetic sensibilities.

That both these elements are present in his verse appreciation of Seeger can scarcely be denied, given the evidence not only of the verse itself, which addresses various points in Seeger's poetry that bear a striking resemblance to passages or ideas in his own verse and prose, fiction and otherwise, but also in his assessment of Seeger as poet. Perhaps the best single expression of this latter point may be seen in his letter to the Kleicomolo correspondence circle of April 1917:

Seeger lacked some of the poetick talent, and most of the delicacy of Brooke; in fact, his verse is in places marked with the low mo-

rality and flagrant pleasure-worship which Parisian dissipation in-
culcated in him; but his strength as a poet is very considerable,
and he exhibits a fidelity to the older models which is truly
commendable. Especially is he willing to use that simple, direct,
and forcible mode of utterance which his contemporaries seem to
have rejected. [. . .] The less martial poetry of Seeger is positively
exquisite in its classick taste, suggesting Mr. Swinburne, though
inexact rhymes and false syllabick values are not wholly absent. [. . .]
I see that I have rambled on about Seeger at great length, thus
proving how marked an admiration I bear for his style. (*LRK* 101–2)

The key, however, is stated by Lovecraft himself in the sentence immediately following: "The secret is to be found in his ar-
chaism of thought and conservatism of expression; things hinted
at in his first sonnet, addressed to Sir Philip Sidney" (*LRK* 102),
which he proceeds to quote. In other words, precisely the same
qualities that so often kept Lovecraft's own poetry of this period
from being a vital expression of select aspects of life in modern
times, or even of an otherwise healthy antiquarianism.

The similarities between the two scarcely stop there, however,
as even a casual reading of Seeger's poetry will show. For example,
Lovecraft's views on pacifism and militarism are well known, but
such verse as "The Aisne," "A Message to America," or "Ode in
Memory of the American Volunteers Fallen for France" show such
marked similarities that even turns of expression may remind one
at times of Lovecraft's own. Most especially, perhaps, is the um-
brage each took to President Woodrow Wilson's oft-quoted "There
is such a thing as a man being too proud to fight"—a statement Seeger scorns in his "Message to America," while Lovecraft ridiculed it
at every opportunity (e.g., "Pacifist War Song—1917").

In connection with "A Message to America," it is interesting to
note an oddity in this respect, as certain passages in that poem
sound uncannily like those in Lovecraft's "The Beauties of Peace,"
especially ll. 15–20 of the latter, which are very close to ll. 17–38 of
"A Message to America," a poem Lovecraft could not have possibly seen at the time of writing; nor, naturally, could Seeger have
seen his—another of those striking instances of parallelism one
encounters with Lovecraft, most dramatically exhibited with "Po-
laris" and Dunsany, but also seen in such instances as "The Green

Meadow" and its resemblances to both Blackwood's "The Willows" and passages in Hodgson's "The Voice in the Night."

There are, in addition, other areas in which the two are notably attuned. While the views expressed on youth and age in the second of Seeger's sonnets, like those stated by Lovecraft at various points in his correspondence, may be said to be fairly common to many poets or writers, especially of a romantic or antiquarian bent, other passages are much more unusual, and may indicate not only why Seeger resonated so with Lovecraft, but perhaps even some degree of influence on one or two of the latter's more well-known works.

One such instance is from the first piece in Seeger's *Poems*, "An Ode to Natural Beauty" (3–9):

> There is a power whose inspiration fills
> Nature's fair fabric, sun- and star-inwrought,
> Like airy dew ere any drop distils,
> Like perfume in the laden flower, like aught
> Unseen which interfused throughout the whole
> Becomes its quickening pulse and principle and soul. (ll. 1–6)

> When half-forgotten sound and scent are wooing
> From their deep-chambered recesses long sealed
> Such memories as breathe once more
> Of childhood and the happy hues it wore,
> Now, with a fervor that has never been
> In years gone by, it stirs me to respond,—
> Not as a force whose fountains are within
> The faculties of the percipient mind,
> Subject with them to darkness and decay,
> But something absolute, something beyond,
> Oft met like tender orbs that seem to peer
> From pale horizons, luminous behind
> Some fringe of tinted cloud at close of day [. . .] (ll. 9–21)

> [. . .] As oft for one brief second
> The veil through which those infinite offers beckoned
> Has seemed to tremble, letting through
> Some swift intolerable view
> Of vistas past the sense of mortal seeing,

> So oft, as one whose stricken eyes might see
> In ferny dells the rustic deity,
> I stood, like him, possessed, and all my being,
> Flooded an instant with unwonted light,
> Quivered with cosmic passion [. . .] (ll. 78–87)

Do we not hear echoes of this in "Background" and "Continuity"? Especially the former's list of "sights that shaped my childhood dreams" (l. 8) or the latter's "slanting sunbeams" (l. 9) or the poem's first stanza:

> There is in certain ancient things a trace
> Of some dim essence—more than form or weight;
> A tenuous aether, indeterminate,
> Yet linked with all the laws of time and space.
> A faint veiled sign of continuities
> That outward eyes can never quite descry [. . .] (ll. 1–6)

There are also the opening stanzas of Seeger's "The Deserted Garden" (10–26), which strongly seem to mirror parts of Lovecraft's "Ex Oblivione" and "The Gardens of Yin"; or Seeger's fourth sonnet, which bears a notable resemblance to the unfinished fragment "Azathoth." There is even Seeger's penchant for the word "cosmic" to indicate the numinous, the supernal, or the Burkean sublime—a penchant shared by Lovecraft, as seen throughout his fiction and letters, and notably in "Supernatural Horror in Literature" (which last prompted a scornful response on his use of the word from M. R. James). This peculiar usage common to both may be seen, for instance, in Seeger's letters (see, e.g., *Poems* xxvii) as well as in lines such as the following, from "The Hosts" (138–40): "They are big with the beauty of cosmic things" (l. 19). All of which would indicate Seeger's possible influence on Lovecraft far beyond what has previously been considered. While not definitely proven, it would appear to be a matter worth investigating.

On the other hand, one item that would seem beyond dispute is the partial modeling of the character of Randolph Carter on Seeger; for, like the real-life dreamer and poet, Lovecraft has Carter precede his country into the Great War, with interesting results. Following his doubling back on the track of time, "It was as early as 1897 that he turned pale when some traveller men-

tioned the French town of Belloy-en-Santerre, and friends remembered it when he was almost mortally wounded there in
1916, while serving with the Foreign Legion in the Great War"
(CF 3.85). Here he has chosen to have Carter follow exactly in
Seeger's footsteps, except that Carter necessarily survives, while
Seeger died. Even this may have its origin in real life, for Lovecraft, in a letter to Rheinhart Kleiner dated 23 May 1917 recounts
the following:

> Before leaving the subject of the *res militaria* I must add an item
> concerning Alan Seeger which has just come to my notice. A re-
> cent rumour declares that the young poet did not die directly
> from his wounds, but shot himself in the temple after having
> been injured so direfully that death was only a few hours off.
> (*LRK* 109)

That Seeger was mortally wounded rather than killed outright is
supported as well by the biographical introduction to his *Poems*,
written by William Archer:

> On July 1st, the great advance began. At six in the evening of July
> 1st, the Legion was ordered to clear the enemy out of the village
> of Belloy-en-Santerre. Alan Seeger advanced in the first rush, and
> his squad was enfiladed by the fire of six German machine guns,
> concealed in a hollow. Most of them went down, and Alan among
> them—wounded in several places. But the following waves of at-
> tack were more fortunate. As his comrades came up to him, Alan
> cheered them on, and as they left him behind, they heard him
> singing a marching-song in English:—
> Accents of ours were in the fierce mêlée.
> They took the village, they drove the invaders out; but for
> some reason unknown—perhaps a very good one—the battlefield
> was left unvisited that night. Next morning, Alan Seeger lay dead.
> (xliv)

Perhaps, if he read this essay (as he likely did), Lovecraft realized
the possibility Seeger might have lived, had he been given timely
medical attention, and perhaps he chose to give, by literary proxy,
another chance at life to the poet of whom he said: "'To Alan Seeger'
[. . .] celebrat[es] the memory of a young American hero of the
French Foreign Legion, who, had the fortunes of battle spared

him, would have been one of our country's great poets. [He] was a bard of the broadest and keenest vision" (*CE* 1.220). If such was the case, he must have also realized, by the time he wrote "The Silver Key" in 1926, how sadly out of step Seeger's approach to poetry, like his own, would have been, for he has his protagonist double back, at that point, on his own timeline; and if the analogy between Seeger and Carter remained as late as "Through the Gates of the Silver Key" (1932–33), he made it quite plain just how alienated such a mind had become by depicting the ultimate in alienation for Carter. (The entire subplot involving the Strontian wizard Zkauba was Lovecraft's invention, being completely absent from the original version, "The Lord of Illusion," by his collaborator, E. Hoffmann Price; see *Tales of the Lovecraft Mythos* 137–52.)

In any event, just as with his identification with the Irish peer at the height of his absorption in Dunsany ("Dunsany *is myself*, plus an art and cultivation infinitely greater" [*SL* 1.234]), it is likely Lovecraft noted the similarities between Seeger and himself and combined the two—as well as Dunsany, who could be said to have provided the stylistic identity—in his depiction of Carter in "The Silver Key," thus both honoring and purging the spiritual presence of two men he admired greatly.

As for the most obvious of Lovecraft's tributes to Seeger: while the verse itself may be of little value either intrinsically or (in the main) biographically, its obvious references to particular works by Seeger show how strongly the man's work impressed Lovecraft, and the likelihood that this impression bore no further fruit would seem to be a rather slender one.

It is an ironic comment on the nature of things that, as with Dunsany for so many years, it is only due to interest in the "pupil" that the "master" is remembered, if at all; but in the case of an almost-forgotten poet of the First World War named Alan Seeger, I fear it may not only be an accurate observation but, perhaps sadly, a just outcome as well.

Works Cited

Joshi, S. T. *I Am Providence: The Life and Times of H. P. Lovecraft.* New York: Hippocampus Press, 2010. 2 vols.

Lovecraft: H. P. *Letters to Rheinhart Kleiner*. Edited by S. T. Joshi and David E. Schultz. New York: Hippocampus Press, 2005. [Abbreviated in the text as *LRK*.]

Price, Robert M., ed. *Tales of the Lovecraft Mythos*. Minneapolis, MN: Fedogan & Bremer, 1992.

Seeger, Alan. *Poems*. New York: Charles Scribner's Sons, 1916.

Shea, J. Vernon. "On the Literary Influences Which Shaped Lovecraft's Works." In *H. P. Lovecraft: Four Decades of Criticism*, ed. S. T. Joshi. Athens: Ohio University Press, 1980.

Wilson, Edmund. "Tales of the Marvellous and Ridiculous." 1945. In *H. P. Lovecraft: Four Decades of Criticism*, ed. S. T. Joshi. Athens: Ohio University Press, 1980.

Gothic Mythology: "The Moon-Bog" and the Greek Connection

Juan Luis Pérez de Luque

Introduction

"The Moon-Bog" has been described by S. T. Joshi as "a very conventional supernatural revenge story" (*IAP* 384). In fact, the tale has a very Gothic tone, in the line of classic genre writers such as Edgar Allan Poe.[1] Apart from aptly showing the Gothic roots of Lovecraft's fiction, the tale includes some of his constant fixations, especially those related with a past that haunts the present. "The Moon-Bog" also raises interesting questions about classic Greek mythology and its relation with the writer's oeuvre, and the importance that Lovecraft gave to folktales and its connections with culture and tradition. Apart from that, nature plays an important role in the narration, in that the main source of conflict is a group of naiads that dwell in the pond. There are no alien invasions, but haunted spirits inspired by Greek mythology that take care of the bog, and the effects produced in the tale, in terms of narration, are the same as in the case of the characteristic amorphous Lovecraftian creature.

This paper aims to explore the Greek twist introduced into the tale and how it provokes several ideological layers that go beyond the classic ecocritical interpretation.

---

1. There are, in fact, many classic elements from the Gothic tradition that can be found in "The Moon-Bog": an unreliable narrator, a lonely nobleman asking a friend to pay a visit (which reminds us of the triggering events of Poe's "The Fall of the House of Usher"), the action based in Europe, the old, medieval, and isolated castle, family heritage, a lonely bog that hides a secret, the ancient ruins in the rural, green landscape, the events taking place during the night . . . For more information on the typical Gothic setting, see Botting (38) and Duncan (20–50).

The Call of Nature

"The Moon-Bog" has been dismissed by some critics as a "medio-cre story of supernatural horror" (de Camp 151), or "unusually trite and commonplace" (Joshi, *Life* 251). Lovecraft himself considered the tale "insufferable maundering" (*SL* 3.296). On the other hand, Burleson extols "The Moon-Bog," noting Lovecraft's efforts in "displaying some of his erudition by making artful use of some relatively little-known Irish legendry" (78). Burleson adds that "although lacking the vast cosmic scope of the later and more significant tales, the work manages to portray a 'local' horror sufficiently rooted in antiquity to make it ponderous and haunting. Lovecraft's descriptive prose and mood-sustaining narration in the tale are quite worthy of him" (77).

The events surrounding the creation of the text are quite different from those pertaining to the vast majority of Lovecraft's tales, since it was written for a special occasion: the celebration of St. Patrick's Day in 1921 by a group of amateur writers, a party to which Lovecraft was invited and asked to write a tale to be read aloud for the audience in a literary contest. Five years after the party, "The Moon-Bog" was published in *Weird Tales*, in its issue of June 1926.

The first thing that is made explicit in the tale is the aristocratic origin of Denys Barry, the narrator's friend who is trying to drain the bog on his property in order to produce fertile land. Those origins are the reason why he comes back to Ireland, in an attempt to reconstruct his ancestral heritage, which is embodied in the immensity of the family castle:

> It was from Kilderry that his father had come, and it was there that he wished to enjoy his wealth among ancestral scenes. Men of his blood had once ruled over Kilderry and built and dwelled in the castle, but those days were very remote, so that for generations the castle had been empty and decaying.[2] (*CF* 1.256)

The word "decay" makes reference to the castle, but probably also to the aristocratic Barry family itself. It is said in the tale that

---

2. According to Pearsall, "Kilderry is occasionally encountered as an Irish surname, which is how HPL may have heard it" (246).

Denys Barry "had grown rich" in America, but it is logical to think that he was unable to keep his noble perks in the United States. So after his arrival back to the place where his ancestors ruled in order to restore the castle, "the peasants blessed him for bringing back the old days with his gold from over the sea" (*CF* 1.256). Barry is symbolically trying to start a process of restoration of his aristocratic past, as a welcomed new lord with a retinue of workers and peasants who bless him for reviving the good old times.

When the narrator arrives to Ireland he is said that the village of Kilderry is "accursed" (*CF* 1.257). Following this piece of advice, the narrator faces this scene: "Barry's motor had met me at the Ballylough station, for Kilderry is off the railway. The villagers had shunned the car and the driver from the north, but had whispered to me with pale faces when they saw I was going to Kilderry"[3] (*CF* 1.257). The breach produced by the supernatural elements, initiated with the superstitious commentaries of the villagers, is enhanced during the talk that Barry and the narrator have during the first evening. When Barry explains the reasons why the peasants are scared of the drain project, he tells the narrator that according to them "[t]here were secrets [. . .] which must not be uncovered; secrets that had lain hidden since the plague came to the children of Partholan" (*CF* 1.257–58).

Barry goes on in his explanation, saying that "In the *Book of Invaders* it is told that these sons of the Greeks were all buried at Tallaght, but old men in Kilderry said that one city was overlooked save by its patron moon-goddess; so that only the wooded hills buried it when the men of Nemed swept down from Scythia in their thirty ships"[4] (*CF* 1.258). This is the first reference to Irish-

---

3. This scene, with the arrival of the narrator, the pickup car, and the superstitious commentaries of the locals, is an abridged imitation of the first steps Jonathan Harker takes before visiting the castle of Dracula in Stoker's novel. Just when he departs in the coach, people from the inn react by making the sign of the cross: "When I got on the coach the driver had not taken his seat, and I saw him talking with the landlady. They were evidently talking of me, for every now and then they looked at me, and some of the people who were sitting on the bench outside the door came and listened, and then looked at me, most of them pityingly" (14).
4. *The Book of Invaders* is a real book, comprising several narrative and lyrical texts, and it gives an account of the mythical history of Ireland. It is said that Partholan invaded Ireland in 1240 B.C.E., and several centuries after this invasion his

Greek mythology made in the text. According to Peter Berresford Ellis, Partholan (or Partholón) was "the leader of the third mythical invasion of Ireland," and he came from Greece (300). So there is an ancient source of conflict in "The Moon-Bog," to be found in the mythological, fictitious Greek invaders of Ireland who were buried in an unknown magical city, protected by a moon-goddess. Some elements of the Greek mythology will play the role of the ghostly entity of the tale, as I will explain later. It is important to remember that Lovecraft was extremely fond of Greece and its mythology from a very early age, as he confesses—referring to himself in third person—in the essay "Idealism and Materialism— A Reflection":

> Then, at an age not much above six, he stumbled on the legends of Greece—and became a sincere and enthusiastic classical pagan. Unlearned in science, and reading all the Graeco-Roman lore at hand, he was until the age of eight a rapt devotee of the old gods; building altars to Pan and Apollo, Athena and Artemis, and benignant Saturnus, who ruled the world in the Golden Age. And at times this belief was very real indeed—there are vivid memories of fields and groves at twilight when the now materialistic mind that dictates these lines *knew absolutely that the ancient gods were true*. Did he not see with his own eyes, beyond the possibility of a doubt, the graceful forms of dryads half mingled with the trunks of antique oaks, or spy with clearness and certainty the elusive little fauns and goat-footed old satyrs who leapt about so slyly from the shadow of one rock or thicket to that of another? (*CE* 5.44)

The presence of Greece in the tale continues the first night. After observing some distant ruins in an islet in the bog, the narrator hears "faint sounds from the distance" that trigger strange visions in his dreams. Barry's friend talks of dreams "more wonderful than any sound of wild pipes in the night" (*CF* 1.258) where his mind "had in slumber hovered around a stately city in a green valley, where marble streets and statues, villas and temples, carvings

---

people died because of a plague, and they were buried in Tallaght. Nemed, on the other hand, invaded Ireland in 910 B.C.E. and had a battle with the Fomorians in which most of the two sides were annihilated. For more information, see *Lebor Gabála Érenn: The Book of the Taking of Ireland*, parts 2 and 3, which narrates the events of the Partholonians and the Nemedians.

and inscriptions, all spoke in certain tones the glory that was Greece" (*CF* 1.259). The Gothic tone of the narration is now clearly infused with Greece and its history. The old superstitious stories about the buried Greek invaders and the dreams of the narrator start to shape what moves "The Moon-Bog" away from the purest Gothic tradition.

The second night the sound of flutes is intensified, a "monotonous piping from afar; wild, weird airs that made me think of some dance of fauns on distant Maenalus" (*CF* 1.260).[5] The narrator looks through the window and recognizes the workers, dancing near the bog, but with the dawn he "became sure that there was no reality in what I thought I had seen" (*CF* 1.260). Nonetheless, he feels uneasy and "for some unknown reason I dreaded the thought of disturbing the ancient bog and its sunless secrets" (*CF* 1.261). At this point he starts to be dubious about dragging the marsh: "that these secrets should be brought to light seemed injudicious, and I began to wish for an excuse to leave the castle and the village" (*CF* 1.261).

The rationality of the narrator, established at the beginning of the tale in the first talk with his friend when the two of them laughed at the superstitions of the peasants, is starting to be shaken. At this point he shares the idea of keeping the truth underwater, without having any rational explanation for this change of mind, apart from the noises and dreams. He now embraces an epistemological point of view radically different from that of Lovecraft himself, who was in favor of knowledge even if it might reveal truths that would dismantle our reality. It is during the third night that the strangest events take place. According to the narrator, these events "transcend anything we dream of in Nature and the universe; yet in no normal fashion can I explain those disappearances" (*CF* 1.261). When he looks through the window and sees the islet, "the aspect of that ruin I cannot describe" (*CF* 1.262): it now looks "undecayed" and "splendid." The sounds of flutes and

---

5. The Mons Maenalus (Mount Mainalo) is a mountain located in Arcadia, and it was supposed to be a place frequently dwelt by the god Pan. Notice that Pan and the fauns are normally represented playing a flute. According to Salonia, "It is possible that Lovecraft intended the drums-and-pipes imagery to portray a sort of musical migraine" (94). However, Wetzel relates the sound of these instruments to the "music that surrounds Azathoth in the Mythos" (62), for instance in the description of the godlike alien in "The Dreams in the Witch House."

drums appear again, and the narrator sees "a procession of beings in such a manner as none ever saw before save in nightmares" (*CF* 1.262). After the workers drown in the bog, he hears the shrieks of his friend, and they attain "a magnitude and quality which cannot be written of" (*CF* 1.264).

Greek Mythology in Ireland

The source of conflict in "The Moon-Bog" lies in some kind of ancient Greek mythological elements. The key passage that exposes what is the real nature of the enchantment is the following: "I noted amidst my fear that half of these tireless, mechanical dancers were the labourers whom I had thought asleep, whilst the other half were strange airy beings in white, half indeterminate in nature, but suggesting pale wistful naiads from the haunted fountains of the bog" (*CF* 1.260). The naiads, also known as waternymphs, ondines or undines, are creatures from the Greek mythological tradition.[6] Jenny March defines them as:

> Female spirits of nature, either immortal or very long-lived, who dwelt in a particular place or natural phenomenon, usually in the countryside (though not always: there was, for instance, a fountain house sacred to the Nymphs in the Agora at Athens). They were visualised as beautiful young girls with an amorous disposition. There were several categories of nymphs, depending on where they dwelt. Oreads were mountain-nymphs (*oros*); Alseids were nymphs of groves (*alsos*); and Naiads were water-nymphs, living in springs, lakes or streams, and were often the daughters of the god of the river in which they lived. (537)

The naiads are then a subcategory of nymphs. According to the description provided by March, the naiads present in the tale by Lovecraft were probably daughters of the "patron moon-goddess" (*CF* 1.258) mentioned in the story, and their task is to defend the bog they are so strongly attached to.

The dancing ritual performed by the workers, perhaps under the enchantment of the nymphs and the sound of drums and

---

6. In his essay "Supernatural Horror in Literature," Lovecraft mentions the novel *Undine* (1811), by Friedrich Heinrich Karl, Baron de la Motte-Fouqué, considering it the "most artistic of all the Continental weird tales" (38).

flutes, is deeply rooted into the Greek tradition. Dodds studied the importance of frenzy dancing in the traditional folklore, and its connections with the classical mythology:

> In the extraordinary dancing madness which periodically invaded Europe from the fourteenth to the seventeenth century, people danced until they dropped, and lay unconscious, trodden underfoot by their fellows. Also the thing is highly infectious. [. . .] The will to dance takes possession of people without the consent of the conscious mind. [. . .] This last fact suggests the way in which in Greece the ritual oreibasia at a fixed date may originally have developed out of spontaneous attacks of mass hysteria. By canalizing such hysteria in an organized rite once in two years, the Dionysiac cult kept it within bounds and gave it relatively harmless outlet.
>
> There are, further, certain resemblances in points of detail between the orgiastic religion of the *Bacchae* and orgiastic religion elsewhere, which are worth noticing because they tend to establish that the "maenad" is a real, not a conventional figure, and one that has existed under different names at widely different times and places. The first concerns the flutes and tympana or kettledrums which accompany the maenad dance in the *Bacchae* and on Greek vases. To the Greeks these were the "orgiastic" instruments *par excellence*: they were used in all the great dancing cults, those of the Asiatic Cybele and the Cretan Rhea as well as that of Dionysus. They could cause madness, and in homoeopathic doses they could also cure it. (272–73)

This idea of musical frenzy, "without the consent of the conscious mind," has also important sexual connotations that have to be considered in the interpretation of the frog scene that I will mention below.

Lovecraft intermingles some other references to the nymphs throughout the tale. The apparition of the Mons Maenalus mentioned above, as well as the music of the pipes, are two elements strongly connected with the god Pan. And Pan, as Ovid narrated in the *Metamorphoses*, falls in love with Syrix the nymph. According to March:

> [. . .] she wished to keep her virginity and so she fled from him until she reached the River Ladon. Here she could go no further.

Desperately she prayed to the river-nymphs to transform her, and just as Pan thought he had at last caught hold of her, he found that instead of the nymph's body he was holding a bunch of marsh reeds. He sighed with disappointment, and the air blew through the reeds, producing a thin, haunting sound. Enchanted by so sweet a music, he cut the reeds into different lengths and joined them into the first set of panpipes, giving them the Greek name of syrinx after his lost love. Such panpipes are still played by shepherds. (715)

Finally, when the narrator escapes from the castle, he sees that the bog is crowded with "a horde of slimy enormous frogs which piped shrilly and incessantly" (CF 1.264). This particular moment is quite obscure, since there are no other references to frogs or any other animal in the text and the appearance of the animals in the middle of the climax seems, at first, quite out of context. There is, however, a reference that connects the nymphs with frogs in the Greek mythology. Pothius' *Bibliotheca of Myriobiblion* includes a summary of Ptolemaenus Chennus' *New History*, a lost collection of six volumes. According to Pothius' records (codex 190), the fourth book of *New History*

> recounts that Helen was the first to imagine drawing lots with the fingers and that she won at chance with Alexander; she was the daughter of Aphrodite. There was born of Helen and Achilles in the fortunate isles a winged child named Euphorion after the fertility of this land; Zeus caught him and with a blow knocked him to earth in the isle of Melos, where he continued the pursuit and changed the nymphs there into frogs because they had given him burial.

Zeus, then, punished the naiads from Melos because they buried Euphorion, son of Achilles and Helen, after his death.

There is a most extended piece of mythology in which frogs have an important role, again as punishment, but not directly connected with the naiads. According to March, Leto, daughter of the titans Phoebe and Coeus, converted some peasants into amphibians: "Leto herself could sometimes be driven to vengeful anger: soon after her children's birth she was travelling with them in Lycia when, hot and weary, she tried to quench her thirst at a lake.

Some peasants not only refused to let her drink, but threatened and insulted her, so she turned them into frogs" (461).

The only coherent interpretation that I can draw from Lovecraft's text is that the Irish nymphs living in the bog are also punished by the moon-goddess because they drown the workers instead of letting the goddess take revenge on them.[7] In fact, the end of Denys Barry is different from that of the northern workers, since at the end of the tale the narrator sees his figure following a moon beam up to the skies, instead of perishing in the marsh. The moon, in the Greek mythological tradition, is the symbol of Selene, which is probably the referent of the moon-goddess named in the text. According to March (695), Pan was one of her lovers, so this might round up the mythical connections in "The Moon-Bog," with the references to the flutes and the Maenalus. However, it is important to consider that the figure of Selene as the moon-goddess was later replaced by that of Artemis, who can be also strongly connected with Lovecraft's text, since "Artemis was believed to roam the mountains and forests with a band of attendant nymphs, all of them delighting in the hunt and vowed to a determined chastity. If this were violated, they would be sternly punished" (March 135). This would lead to another strong moral reading of the presence of frogs in the tale. If the moon-goddess of the bog is identified with Artemis, and the naiads are her chaste fairy retinue, the procession of dancing workers toward the marsh might have a sexual interpretation. The subsequent punishment on the part of the moon-goddess against the nymphs, transforming them into the amphibians that are presented at the end of the narration, is then produced because the nymphs have broken their chastity vows. The dancing performed by the men is described as clumsy and lurching (that of the nymphs resembles "some ancient and solemn ceremonial dance" [CF 1.263]), but the general impression is that the men are completely under the control of the nymphs and the rhythm of flutes and drums:

---

7. Peter Cannon puts forward the notion that the frogs are not the nymphs but Barry's workers (H. P. Lovecraft 18). This interpretation seems also legitimate, but it is somehow blurred by the fact that the workers are supposed to be drowned, "vanished amidst a tiny vortex of unwholesome bubbles" (CF 1.263).

[. . .] a throng of lurching labourers who followed dog-like with blind, brainless, floundering steps as if dragged by a clumsy but resistless daemon-will. As the naiads neared the bog, without altering their course, a new line of stumbling stragglers zigzagged drunkenly out of the castle from some door far below my window. [. . .] The flutes piped horribly, and again I heard the beating of the drums from the direction of the island ruin. Then silently and gracefully the naiads reached the water and melted one by one into the ancient bog; while the line of followers, never checking their speed, splashed awkwardly after them and vanished amidst a tiny vortex of unwholesome bubbles [. . .] (CF 1.263)

So Lovecraft weaves a net of crossed references between the nymphs, Artemis, Pan, and the use of flutes to present his Gothic fiction.

Historically, the Gothic tradition has not been completely detached from classical mythology, so this cannot really be considered Lovecraft's innovation. There are three capital examples illustrating this point. Mary Shelley's most famous work, *Frankenstein; or, The Modern Prometheus* (1818), is obviously inspired in part by the legend of Prometheus. Two years later, her husband Percy Bysshe Shelley wrote the dramatic poem *Prometheus Unbound*. The third reference that has to be considered is the bust of Pallas Athena present in Poe's "The Raven" (1845), which decorates the narrator's library.

However, the active use of the Greek mythological tradition is quite interesting, since the haunting presence in the tale is the figure of the undine or naiad, instead of the classical ghost or typical Irish banshee. The narrator and Barry are attacked by entities that are deeply rooted in the past; but their origins are found in classical antiquity rather than in some kind of genealogical decay (as in the case of "The Shadow over Innsmouth"), or in a period millions of years prior to the appearance of humanity (as in *At the Mountains of Madness*).

There are some good reasons for Lovecraft to mix the Gothic with classical mythology, instead of using the powerful magical Irish folklore. In a 1930 letter in which he discussed the witchcraft tradition, the writer explored its racial origins. At a certain point he asserts that:

> It is true that the Celts share most vigorously the myth-cycle of fairies, gnomes, and little people, which anthropologists find all over western Europe (in a distinctive form marking it off from the general Aryan personification system which produced fauns, satyrs, dryads, etc.) and attribute to vague memories of contact with the Mongoloids which was wholly prior to their invasion of Britain.[8] (*SL* 3.162)

According to Guarde Paz, Lovecraft dismissed the Celtic tradition because of its likely Mongoloid origins, far from the Aryan mythological tradition (30). This might be an interesting ideological point of view in order to consider why Lovecraft preferred to use an obscure Greek connection in his Irish tale rather than assimilate the local folklore. The writer, in spite of being familiar with the strong Celtic folklore, is aware that the origins of the weird are to be found in classic texts. He explains it in "Supernatural Horror in Literature":

> Just as all fiction first found extensive embodiment in poetry, so is it in poetry that we first encounter the permanent entry of the weird into standard literature. More of the ancient instances, curiously enough, are in prose; as the werewolf incident in Petronius, the gruesome passages in Apuleius, the brief but celebrated letter of Pliny the younger to Sura, and the odd compilation *On Wonderful Events* by the Emperor Hadrian's Greek freedman, Phlegon. It is Phlegon that we first find that hideous tale of the corpse-bride, "Philinnion and Machates", later related by Proclus and in modern times forming the inspiration of Goethe's "Bride of Corinth" and Washington Irving's "German Student". (25)

To complete the dismissal of the Irish tradition (and in fact of most of the cultural artifacts that are not directly derived from the classical heritage) in favor of Greek mythology, Lovecraft provides the following enlightening passage in one of his letters from 1931:

---

8. Prior to that letter, in 1927, he already focused his attention in this issue in "Supernatural Horror in Literature": "Much of the power of Western horror-lore was undoubtedly due to the hidden but often suspected presence of a hideous cult of nocturnal worshippers whose strange customs—descended from pre-Aryan and pre-agricultural times when a squat race of Mongoloids roved over Europe with their flocks and herds—were rooted in the most revolting fertility-rites of immemorial antiquity" (24).

The civilizations of Egypt, Persia, Greece & Rome undoubtedly excelled ours—in fact, virtually everything of value in ours was borrowed or inherited from Greece & Rome, so that it is really a prolongation of the Graeco-Roman stream rather than a new & separate affair. Probably the next civilisation will be a sort of continuation of this as this is of the Graeco-Roman.[9] (SL 3.384)

It would be a serious mistake to think that Lovecraft rejected all kinds of folklore and tradition. As can be seen from the previous quotation, he supported any cultural artifact that was clearly connected with the Greco-Roman heritage. In fact, Timothy Evans supports the theory that Lovecraft tried to reinforce America's tradition by borrowing ideas from others and incorporating them into his own texts. This characteristic, according to him, brings the writer close to postmodernism (127).[10] In words of John Salonia:

Lovecraft's overwhelming sense of the past led him to take great pains to invest his horrors with a shadowy omnipresence throughout history and in a variety of cultures, lending his fictional creations verisimilitude by subtly weaving them into known chronologies. He also sought inspiration in actual legends, to give his fiction reflected believability by imitating the forms of real myths handed down from preliterate cultures. (95)

---

9. In the 1935 essay "A Living Heritage: Roman Architecture in Today's America," Lovecraft reinforces the idea that everything worthy in modern Western society has its origins in the ancient Greek and Roman tradition, through the analysis of architectural influences of the classical arts in contemporary buildings: "Whether the radicals admit it or not, our genuine stream of art and civilization is still the ancient western one which took its general form in Greece and Rome" (CE 5.124).

10. Fritz Leiber believes that Lovecraft, after realizing that "the universe revealed by materialistic science is a purposeless, soulless place" (9), had to find a shelter from these discoveries: "In his personal life Lovecraft met the challenge of this hideous realization by taking refuge in traditionalism, in the cultivation of mankind's time-honored manners and myths, not because they are true, but because man's mind is habituated to them and therefore finds in them some comfort and support" (9–10). Salonia shares Leiber's ideas about Lovecraft's intellectual acceptance of universe's indifference toward mankind and his emotional rejection of it: "The past became the haven of security, of ordered things; the present, the inescapable crumbling, the breaking-down; the future, the inevitable downfall into complete collapse. Out of this conflict between bleak intellectual conviction and blazing emotional rejection was born his compelling literary works" (100).

The consequences of the events that take place in the bog and castle have been described by Joshi in terms of a basic moral: "the spirits of Nature avenging or warding off desecration by human beings" (*IAP* 384). However, it is interesting to explore this aspect a little further. The portrayal of Denys Barry, the man who tries to drain the Moon-Bog, is poor. It is known that "he had grown rich" in America (*CF* 1.256), and that he does not care about the superstitious rumors about the marsh told by the peasants. He is depicted as the typical Lovecraftian rational mind, who "gave his resounding laugh" (*CF* 1.261) when told about the narrator's suspicions and uneasiness. The most enlightening observation about Barry occurs when the narrator explains the motivations his friend has for draining the bog: "For all his love of Ireland, America had not left him untouched, and he hated the beautiful wasted space where peat might be cut and land opened up" (*CF* 1.257).

The wealthy Barry represents the decadent aristocracy of the United States. This plutocracy was well described by Lovecraft in his 1933 essay "A Layman Looks at the Government." After drawing a timeline of the history of aristocracy in that text, the writer reaches the 1920s, when the tale is probably set. From this particular period of history, Lovecraft remarks:

> But the plutocrats were, by the second decade of the twentieth century, manifestly in decadence. Greed had become utterly paramount, and the sense of responsibility toward weak dependents which the aristocrats had possessed was largely atrophied save for sporadic cases of capricious and often well-advertised philanthropy. Callousness and oppression toward the masses became exaggerated to the point of murderous grotesqueness—egged on by a steadily increasing mechanization which made the resource-holders more and more independent of their slaves and victims. All the ability of the competent class became canalized in the one sterile channel of grabbing increased material resources for those already holding them, and inventing new material luxuries for the trivial and meaningless pleasure of the few resource-holders and their larger but still limited penumbra of essential higher employes. Meanwhile the natural growth of mechanization made more and more persons become permanently unemployable and dependent on grudging and capricious charity to save them from starvation,

whist the suffering from cyclic depressions became acuter and acuter. (*CE* 5.107)

This attack against modern aristocracy might be surprising at first, considering Lovecraft's own political ideas. However, it should be recalled that Lovecraft's ideal aristocracy is far from the conception that was contemporary to him. In fact, he appreciated the classic concept of aristocracy, the one that "made possible the evolution or refinements which colour the lives of increasing numbers of people today" (*CE* 5.104).

For Guarde Paz, "Barry must travel to Ireland to confront his past" (25). As a result of the plans for draining the bog, "the killing of beauty leading to some nameless horror of past naiads in the bog transforms the transgressor into 'a nauseous, unbelievable caricature'" (26). So both Guarde Paz and Joshi share the idea that the tale's moral connotations are related to the revenge of the wilderness against human profanation of the natural environment and beauty. In my opinion, "The Moon-Bog" has a deeper social and political reading that transcends the mere ecological interpretation, but which is still compatible with that reading. When the narrator asserts that Barry has been touched by America, because of his hatred of the wasted space that might be used for labor, the criticism to America's excessive focus on production is explicit. Lovecraft's attacks against excessive urbanization were clear, as exemplified in this 1931 letter:

Now it is perfectly possible that the norm of a mechanised future may be so impersonal & objective that mechanical stresses will be, for that future, a truer & more artistic form of expression than the humanly felt stresses of oral speech & its hand-written transcript. Very well & good. But the man who practices the methods of that future belongs to it—& not to the traditional past. As for city apartments—who ever said Grandpa was *blaming* you for living in one? I merely said that the accidents of fortune which have so reared you have unalterably changed your relationship to the soil & landscape from that relationship which was your grandparents'. It may be all in the normal direction, if mechanised urban life is the norm of the future. But how can you fancy yourself a traditionalist if you do not long constantly for the sweep of green fields & delicate spring odours & the sight of cottage roofs embowered among blossoming orchards? As we were environed before the age of seven, so are our tastes for the rest of our lives. The lack of access to the green fields & cycle of rural nature would simply drive me mad . . . an apartment out of reach of Nature would be simply the antechamber to a still more cramped padded cell. Thus I belong to the early-American setting in a way that urbanites cannot belong. (*SL* 3.336)

For Lovecraft, the benefits of the rural life, or at least of a life apart from big metropolises such as New York, were evident. He considered that direct contact with Nature was essential in order to produce artistic and cultural artifacts, and that this was the task of the aristocratic class that should rule over a majority of workers:

I believe in an aristocracy, because I deem it the only agency for the creation of those refinements which make life endurable for the human animal of high organization.

Since the only human motive is a craving for supremacy, we can expect nothing in the way of achievement unless achievement be rewarded by supremacy.

We cannot expect justice—justice is a mocking phantom— and we know that aristocracy has many undesirable features. But we also know—sadly enough—that we can never abolish the evils without abolishing everything of value to civilised man.

In an aristocracy some persons have a great deal to live for. In a democracy most persons have a little to live for. [. . .]

Aristocracy alone is capable of creating thoughts and objects of value. Everyone, I fancy, will admit that such a state must precede democracy in order to build the original culture. Fewer are willing to admit the cognate truth that democracies and ochlocracies merely subsist parasitically on the aristocracies they overthrow." ("Nietzscheism and Realism," *CE* 5.70)

So the triumph of the nymphs and the moon-goddess over the plans of Barry symbolizes not only Nature overcoming mankind, but something deeper: the defeat of industrialization against tradition and, ultimately, the defeat of machinery and work in favor of pastoral landscape. There are no time references that place the action in a very specific period, but considering the fact that Barry owns a car that picks the narrator up in the station, it is clear that the text was intended to be set at a time contemporary to Love-craft, in the first decades of the twentieth century. So nature reigns not just over mankind, but over science and progress, and the attempts to domesticate it fail and bring terrible consequences for men.

On a second level of analysis, "The Moon-Bog" also shows Lovecraft's preferences regarding the mythical tradition. As has already been explained, the writer neglected the rich Irish folklore and preferred to expand a brief Greek mythical reference in order to create the haunting atmosphere of the tale. This cultural dis-dain, inspired by the Mongoloid origins of the Celtic tradition, also arises from the text. However, this is more a metatextual reading: since there are no elements of the Irish (or American, considering the origins of the main characters) folklore in the narration, there is no direct conflict between the two traditions in the text. Denys Barry and the narrator personify rationality rather than a particular modern Western folklore tradition.

If we consider "The Moon-Bog" under the previous perspec-tive, it would be, from an ideological point of view, one of few Lovecraft's tales with a positive reading. It is hard to find, among all the writer's oeuvre, a piece of fiction in which the results are clearly positive from the ideological perspective of the writer. The triumph of the naiads is a concession to Lovecraft's taste for the ancient Greek culture over his contemporary materialistic human beings. Five years before writing "The Moon-Bog," the writer was pessimistic about the future of the contact with the pastoral side of mankind, as he himself expressed in 1916:

Much has been said of "the sheer joy of living", an ebullient sensa-tion enjoyed by those in close communion with Nature. This feel-ing undoubtedly exists, but it is in itself a sinister thing, since it is but an atavistic delight in prehistoric things which the intelligent are leaving behind. It is, indeed, a sort of warning against the con-tinued progress of mankind; a finger beckoning us back to the simpler ages we have survived. I have often wondered if mankind would not be happier for a deliberate destruction of learning and civilisation—an absolute and unqualified return to the happy pas-toral barbarism of our legendary ancestors! (*Letters to Rheinhart Kleiner* 38)

As has been proved in my analysis, the discordant element for Lovecraft is not the Greek tradition but Denys Barry himself. He represents the decay of the aristocracy that Lovecraft is unable to accept, an aristocracy that has changed its taste for refinement and the arts by the greed of capitalism.

Conclusion

"The Moon-Bog" possesses some features that make it a typical Gothic tale for a casual reader. However, the Greek component of the narration summons different layers related to profound ideological issues and give the story some characteristics that move it away from a the classic Gothic tradition.

The few readings that have been made of the text propose a quite superficial analysis that I have tried to refute in the present paper, proving that the tale has several levels of analysis that go beyond the mere ecological reading. The triumph of Greek myth over contemporary men is different from any horror coming from the past in other Lovecraftian pieces of fiction, since this time the past invoked by the author is deeply esteemed and valued by him. So the tale is a landmark in his oeuvre from the point of view of the positioning and sympathy of the author toward the fairy and monstrous world.

The naiads reign not only over men, but also over the traditional Irish folklore, which is fully neglected in a tale that would have been perfect for its use. The Mongoloid origins of the Irish popular tradition forestall its value in Lovecraft's eyes, since the most valuable cultural artifacts must be derived from the ancient Greek and Roman traditions.

Barry, with his attempts to destroy the natural landscape in order to create a vast tract of land to be exploited, is the personification of Lovecraft's fears of the aristocratic decadence of his age. At the same time, the attack that Barry is leveling at the natural landscape is an assault on the natural order. Draining the Moon-Bog, he is trying to reformulate the rules of nature.

In "The Moon-Bog" the human counterpart of the monster is depicted as the negative force in action. The naiads and the moon-goddess are not the symbolization of foreign elements, detached from Lovecraft's beloved Teuton's origins; on the contrary, they are the origins of modern civilization and culture. The conflicting element this time is Barry, who arrives to the pastoral landscape with American ideas of industrialization and capitalism. He is the personification of the excesses of the decayed aristocracy and the growing technological advances that Lovecraft attacks when referring to architecture:

> They claim that the Athenians who conceived the Parthenon, the Choragic Monument of Lysicrates, and the Olympian Zeus, the mediaeval Nordics who conceived the cathedrals of Chartres and Lincoln, and the Georgian cabinet-makers who conceived the magnificent furniture of two centuries ago, were precisely on a par with the depression-age theorists who laboriously reared the steel-and-glass horrors of the late Chicago "Century of Progress", and who continue to plan and perpetrate nightmares in chromium, bakelite, glass, concrete, and other media—calling upon corkscrews, factory refuse, gas-tanks, oil derricks, chicken-coops, radio masts, and other "typical forms of our twentieth-century machine 'civilization'" as models for what they ironically term chairs, tables, buildings, and the like. ("A Living Heritage," CE 5.120–21)

The decay of the higher classes of his society was undoubtedly another source of conflict for the writer, and "The Moon-Bog" offers an underlying idea that exposes it and punishes Barry for his greed. In fact, at the end of the narrative Barry becomes "a nauseous, unbelievable caricature—a blasphemous effigy of him who had been Denys Barry" (CF 1.264). The decadent aristocrat is now the "unbelievable" creature, the monster itself. The order is reestablished for Lovecraft.

Works Cited

Botting, Fred. *Gothic*. New York: Routledge, 1996.

Burleson, Donald R. *H. P. Lovecraft: A Critical Study*. Westport, CT: Greenwood Press, 1983.

Cannon, Peter. *H. P. Lovecraft*. Boston: Twayne, 1989.

de Camp, L. Sprague. *Lovecraft: A Biography*. 1975. New York: Barnes & Noble, 1996.

Dodds, E. R. *The Greeks and the Irrational*. Boston: Beacon Press, 1957.

Duncan, Ian. *Modern Romance and Transformations of the Novel: The Gothic, Scott, Dickens.* Cambridge: Cambridge University Press, 1992.

Ellis, Peter Berresford. *Dictionary of Celtic Mythology.* Santa Barbara: ABC-CLIO, 1992.

Evans, Timothy H. "A Last Defense against the Dark: Folklore, Horror, and the Uses of Tradition in the Work of H. P. Lovecraft." *Journal of Folklore Research,* 42 (2005): 99–135.

Guarde Paz, César. "Race and War in the Lovecraft Mythos: A Philosophical Reflection." *Lovecraft Annual* 6 (2012): 3–35.

Joshi, S. T. *I Am Providence: The Life and Times of H. P. Lovecraft.* New York: Hippocampus Press, 2010. [Abbreviated in the text as *IAP.*]

Lebor Gabála Érenn: Book of the Taking of Ireland, Parts 1–5. Ed. and trans. R. A. Stewart Macalister. Dublin: Irish Texts Society, 1941.

Leiber, Fritz. "A Literary Copernicus." 1949. In *Discovering H. P. Lovecraft,* ed. Darrell Schweitzer. Rev. ed. Holicong, PA: Wildside Press, 2001. 7–16.

Lovecraft, H. P. *Letters to Rheinhart Kleiner.* Ed. S. T. Joshi and David E. Schultz. New York: Hippocampus Press, 2005.

———. "Supernatural Horror in Literature." 1927. In *The Annotated Supernatural Horror in Literature.* Ed. S. T. Joshi. New York: Hippocampus Press, 2000; rev. ed 2012. 25–96.

March, Jenny. *Cassell's Dictionary of Classical Mythology.* London: Cassell & Co., 1998.

Pearsall, Anthony. *The Lovecraft Lexicon: A Reader's Guide to Persons, Places and Things in the Tales of H. P. Lovecraft.* Tempe, AZ: New Falcon Publications, 2005.

Pothius. *Bibliotheca of Myriobiblion. Codex 190.* In *The Tertullian Project, Codices 186–222 [extracts].* Web. 10 Jun. 2014. http://www.tertullian.org/fathers/photius_copyright/photius_05bibliotheca.htm.

Salonia, John. "Cosmic Maenads and the Music of Madness: Lovecraft's Borrowings from the Greeks." *Lovecraft Annual* 5 (2011): 91–101.

Wetzel, George T. "Genesis of the Cthulhu Mythos." 1975. In *Discovering H. P. Lovecraft,* ed. Darrell Schweitzer. Rev. ed. Holicong, PA: Wildside Press, 2001. 54–62.

Reviews

JACK KOBLAS. *The Lovecraft Circle and Others as I Remember Them.* Eugenia, ON: Battered Silicon Dispatch Box, 2012. 385 pp. $30.00 tpb. Reviewed by S. T. Joshi.

I wish I had read, and reviewed, this book before its author died on March 8, 2013. I can at least say that I met him—one of the key figures in the Lovecraft fan movement of the 1970s and 1980s—only a few months before his death, when I was guest of honour at Arcana 42, the successor to the private MinnCons dating back to the early 1970s. This book—arranged rather oddly in alphabetical order by the author or artist discussed, as if it were some kind of reference work—is an utterly charming account of the many distinctive personalities, from Robert Bloch to Jack Williamson, whom Koblas knew in the course of his long career. Many of them had direct, or at least tangential, associations with Lovecraft, and others were central players in the worlds of weird pulp fiction (many of them contributed to *Weird Tales*) or weird art from as early as the 1920s to the present day.

One of the more surprising details that emerge out of this book is the number of individuals who were based in, or had become transplanted to, the Twin Cities region of Minneapolis–St. Paul. It was, of course, largely this fortuitous collocation of both fans and professional writers that led to the formation of the MinnCon gatherings, which began in a loose and casual manner and later became a more formalised convention where notable figures were brought in as special guests. The core of the group—which paralleled the contemporaneous MadCon gatherings in Madison, Wisconsin—were Koblas, Carl Jacobi, and Donald Wandrei (whom Koblas declares was "my mentor and perhaps closest friend"), but included many others, either as one-time guests or as regulars. The agent Kirby McCauley was in frequent attendance, as were Richard L. Tierney, the artist Joe West (who curiously has no chapter dedicated to him), E. Hoffmann Price, and many others.

A number of interesting tidbits emerge from this book. I don't recall hearing before that Robert Bloch first heard of Lovecraft's death while listening to Stravinsky's *Firebird Suite*. "That music has always signified death and funerals ever since," Bloch testifies in an interview. Koblas had a long and involved association with Mary Elizabeth Counselman, many of whose letters he prints here. Those letters are written with a liveliness and pungency that frequently equals Lovecraft's own; and what is more surprising are the numerous references to Lovecraft and his creations found in those letters, written by one who to my knowledge never wrote a truly "Lovecraftian" story in her decades-long career. Still more surprising, Counselman notes that in "my Callow Teens, in Tallahassee," she had written a fan letter to Lovecraft after reading "The Rats in the Walls" in *Weird Tales;* but she had never received a response. This seems very odd—Lovecraft would surely have written back if he had received the letter, especially as it was from a young woman. This probably was in the late 1920s (Counselman was born in 1911).

Another fascinating chapter deals with Raymond B. Nixon, an old amateur journalist whom Koblas one day found in his local telephone book. Nixon was the editor of the *Dixie Booster*, the amateur journal that in 1916 published Lovecraft's "Temperance Song." He of course never met Lovecraft, but his impressions of Lovecraft and the amateur movement of the day are fascinating. Nixon went on to become a longtime editor of the Emory University alumni magazine and a professor of journalism at the University of Minnesota.

Koblas established a close relationship with E. Hoffmann Price, whose letters (reprinted here *in extenso*) are also vivid and at times acerbic. Price roundly abuses the fans of his day for misplaced nostalgia for old-time writers of the 1920s and 1930s while ignoring the good work being done by their contemporaries. And he has a touching tribute to August Derleth, written about a year after Derleth's death:

> While I do not pretend to be sitting around, either in mourning or
> despair, I have not yet recovered my emotional equilibrium, and I

think I shall for a long time remain keenly aware of the gap created by his death. August had for so long been part of my scene—
through our correspondence, since 1932; through our sharing of
the impact of HPL's death; through other deaths, and, through our
working together in producing my first and thus far, only hard
cover book—and, finally, our two meetings in Sauk City clinched
the bond, although a prior meeting in Redwood City had done
much to strengthen it. I realized his importance as a friend, as a
long time associate, as a fellow pioneer of W.T.['s] early days—yet
until his death, I did not suspect how important August had become in a purely personal way, through our long sustained exchange of thoughts on life and living, things and people, friends
and their opposites we shared!

More recent members of the extended Lovecraft circle—many
of whom are still alive—also come in for discussion. The larger-
than-life Wilum Hopfrog Pugmire made an impression on a number of the people with whom Koblas associated, and from an early
age. Mary Elizabeth Counselman charmingly refers to him at one
point as "Wilum the Wampyr, from Seattle." Pugmire naughtily
told J. Vernon Shea that he had written the screenplay to the
dreadful horror film *Dracula vs. Frankenstein* (1971). The screenplay is credited to one William Pugsley, and Wilum (who at times
went by the nickname "Count Pugsly") maintained that this was
his own pseudonym. Shea fell for the playful deception in toto,
repeating it soberly (although with due incredulity) in a 1976 letter to Koblas. Given that Pugmire would have been only twenty
years old at the time of the film's release, and that he had (and still
has) not the slightest experience as a screenwriter, Shea should
have been a bit more skeptical.

There are discussions of other writers not associated with the
Lovecraft Circle, but these prove to be entertaining and informa-
tive as well. John Arfstrom, for example, was a Twin Cities–based
artist who did some illustrations for *Weird Tales* but mostly for
other science fiction or adventure pulps; he also did some dust
jackets for early Fedogan & Bremer titles. Then there is Tommy
Thompson, a prolific writer of westerns who was elected a life
member of the Cowboy Hall of Fame. Who knew there was such
a thing? But even he proves to be of interest.

This book is not in any sense a formal treatise but more a mine of information that others might quarry for treatises of their own. Koblas prints many letters by his associates (and does so, insofar as I can tell, without permission), including more than 80 pages of letters by Counselman and dozens of letters by Price, Shea, Wandrei, Jacobi, and others; he even prints the entire text of Edmond Hamilton's early story "The Monster-God of Mamurth." The book could inevitably have used a professional copyedit, and Koblas's chapter on Wandrei would have benefited from his consultation of recent publications by and about Wandrei, including *Mysteries of Time and Spirit* and Wandrei's *Collected Poems* (revised as *Sanctity & Sin*). But these are cosmetic matters. Overall, this book is a delightful and, at times, poignant look at some of the personalities over the past several decades, stretching back almost a century, that have made the worlds of pulpdom, fandom, and Lovecraftdom so appealing. To those of us of a certain age who lived through at least some of that period, this book will evoke many echoes of friendships, feuds, and distinctive characters now gone forever—gone, that is, except in our memories and in the abundant writings they left behind.

H. P. LOVECRAFT. *The New Annotated H. P. Lovecraft*. Edited with a Foreword and Notes by Leslie S. Klinger. New York: Liveright, 2014. lxx, 846 pages. $39.95 hc. Reviewed by S. T. Joshi.

This mammoth tome is one of the most impressive volumes ever published relating to the work of H. P. Lovecraft. In its more than 900 pages (including a lengthy "foreword" [i.e., introduction] that provides both a compact history of weird fiction up to Lovecraft's time and a sound bio-critical overview of the author) are contained nearly all the tales for which Lovecraft is best known. The annotations are almost unfailingly intelligent, copious, and pertinent.

Leslie S. Klinger may not have been one's most likely choice to compile such a book, since nearly all his previous books relate to Sherlock Holmes (he has co-written one book on nineteenth-century vampire fiction); but, as his copious bibliography attests, he has been a quick learner of all things Lovecraftian and has absorbed the best scholarship old and new on the Providence writer.

His annotations also include an abundance of illustrative matter ranging from photographs of sites mentioned in the tales (especially the plethora of Providence sites in *The Case of Charles Dexter Ward*), illustrations of Lovecraft's stories by artists in *Weird Tales* as well as contemporary artists such as Jason C. Eckhardt, and numerous covers of Lovecraft books (both US and foreign), posters of Lovecraft films, and all kinds of other interesting matter.

The evaluation of a book of this size and complexity must proceed in stages. The first order of business is to determine what stories were selected. In a book that is approximately the size of the Library of America edition of Lovecraft's *Tales* (2005), it would seem possible to include just about every tale that is generally considered top-notch. But a stark omission meets us almost at the outset. Where is "The Outsider"? Could Klinger not spare 7 pages for this signature story? To be sure, it perhaps offers relatively little fodder for the annotator (although the multifarious literary influences—Poe, Hawthorne, Mary Shelley, etc.—might have been of interest to point out), but it surely deserves inclusion more than the mediocre early story "Beyond the Wall of Sleep." That story has some minimal interest as a kind of predecessor to "The Shadow out of Time" (although Klinger makes the odd comment that "The Whisperer in Darkness" "may be seen as a more mature version of 'Beyond the Wall of Sleep'"), but that is about all. And then there is the cavernous omission of "The Rats in the Walls," which—as anyone can see from my version of the story in *The Annotated H. P. Lovecraft* (1997)—is extraordinarily rich in annotation possibilities. I suppose we should now be resigned to the inclusion of "Herbert West—Reanimator" among Lovecraft's "best" stories (too bad Klinger used a colon instead of a dash in the title), and we should perhaps be grateful for the small mercy that "The Horror at Red Hook" is omitted (it is unfortunately embalmed in the Library of America edition, chosen by Peter Straub). Otherwise, every major story Lovecraft wrote—especially in his last decade of writing—is included here.

I provided the texts of the stories, although these are not the slightly revised texts that I have prepared for my new variorum edition of Lovecraft, due out later this year. The publisher has apparently made some deliberate format changes—such as printing most extracts (e.g., the letters between Curwen and his cohorts in *The Case of Charles Dexter Ward*; the letters between Wilmarth and Akeley in "The Whisperer in Darkness") in italics. This is nothing to get all hot and bothered about, but it would have been nice to have printed the tagline to the epigraph to "The Haunter of the Dark" ("—*Nemesis*"), as Klinger is forced in a note to identify the epigraph as coming from Lovecraft's poem. Speaking of epigraphs, many readers will be startled to find one at the head of "Herbert West—Reanimator"; it reads: "To be dead, to be truly dead, must be glorious. There are far worse things awaiting man than death."—COUNT DRACULA. Well, what can this possibly be? It turns out to be a paraphrase from the *film version* of *Dracula* (1931), which Lovecraft is on record as despising! No such epigraph, needless to say, appears either in Lovecraft's surviving typescript nor in the only publication (*Home Brew*, February–July 1922) of the story in Lovecraft's lifetime. When I raised the matter with Klinger upon seeing the proofs, he informed me that he had found it in several online versions of the story. I gather this is one of those instances where, in Klinger's opinion, he has "noted errors in Joshi's work or expressed a different opinion about the 'best' text." Klinger admitted to me that the epigraph did not in fact belong in the text, but it was too late to do any major surgery, so he ended up revising his footnote to declare that the epigraph is "apocryphal."

Toward the end of *The Case of Charles Dexter Ward*, Klinger fails to print the "Saxon minuscules" that a nameless denizen of the eighth century scribbled to Willett in the basement of the Ward/Curwen bungalow. The omission is particularly odd, since my Arkham House edition (and every other text I have ever seen) does print it, and the paragraph preceding it states explicitly: "The briefly scrawled message was this . . ." (In my electronic file I have a placeholder for the minuscules, since I feel that the only way to reproduce them accurately is to print a facsimile of Lovecraft's manuscript at this point. His manuscript shows his numerous attempts to get this inscription exactly right.)

One other small point in which Klinger disagrees with my texts is in printing "out" with a capital O in the titles "The Colour out of Space" and "The Shadow out of Time." (Oddly enough, he does not use a capital O in "over" in "The Shadow over

Innsmouth.") This variant occurs frequently in many Lovecraft editions, including my own corrected Arkham House editions of 1984–86, where Jim Turner overruled me on this point (the "out" is lower-cased in the electronic files I sent to Klinger). To put an end to this insignificant matter, *out* in these titles is a preposition, and by contemporary rules for printing titles prepositions are not capitalised. Lovecraft himself did not pay much attention to these matters (for which, in any case, there was no standard usage in his day), so one can find "out" capitalised or uncapitalised when he cites these titles in letters.

It is understandable that Klinger, aiming for a general audience, seeks to define words that some readers might find difficult. I was asked to go easy on this point when compiling my Penguin editions, but I did define a few. Klinger's definitions are for the most part unexceptionable, but he stumbles on a few occasions. He defines "Cyclopean" as "huge, massive, like the Cyclops of classic mythology" (the definition is quoted from Brewer's *Dictionary of Phrase and Fable*); but this is not quite right. The *Oxford English Dictionary* (*OED*) supplies two definitions, one specifically applied to architecture (which is almost always how Lovecraft uses it): "Applied to an ancient style of masonry in which the stones are of immense size and more or less irregular shape ..." This seems to me an important distinction.

Klinger supplies a long note on the word "alienist," which he at the outset defines merely as a "'mad-doctor' who treated mental disease." This is not so much inaccurate as inadequate; for the term gained currency in the later nineteenth and early twentieth centuries as referring to a physician who was specifically brought in to gauge whether a potentially "mad" person was to be confined in an asylum or mental hospital; all Lovecraft's usages (especially in *The Case of Charles Dexter Ward*) are of that sort. And does "infandous" really mean "too terrible to be described"? Not quite; *OED* says: "Unspeakable, not to be spoken of, nefarious." The Latin derivation (from *fari*, to speak) is critical here.

Klinger's decision to focus almost exclusively on historical and literary elements in the tale, with little discussion of their origins in Lovecraft's own life and career, sometimes carries him too far. I acknowledge his courtesy in not treading ground that I covered in my annotated Penguin editions, but I think he could have added certain critical bits of information with little difficulty. For example, is it not significant that Lovecraft derived the inspiration for "Beyond the Wall of Sleep" from an article in the *New York Tribune* (April 27, 1919) about backwoods denizens in the Catskill Mountains? Instead, we have a long note citing other articles about such denizens that Lovecraft probably did not read. Both he and I have missed the fact that, in the resonant opening paragraph of "The Picture in the House," the phrase "catacombs of Ptolemais" probably comes from Poe's "Shadow—A Parable" (where Ptolemais is mentioned). He and I are also remiss in not identifying the name Keziah Mason as probably deriving from Hawthorne's *Septimius Felton*, where an Aunt Keziah is cited. And would it have been so much trouble for Klinger to have mentioned, in his note on the Endless Caverns in Virginia (alluded to in "The Shadow out of Time"), that Lovecraft had visited the site in 1928 and written extensively about it in "Observations on Several Parts of America"? And Klinger not only erroneously defines "Magnum Innominandum" (cited without explanation in "The Whisperer in Darkness") as "The Great One Who Is Not to Be Named" (the term is a neuter singular, hence must mean "The Great *Thing* That Is Not to Be Named"), but cannot be troubled to note that the term occurred in Lovecraft's great "Roman dream" of 1927 (where the reference is indeed to some kind of entity—but the fact that it is neither masculine nor feminine is significant).

In other cases, Klinger simply errs in his understanding of certain phases of some stories. Some of these matters relate to points of *interpretation* that, generally speaking, should probably not have been the subject of annotation at all; I specifically avoided such notes in my Penguin editions, leaving these matters to readers, critics, and scholars. For example, in reference to the poignant line in "The Festival," "For though the wind had not left much snow, a few patches did remain on the path near the door; and in that fleeting backward look it seemed to my troubled eyes that they bore no mark of passing feet, not even mine," Klinger remarks: "This makes no sense," and goes on to berate Lovecraft for irrationality. Alas, this is the intemperate comment of a critic whose preference for the cut-and-dried reasonableness of detective fiction has made him insensitive to the subtleties of the weird tale. Perhaps we are to understand the image as an indication that the entire episode of the narrator's wandering through Kingsport was a dream? Lovecraft himself suggests as much when recounting his trip of December 17, 1922, that inspired the story (a trip that, needless to say, Klinger fails to mention). Other interpretations are possible.

Klinger fails to note that Lovecraft erred in dating the Danish scholar Olaus Wormius (the translator of a Latin version of the *Necronomicon*) to the thirteenth rather than the seventeenth century. The issue is not specifically addressed in "The Festival" ("the unmentionable *Necronomicon* ... in Olaus Wormius' forbidden Latin translation"), but it most emphatically is in "History of the *Necronomicon*," which is printed in one of the seven (!) appendices to Klinger's book.

In regard to the passage in "The Call of Cthulhu" where the narrator notes that "in some way the second of April had put a stop to whatever monstrous menace had begun its siege of mankind's soul," Klinger notes: "This is wishful thinking" (he cites one Justin Taylor for this remark), saying that threats to mankind still exist. But the comment refers specifically to the second sinking of R'lyeh after its temporary emergence a few days before: the point that Lovecraft is making is that the stars are not "right," and therefore it is not yet time for Cthulhu's definitive re-emergence in the world.

In correctly identifying Borellus in *The Case of Charles Dexter Ward* with Pierre Borel, Klinger curiously refers readers to Roger Bryant's old article "The Alchemist and the Scientist" (*Nyctalops*, January–February 1975), which erroneously identifies Borellus as Giovanni Borelli.

At the end of "The Whisperer in Darkness," in regard to the climactic utterance ("For the things in the chair, perfect to the last, subtle detail of microscopic resemblance—or identity—were the face and hands of Henry Wentworth Akeley"), Klinger states oddly that "the use of the word 'identity' here suggest[s] that the mask is a representation of Akeley's actual face." Well, no—what is suggested (even more horribly) is that it *is* Akeley's actual face!

Finally, in noting the seemingly peculiar mention of "Roderick Usher" toward the end of "The Haunter of the Dark," Klinger says that the name was mentioned to refer to "Usher's hypersensitivity to distant sounds." Again no: as Klinger (who otherwise seems well familiar with "Supernatural Horror in Literature") should have known, the reference points to the psychic union at this point of Robert Blake and the haunter of the dark ("I am it and it is I"), since Lovecraft is referring to his own pioneering interpretation of "The Fall of the House of Usher" as suggesting the psychic union of Roderick, Madeline, and the house itself. This point was made as long ago as the 1950s by George T. Wetzel.

But Klinger does make a number of advances in Lovecraft scholarship. He identifies the "Dr. Anderson" cited in the quotation from Garrett P. Serviss at the end of "Beyond the Wall of Sleep." He suggests an intriguing source for Alhazred's "unexplainable couplet" in the work of John Donne ("One short sleep past, we wake externally, / And Death shall be no more; Death, thou shalt die"). He works out a detailed chronology of events in "Herbert West—Reanimator," which begins so early as the year 1903. He corrects me on the origin of the concept of Lemuria, which dates to the work of one Philip Sclater in 1864, not Ernst Haeckel, as I had stated. Sometimes, though, Klinger goes a bit overboard. He has discovered that Narath (as in "the peerless beauty of Narath" in "The Silver Key") is a town in southwestern India; but I suspect Lovecraft thought he had made it up. And Klinger seems to fancy that *everything* in *The Case of Charles Dexter Ward* is based on some real person or event, so he states blandly, in reference to "Melville F. Peters, Esq., of George St.": "There are no records of this individual." No surprise!—he is fictitious. Perhaps this is an instance of annotator's humour.

Klinger is pretty good on citing up-to-date sources for both primary and secondary texts; but it would have been nice to have noted that the notes to *At the Mountains of Madness*, "The Shadow out of Time," and "The Shadow over Innsmouth" (complete with Lovecraft's illustrations) are included in *Collected Essays*, Volume 5 (the series is indeed cited in his bibliography), rather than referring readers to the almost inaccessible *Something about Cats and Other Pieces* (1949).

If many of the above criticisms seem picayune, that is because, for the most part, they are. Aside from the actual errors cited above (not numerous), some of my comments merely relate to different philosophies or practices in preparing annotated editions. No one can deny the diligence and intelligence that Leslie S. Klinger has brought to his chosen task, and it is safe to say that this volume contains more hard information relating to H. P. Lovecraft's stories than any book ever published. It deserves the widest possible audience.

GAVIN CALLAGHAN. *H. P. Lovecraft's Dark Arcadia*. Jefferson, NC: McFarland, 2013. 288 pp. $40.00 tpb. Reviewed by Michael J. Abolafia.

The modern scholar of the writings of H. P. Lovecraft has no dearth of secondary sources to which he or she can refer. This is an immediate consequence of the critical renaissance fomented by luminaries like S. T. Joshi, Barton Levi St. Armand, Dirk W. Mosig, and a whole host of other scholars whose exegeses of Lovecraft's corpus throughout the 1970s and '80s were formative influences on the vast body of scholarly discourse produced in the following decades. The sheer volume of critical work being done on Lovecraft's fiction (and, to a lesser extent, nonfiction and poetry) today would have probably been unthinkable to the field's pioneers, whose tireless efforts to bring to light obscure biographical details, textual histories, and ignored or forgotten stories, poems, and essays by Lovecraft have elevated the once-maligned scribblings of an ostensible "pulp horror writer" to the realm of high philosophy and serious literature.

Today, the depth and breadth of Lovecraft scholarship is staggering, with critics examining the writer's fiction and poetry through nearly every conceivable literary-critical methodology and lens. He has, after decades of consternation and neglect on the part of the academy, been co-opted by both critics of Modernism and Postmodernism. His literary output has been examined, too, by feminists and Marxists, historicists and poststructuralists, by the followers of Foucault, Derrida, Žižek, Blanchot, and Kristeva, and by philosophers of science and religion. And, perhaps not surprisingly, the bleeding-edge theoretical angles gaining momentum in university English departments—frameworks that deploy critical terminology like spectrality, hauntology, ecocriticism, psychogeography, trauma theory, and hybridity (in the field of cultural studies)—have all been applied to Lovecraft's oeuvre by the next generation of literary critics and academicians. All this is to say that the academic mythologization of Lovecraft is well under way, and he has become canonical—if, indeed, canonicity in the academy is reflected by the sheer number of master's and doctoral dissertations written annually on Lovecraft and the weird.

There is a particular strain of Lovecraftian criticism that has been robustly present since the very first critical essays about Lovecraft appeared in the 1950s and '60s: the psychoanalytic, in which the followers of Freud, Jung, and Lacan examine the unconscious desires, dreams, and sublimated anxieties of both the author and his or her fictional creations. Dirk W. Mosig (*Mosig at Last: A Psychologist Looks at H. P. Lovecraft*), Barton Levi St. Armand (*The Roots of Horror in the Fiction of H. P. Lovecraft*), Michel Houellebecq (*H. P. Lovecraft: Against the World, Against Life*), and various essays by Robert M. Price (largely in *Crypt of Cthulhu* and *Lovecraft Studies*) and others all explore and problematize, with varying degrees of success, the psychological component of Lovecraft's dream-hazed life and work. And much like Lovecraft and his writing, Gavin Callaghan's recent study, *H. P. Lovecraft's Dark Arcadia: Satire, Symbology and Contradiction*, is limned with tension and internal incongruity. Callaghan's self-described aim in *Dark Arcadia* is one of re-imagination: in his view, "received ideas and secondary texts" have "obscure[d] the primary sources" themselves (i.e., Lovecraft's actual writings), which has resulted in the widely held but erroneous (as Callaghan claims) exaltation of a "vaunted cosmicism" that is only *part* of Lovecraft's project as a horror writer.

The book is comprised of six interconnected essays, ranging in length from ten to ninety pages, that wax psychoanalytic on everything from Lovecraft's Romantic satirization ("following Cicero") to the Decadents' aestheticization of hedonism (often homosexual and/or pederastic in nature). Callaghan operationalizes Lovecraft's "sadistic horrors" (lycanthropy, bestiality, cannibalism, etc.) as functions of his "inverted Hellenism"—a rejection of the Arcadian, Pan-haunted aesthetics he embraced viscerally as a boy. Lovecraft's fiction and poetry are, in effect, obsessed with enacting a balancing act—with mediating the underlying tensions—between his New England aristocratic Puritanism and his ensorcelment with Greek mythology and art, with its underlying substratum of epicurean bacchanalia. Callaghan's meditations on Samuel Loveman, whose Decadent Hellenism and sylvan classicism Lovecraft somewhat paradoxically admired, are insightful and well-conceived.

For Callaghan, Lovecraft is a Roman caricaturist of the twentieth century who turned his satirist's steely gaze toward the Decadent and the Hellenistic, in an attempt at reconciling his own dissociated artistic, literary, and even sociopolitical ideals. In other words, there is the "classical grandeur" of Rome on the one hand, and the "bacchanalian decay" of the Greeks (and the Decadents who later appropriated their imagery) on the other. Callaghan concludes that "Cosmicism merely forms the backdrop for a basically Roman satire"—a genuinely unique perspective, and one that Callaghan succeeds in buttressing and arguing for. Some of his observations are doubtless true, and the value of his essay lies precisely in his assertion that "blindness on the part of some of Lovecraft's readers is . . . facilitated by the dearth of classical education in the United States, which has rendered many of his classical references incomprehensible to the modern reader," a roadblock to understanding that his work actively (and usually fruitfully) attempts to clear. *Dark Arcadia* debunks commonly held assumptions about the prevalence of cosmicism in Lovecraft's fictional oeuvre, a valuable argument that is not without merit, and which, in the hands of Callaghan, with his rhetorical aptness and vast repository of historical, sociological, and literary knowledge, demands further attention.

Callaghan's book is an academic *tour de force*, animated by a scholarly *joie de vivre*. He revels in the obscure, the recondite, and the arcane, drawing from a breathtaking array of historical and literary primary sources, and his knowledge of Lovecraft's corpus—from the most obscure of political propagandist poems to his little-read travelogues and fictional collaborations—is indicative of a scholar whose dedication to the source material is evident in every endnote, bibliographical citation, and occasional musing, questioning, or aside. His academicisms and occasionally stilted exegeses are tempered, at least marginally, by the book's germane illustrations, charts, and epigraphs. The cumulative effect is one of striking academic richness and extensivity—which is not to say that Callaghan's claims are all entirely and ubiquitously well-made. Throughout the book, the critic's seemingly "objective" (by virtue of its dedication to citing the stories, poems, essays, and letters themselves) tone is hampered by misplaced suggestions, muddled thinking, and bewildering "value judgments" that are all the more ironic given Callaghan's use of Jungian (and Freudian) theoretics as critical praxis.

In the introduction, Callaghan remarks, with a distinct note of unrecognized irony, that Lovecraft's "ongoing anti-bacchanalian critique accurately predicted the worst excesses of the 1960s counterculture and the insanity of the sexual revolution" (8). The use of a word like "insanity" to describe the sexual revolution—a liberatory movement that was, ironically, spurred by the same psychoanalysts of the late nineteenth and early twentieth centuries whom he uses as his focal interlocutors, directly or indirectly—is hyperbolic at best and misinformed at worst. At the essay's end, Callaghan proceeds to launch into a bewildering, half-formed "critique" of contemporary society: "The lascivious rites of Cthulhu's animalistic followers are now broadcast every night on TV ... And that bacchanalia from which Lovecraft so recoiled, has, in the form of the sexual revolution, spawned an epidemic that is just as unspeakable, and just as unnamable, as anything he, in his paranoia, could have created." It is difficult to ascertain exactly what "unspeakable epidemic" Callaghan is referring to here; the entire paragraph reads like a vague, schizoid, Spenglerian condemnation of those aligned with the "environmentalist, feminist, luddite, leftist, gay liberation" movements, "radical organizations" that Callaghan is evidently at odds with (207). At other moments, he gives short shrift to occultists like Aleister Crowley, whom he dismisses summarily (and quite bizarrely) as a "pathetic magician," notwithstanding his contributions to the Western mystery tradition, his uneven, but interesting, fiction, nonfiction, and poetry, his influence on popular culture, and his pioneering work on consciousness research.

These polemical declarations are hardly useful, or even relevant, within the actual milieu of his argument, and their presence unfortunately hurts Callaghan's authorial and scholarly ethos. There are brief, but fortunately not disastrously distracting, hiccups in Callaghan's prose in the form of repeated words and estranged or unnecessary commas. The book could have benefited from a more eagle-eyed editor. There are historical assertions, too, that are of questionable or suspect accuracy. At one point, Callaghan remarks, "Known to the Romans as Diana, Artemis figured prominently in the Dianic fertility cults of the Middle Ages, which also played so large a role in Lovecraft's weird fiction." This statement, a summary of Margaret Murray's thesis as she presents it in *The Witch-Cult in Western Europe* (and which was later advanced, in slightly modified form, in Carlo Ginzburg's *Night Battles*), is widely discredited, and it is unclear if Callaghan himself believes this outdated scholarship on medieval history to be true, or if he is referring to Lovecraft's interest in that particular text.

Three of the book's essays are centered on revealing the polysemic meanings of a particular group of symbols, or images, that recur in Lovecraft's writings: the bee/apiary motif; "The Shadow over Innsmouth" and its thematic-psychological relation to Lovecraft's cousin, Phillips Gamwell, who died of tuberculosis; and the "moon-ladder," which appears in Lovecraft's writings, variously, "as a beam, a path, a road, a bridge, and simply as a rapid rising and falling." These pieces attempt a (mostly Jungian) hermeneutical analysis of these very particular, and very specific, threads that run concurrent throughout the Lovecraftian imaginary, and they are deeply learned, with well-made and well-argued claims. Callaghan's skillful vacillation between the minute (textually, that is) or the microcosmic and the broader, more macrocosmic aims of Lovecraft as a writer makes for penetrating and revelatory reading. Callaghan brings his trenchant interpretations to life through well-selected historical, literary, and biographical source matter, making connections between the stories and Lovecraft's life (in typical Freudian/Jungian fashion) that seem plausible: Danforth's delvings into the *Necronomicon*, for example, "suggest to us the role played in his own weird fiction by Lovecraft's course of early reading in Edgar Allan Poe."

Even longtime Lovecraft readers and scholars are likely to find Callaghan's acute observations interesting (and necessarily controversial), regardless of one's relationship with the school of psychoanalytic criticism. The textualist or post-structuralist who believes firmly that the writer is dead and buried once the text is written, that nothing—least of all the writer's biography—should be read into the work itself, will likely find fault with Callaghan's arguments. This, however, is ultimately a disagreement about theory, but in practice, and as a work following the psychoanalytic approach, Callaghan's book is admirable and evinces a clear understanding of the animating forces behind the Freudian and Jungian literary worldview.

"Behind the Locked Door" and "H. P. Lovecraft and the Magna Mater" are more substantial essays, length-wise, and they concern the Jungian archetypes of Theseus' trapdoor and the figure of the Great Mother. The former is a wide-ranging explication of Lovecraft's paternal anxieties and their manifestations in his fictions, while the latter, perhaps the book's crowning achievement, explores the nature of the Feminine as it is represented and imagined in the oeuvre. Callaghan traces Lovecraft's strange and deeply convoluted depiction of the Magna Mater figure to his earliest and most deep-seated ideological, psychological, and political anxieties, arguing that his cosmogony is as "firmly rooted in primal ideas of the "Mother Goddess" as the anti-witch fulminations of Cotton Mather." He cites anthropologists, fellow psychoanalytic theorists, and historians in his advancement of a hermeneutics of the Feminine in Lovecraft's fiction, which he meticulously organizes, collocates, and systematically investigates and presents via charts and tables (e.g., Table 4. Benevolent vs. Malevolent Wives and Mothers in HPL's Weird Fiction). Parental giganticism, racial angst (particularly with regard to Jews), and queer/sexual/feminine anxiety are, as Callaghan argues, the galvanizing energies fueling the "mundane" psychological and deeply physicalist/bodied assemblage of horrors at work in Lovecraft's fiction.

Gavin Callaghan has presented, in *H. P. Lovecraft's Dark Arcadia*, a wide range of insights, far too great in number even to attempt to summarize. Suffice it to say that this text stands alongside the works of St. Armand and Mosig in its undeniable contributions to the psychoanalytic tradition of Lovecraftian scholarship. Although, at times, the book is mired in the thorny thickets of political, moral, and historical polemic, Callaghan has assembled a text that is prodigious in depth and breadth, panoptic in scope, and certainly worth reading, thinking about, and considering. This is a book to be read slowly, admired for its academic and scholastic rigor, and contemplated with the seriousness and thoroughness that it deserves. *H. P. Lovecraft's Dark Arcadia*, despite its flaws, is an enlightening study sure to bring *jouissance* to the academic-minded aficionados of Lovecraft. Freud once said, in *Moses and Monotheism*, that "The distortion of a text resembles a murder: the difficulty is not in perpetrating the deed, but in getting rid of its traces." Callaghan uncovers the hidden traces of distortion in the writings of H. P. Lovecraft, and through his excavation of the recesses of Lovecraft's psyche and the texts themselves, he sheds light on the great darkness of one of the twentieth century's most enigmatic writers and thinkers.

www.ingramcontent.com/pod-product-compliance
Lightning Source LLC
Chambersburg PA
CBHW051824090426
42736CB00011B/1629